WHY DO YOU STAY?

Based on one survivor's true story from abused, to leaving, rebuilding and finally thriving

Carly Lee

ISBN: 0692884459
ISBN 13: 9780692884454
Library of Congress Control Number: 2017936378
Bond Press, LLC, Melbourne, FL

FOREWORD

I write my story not to show how different or unique my story is but rather the exact opposite. I write to show how domestic-violence stories have a common thread. In my own journey and healing, I often gained strength knowing others had made some of the same choices and mistakes I had made, and that they were still able to come out the other side to a better place. I tell my story for other individuals who are going through domestic violence and are looking for understanding and change. I also write for people who want to help domestic-violence victims—therapists, friends, family members, employers, or anyone who wishes to understand the answer to that hardest of all questions: *Why do you stay?* This is a question I asked myself many times.

My story is not a fun, easy read and will not be of interest to every member of the general public. I am not looking for everyone to agree with me, but my hope is to shed some understanding about how victims think and to promote hope and healing.

Names of people and locations have been changed to protect the identities of the people in my story. The events are real and happened the way I have written—to the best of my ability to remember. By design, the telling of my story is not to recount every detail of all of my experiences or my family's experiences but rather to paint a picture of the overall environment in which I was raised and how these childhood experiences molded and affected me. That will, in turn, I hope shed light on why I made the choices I made that led me to experience an adult life filled with violence. I also hope it will show how I was finally able to change my thinking as an adult. By changing my internal thinking, I was at long last able to create the life I had dreamed of as a small girl.

In a nutshell, I hope to explain why I did what I did and *why I stayed*.

TABLE OF CONTENTS

Section I

1. My First Memory

My first memory of Russell is not a good one. But then, none of my memories of Russell are good ones.

Tuesdays mean church night—in addition to Thursdays and Sundays. As a Jehovah's Witness, if church is open for business, Mom is there with as many of her children as she can commandeer for the event. It's 1973. Mom and Russell's marriage of seventeen years has produced five children: Terri, Lily, Ernie, Robin, and me (Carly). The age spread runs from Terri (fifteen years old) to me (seven). I should note Russell is my biological father although I can't remember ever referring to him as Dad—a title I don't believe he has earned or deserves. I am the only child that calls him by his given name: Russell. But the truth be told, I try to avoid any interaction with him at all times.

My older siblings often complain about attending church, but I don't mind. The people are friendly and nice. I particularly like the elderly people who always seem to take the time to notice me. It is a safe and predictable place—a stark contrast to my home environment.

Church is a sanctuary that allows me to let my guard down and be a child, if only for a short time. It is not so much that I am consciously connecting with God, but it's a place where I don't have to be on high alert for unanticipated explosions from Russell.

1

On this particular Tuesday night, the church posse consists of Mom, Robin, and me. As the two youngest children, our attendance is required without question.

Russell hates church. He holds "believers" of all faiths in contempt. But Russell hasn't been home for months, so I'm not worried. Russell never lived full-time in our house. Like bad weather, he might stay a few days, but he never stays for long before he leaves again. He might return two days later—or not again for six months. It is part of how he controls all of us, the element of surprise. Varying levels of states of emergency defined our lives.

Twelve rows of chairs sit neatly in the small church building. As usual, Mom, Robin, and I sit near the front in the second row. All is well—and predictable—as the preacher settles into his sermon. Everything is ordinary and normal until the back door opens.

The congregation collectively turns to observe the late arrival. To my knowledge, no church members have ever met Russell, and yet everyone in the room seems to instantly sense trouble. It feels like the air has just been sucked out of the room—I suddenly can't breathe. My clothes dampen as I begin to sweat; fear flushes my face and rushes to settle in every cell of my small body.

Russell's presence looms large as he stands stiff and scowling in the back of the tiny church, hands clinched in tight fists at his sides. The preacher hesitates for a moment, looks down at his podium, clears his throat, and then resumes preaching. Toxic air and emotions poison this once-safe place.

Mom stands without saying a word to Robin or me and quickly walks to the back of the church. My head turns to watch my mother as she moves away from me and toward Russell. Even at a young age, I understand keeping Russell in my line of sight is very important. Terrified, I want to know the second he explodes. Keeping my focus on Russell allows me to be ready to react if and when the violence starts. I will then know which direction to run to avoid being the target—or even a witness—of his terror.

As Mom approaches, Russell draws a gun from his jacket pocket, points it toward the ceiling, and waves it ominously in the air.

Incredibly, the preacher continues preaching. It is as if the entire congregation is suddenly struck deaf, dumb, and blind. Doesn't anyone else see this?

I can see Mom desperately trying to calm Russell down.

This is not an empty threat. This is very real. The tension makes my stomach hurt. I am afraid I am going to throw up.

I suddenly begin to feel like I am fading away. My child's mind does not have the words to express my terror, nor do I have the life experience to effectively process what is happening. As I would later learn, this is likely the first time I consciously remember disassociating from my body. Disassociating can occur when someone experiences a traumatic experience. The events are so overwhelming that the individual cannot fully process or comprehend the situation. As a survival mechanism, the conscious self-will detach from the physical body as a way to protect itself. This is an involuntary, unconscious human reaction used as a way to deal with intense emotions.

But the situation gets worse...much worse.

As the preacher perseveres, the congregation appears frozen. In desperation, I concentrate on showing no emotion as well. Previous violent episodes with Russell have taught me it is better to show no emotion in these situations. Reactions shift Russell's attention and I did not want Russell's focus turning to me. No, I did not want to become the next target.

After what feels like an eternity, I see Mom gingerly lead Russell to an empty back pew where she convinces him to sit down.

I cannot hear the words spoken between them, but I am completely riveted to Russell's face. His brows are tightly pulled together, and his mouth is drawn into a deadly sneer. His short black hair is greased close to his head. The veins in his neck are bulging out. His deep anger and evil are on full display.

Finally, Russell and Mom get up and walk out the back door. Mom appears so small behind his six-foot-five-inch height. Without instruction, Robin and I quickly get up from our chairs and silently follow them to the car. We know the drill. No one needs to instruct us. From past experiences, we know our parts well—to be submissive and go along with whatever Russell wants...or incur whatever wrath he decides to bestow upon us. As I walk out of the church behind Robin into the parking lot, the cool night air washes over me. Although I know it isn't over, I do feel relieved that nothing happened inside the church. At least no church member was hurt.

Astoundingly, no one in the congregation intervenes or even questions any of what has just transpired. The only sound that remains is the preacher's sermon.

The four of us—Russell, Mom, Robin, and me—climb into Mom's car. Mom drives with Russell beside her, while Robin and I sit perfectly silent in the back seat. Russell's car, left behind in the parking lot, warrants no comment.

Robin and I remain stone still and deathly silent. We are both in hyper-vigilance mode as we know any word, any movement, or any change in our breathing might be the trigger that could push him deeper into the rage that currently consumes him.

When others refuse to offer triggers, Russell provides his own. He begins yelling at Mom, accusing her of having an affair with someone at church. Convinced Mom is involved with another man, Russell continues to hurl accusations, working himself into a blind rage.

About halfway home, he starts screaming, "Stop the car, you whore! I am going to make you tell me the truth if it's the last thing I do!"

Mom, as ordered, stops the car. We are near the top of a hill, and it is pitch black outside. I see the headlights as they glare against the dark pavement. In the parked car on the hill and without any warning, Russell grabs Mom by the hair and pulls her toward him. He jerks open his passenger door as he drags her across the seat and out of the car onto the pavement. He drags Mom around to the front of the car. In the dark, icky night, the glare of the headlights on the dark pavement creates stark silhouettes of my parents.

All the while, Mom pleads, "Russell, please let me go! Stop this!"

"You are a nothing but a whore, sleeping with those men over there! Tell me which ones you are having an affair with!" he screams through gritted teeth.

Then Russell, as if he were taking his arm back to swing a sledgehammer, raises his arm to the sky and swings it down. He strikes Mom across the face and knocks her to her knees.

Remaining crouched on the pavement with the headlights shining on her, Mom slowly raises her head and softly begs, "Russell, please stop this! I am not sleeping with anyone! I love you!"

Her pleading voice never penetrates the deep layers of his anger. He stares at her for a moment and then strikes her again, like a predator slamming his prey to the ground before devouring it. With his second blow, Mom falls flat onto the pavement. Russell now jumps onto her and grabs her head. He repeatedly bangs her head against the unforgiving pavement, over and over again. I suck in my breath. I stop breathing. I am frozen with terror!

My mind races with a thousand thoughts. "What can I do? Don't kill my mom! What can I do?"

At first, Mom fights back, attempting to defend herself. But Russell just keeps banging her head again and again on the hard asphalt. After what seems like an eternity, Mom's body goes limp. Her body is like a worn rag doll being tossed around by Russell.

Without warning, Russell suddenly stops. Mom's body lies completely motionless on the road. It's as though time is standing still. I can hear Robin taking shallow breaths beside me. Too afraid to speak or move, I dare not look at Robin. I can't take my eyes away from my mother.

I can see her perfectly still and lifeless body in the headlights. Blood is running from her body onto the pavement.

Oh, God, this can't be happening—my mom!

I do not know the word *murder* yet, but I do know the word *kill*. And I believe Russell has just killed my mom.

Russell has now stopped smashing her head on the pavement, but he continues to yell accusations at her. When Mom doesn't respond, Russell stands up straight and stares down at her.

Oh, God, please let him stop. Please let him stop!

He kicks her. She never moves; her lifeless body simply absorbs the attack.

Doesn't Russell realize she may be dead? He bends down to get a closer look.

He starts to gently shake her. His shoulders have softened, and his whole body seems less tense now. Trying to stir her, his voice sounds calmer now. It even seems as if he is concerned for her.

The Jehovah's Witnesses say that Jesus came back from the dead, so I pray as hard as any seven-year-old can that my mom will come back too. Russell now also appears worried that she is not responding. Perhaps the possibility he has killed her pierces his rage. As an adult, I now realize that he was indeed concerned, not for my mother, but for himself!

This does not feel real to me; it's more like a nightmare. I want to wake up, but I can't. There are no words spoken between Robin and me. The interior of the car is eerily silent.

Time seems frozen…but then amazingly, like a roadside Lazarus, Mom begins to lift herself up to her knees, and then slowly, unsteadily, she rises to her feet. Russell offers to help, but Mom waves him away. They talk for a moment although I can't hear what they are saying. Then Russell walks back to the car. Mom follows her head hanging between her shoulders like a wilted flower.

Russell takes over the driver's seat while Mom slowly climbs into the back seat with me and Robin. Neither Robin nor I have spoken since Russell appeared in the back of the church.

I remember the blood. How much blood can you lose before you need to go to the hospital? Are we going to the hospital?

But the hospital is never mentioned. Then I hear her say it.

"I am sorry for making you so mad."

What? Why is my mom apologizing to Russell? "God, why is Mom apologizing to *him*?"

"Please forgive me for upsetting you. I am so sorry. I love only you," Mom says.

I whisper, "Mom, why are you apologizing to him?"

"Be quiet! Don't say anything," she mutters to me under her breath as she squeezes my arm.

"But, Mom, why are you apologizing to him? I don't understand."

My little girl's mind struggles to comprehend that Mom is apologizing to Russell after he has just viciously beaten her. It is at this moment I decide the world is not a safe place. The person I trust the most—my mom—isn't making any sense. What I just witnessed does not match what my mom is telling me.

Something important is slipping away from me. I am desperately trying to make sense of this experience but can't. I am too young. I have to ask her again. "But Mom, why are you apologizing? You didn't do anything wrong."

"Be quiet, Carly," she whispers in a low, deep voice.

I feel my hope and any sense of safety slip away. I feel completely and utterly vulnerable. I am alone.

My hope of understanding simply vanished that night. In one fell swoop, my two sources of safety were lost: my mom's ability to protect me and my belief that church was a safe place. I had no way of knowing that I had just cut off my natural instincts. My internal voice (my instinct) told me Russell had just committed a violent act and was a bad person. But in my physical reality, I had just witnessed my mother—the one person I trusted—apologize for the pain Russell had inflicted on her, and this was very confusing to me.

As stated in Melody Beattie's book *Making Miracles in Forty Days*, denial damages our intuition. Mom's denial made no sense. Something was wrong. I knew this as a seven-year-old child.

When I tried to get Mom to help me understand, she told me to be quiet. I trusted her; I loved her. She must be right, so I needed to be quiet. My internal voice must be wrong.

My thoughts were incompatible. Instinct informed me that Russell was bad. Yet Mom's apology claimed responsibility for instigating the incident. Which one was true? I could not believe my instincts and my mother at the same time. These two competing thoughts could not both be true.

I was desperate to try to figure out which one was the truth. I could not believe or comprehend that my mom could be so wrong, since she was the grown-up and my source of knowledge about the world. Therefore, I came to the conclusion that my instinct was wrong. I could not believe or trust my own gut reaction to situations. So I denied my natural instincts, and by denying them over time, I slowly and methodically shut them down. This was a critical emotional turning point for me although at the time I was completely unaware of the internal shift that had taken place.

Today I realize that my mother did the best she could. Struggling to simply survive, she did what she believed she needed to do to end the violence in that moment and keep herself and her two small children alive. But I left that experience with a new and strong emotional conviction: it was better—safer—to take care of myself and rely on no one. Self-reliance was my key to staying safe.

Another emotional casualty of this incident for me was the destruction of responsibility for one's actions. Russell did not experience any repercussions for his violent actions that night. This lack of accountability communicated to me that those who are violent always get their way. They are not to be challenged. They must get their way at all costs. Compliance is the way to safety, regardless of the cost: emotional or otherwise.

This incident was a game changer. As a result, my internal voice suffered severe and lasting damage. I no longer had strong convictions or belief in my own gut reactions. Maybe I really did see it wrong, or maybe I, myself, caused the incident to happen. This destruction of an internal belief in myself set the stage for my vulnerability, which would allow me to be exploited by predators as an adult. But at that moment, my seven-year-old mind had no way of knowing this realization. It would take more than thirty years for understanding to penetrate my consciousness.

Many events would play out in my adult life in a most unexpected way before I would be able to connect the dots regarding the influence of my childhood experiences on my adult choices decades later.

From that moment on, I simply knew I would hold onto my own spirit as best I could. That also meant that parts of myself would have to be kept secret from others to allow me to feel safe. Unfortunately, it also meant that parts of me were even hidden from my own conscious self.

Gardeners will tell you that the strongest seeds are those that lie dormant over a long hard winter. When they bloom, they bloom big. I was in a very, very long and harsh winter season, but I would live to see this parable play out in my own life many, many years later.

2. What is Love?

Even now, as I write this story, I can't call Russell, "Dad."
He was never a father but an enforcer. Someone to be feared
and avoided.

Russell drives us home that night. When we arrive at the house, Robin and I immediately go to our bedroom and get into to bed. We never mention the incident again.

The pattern for violent episodes repeats in a cyclical rhythm. Following big blowups, eerie silence wafts through the air like death wandering around looking for corpses. No one dares ask questions, afraid of sparking yet another round of terror.

You wait for the aggressor to speak or act. When the aggressor shows signs of calm behavior in whatever ways fit their personality—joking or maybe asking questions—you know the storm has temporarily passed, and it is okay to speak. This is the only normal I know. I have exposure to no other way of life.

My mother often says, "All of you kids were accidents. I never planned to have any of you." After giving birth to five kids in a span of eight years, with me born in 1966, Mom says the doctor asked her if she knew about birth control. Mom told the doctor she had never heard of birth control, but if she could get this thing called birth control, she would never have any more kids. And she is true to her word. I am her last child.

Mom is a practical parent. She doesn't show affection in public or private. She works hard at trying to keep the house clean and cook what meager meals she can rustle up. She is also a very private person, even with her own children. We all know better than to ask her how she is feeling. She gives you a sharp look that makes you feel ashamed that you asked the question. Thoughts, fears, and dreams are items you keep to yourself.

My older sister is often tasked with babysitting me. Now that I no longer associate safety with church or my mother, I gravitate to my oldest sister, Lily, for protection. She is like a second mother to me. Lily teaches me to tie my shoes, count my numbers, and write my ABCs. I feel happiest when I know Lily is at home.

When I am nine years of age, we move to a tiny house in rural southern Tennessee. Eviction, not choice, forces frequent moves from one ramshackle house to another.

In this house, I am thrilled to share a bedroom with Lily. This is the first time we have shared the same bedroom. As the two oldest siblings of the same gender, Lily and Terri usually share a room, but this time, Lily asks me to share a room with her.

I love Lily, so I am thrilled! Sometimes she sings me to sleep. I love watching her sing as her soft brown eyes twinkle and her soft voice floats through the air like a beautiful butterfly. I feel safe when Lily is around. I knew that she watches out for me.

Two twin beds dwarf our small room, but that's okay with me. Our little oasis is the safest place in the house for me. Or it is until one night, just as I have slipped under the covers to go to bed, when Lily walks over and sits on my bedside.

Looking me straight in the eyes with a focused, determined, un-wavering gaze, she flatly states, "I am leaving tonight. I am moving out, and I won't be back."

"What do you mean you won't be back?" I am scared and worried.

"I am moving out; I am going to go live with Stevie."

Stevie is Lily's boyfriend. She has been dating him for two weeks.

How could she move out—just like that? She doesn't even know Stevie that well. Where will she live? What am I going to do without her? These thoughts race through my mind as I sit stunned and con-fused on my little twin bed.

Lily and Terri leave sometimes for brief periods to stay with Nellie, our paternal grandmother. I am always sad when Lily leaves. But she always comes back—always.

Lily insists, "Promise me you won't tell Mom where I am. I am only telling you, Carly, because I don't want you to worry about me when Mom finds out tomorrow that I am gone."

"No, I won't tell Mom. I won't say a word." I don't know where Stevie lives anyway.

I don't fully understand that Lily is leaving for good. I simply think she is going away for a while, just like she does when she goes to Nellie's.

The love Lily and I share matters more to me than anything else. She makes home life more bearable—of course I will keep Lily's secret.

Lily hugs me. "Know that I love you, Carly."

"I love you too, Lily."

I pull the covers up over my head, ready to go to sleep. In the fog just before sleep envelops me, I think, "I hope Robin or Terri won't get to share this room with me because when Lily comes back, I want her to be in here with me."

After I fall asleep, Lily crawls out the bedroom window and leaves home. I never hear her leave. Lily is fifteen.

Sometime later that night, Mom comes into our bedroom. Flipping the light on, she strides over to my bed and starts shaking me.

"Wake up. Wake up, Carly."

I bolt upright in the bed, still bleary eyed, not sure what is happening.

"Where is she? Where is she?"

I just look at Mom. I don't speak. She shakes me again. "Where is Lily? You better tell me where she is or else!"

"I don't know."

Mom repeatedly tries to get me to tell her where Lily is, but I just continue to look at Mom and say nothing.

The truth is I don't know where Lily is. I only know that she left with her new boyfriend, Stevie. My loyalty resides with Lily, not Mom, and I promised Lily I would not say anything to Mom about her leaving.

No, I will not tell Mom what I know. Yes, she is my mother, but I learned that safety is found in keeping your mouth shut when people are angry, and Mom is plenty mad!

No threat looms large enough to convince me to tell Mom that Lily has left with Stevie. Mom, finally realizing I have nothing to say, leaves the bedroom, and I am alone. Totally alone.

I am now more scared and worried about Lily. Mom's mixture of anxiety and anger makes me worry even more about Lily. "Is Lily okay?" I wonder. When will Lily come back? Will Lily come back? I say a silent prayer. "God, please let Lily come back today."

Family Dynamics

Russell is the elder of two boys. His mother—my grandmother—Nellie, made no secret that she longed for a girl. Terri and Lily, my two older sisters, arrived as the first two grandchildren—grand*daughters*—in Russell's family. When Terri arrived, Nellie offered to rear Terri as her own daughter. Although I do not understand the dynamics of their relationship, it is clear neither Russell nor Mom gets along with Nellie.

Nellie's enchantment does not extend beyond Terri. Lily is tolerated, while the three remaining grandchildren are an annoyance when they are not nonexistent.

I have a few memories of Terri, but they are dim. From my point of view, Terri lives in a different world from the rest of us. She is different from my other two sisters and my brother. For as long as I can remember, Terri has been Nellie's favored one. Because Nellie has money, her special relationship with Terri carries with it certain privileges. I am not jealous of Terri, but instead I accept the fact that my grandmother loves only one of her grandchildren—and that is always and only Terri.

A rare old photo reveals all five siblings posed in Nellie's backyard, so I must have been there at least one time, but any specifics are lost in the fog of my past.

Although probably not wealthy by today's standards, in comparison to the extreme poverty my family experiences, Nellie has a "comfortable" lifestyle. Terri's frequent extended stays with Nellie result in her returning home with new clothes and pretty toys. I know things are different for Terri, and this may be the underlying reason why I never feel connected to her. Terri acts differently from my point of view than the rest of the family.

Sometimes, if not most times, Russell and Mom force Lily to accompany Terri on the trips to Nellie's house. Lily also returns with nice things. But unlike Terri, Lily shares her items with us. Terri appears selfish, self-centered, and aloof from the rest of us.

Although Terri and I share the same gene pool, it never feels like she is my sister.

Nellie dies when I am eleven years old. Although it is never discussed, Nellie's favoritism irrevocably impacts interactions between Terri and the rest of the family. We never talk about it as a family; as usual, difficult subject matter is not a topic open for discussion.

Enveloped in a thick blanket of ongoing poverty, crisis, and cycles of abuse, the family focus never wavers from daily survival. The nuances of privilege, although observed through Terri, represent a philosophical debate for which we do not have the luxury or emotional understanding and ability to discuss.

The abusive storm cycles roll in like clockwork. Survival is the primary directive. The calm following each blowup lasts just long enough for me to catch my breath before the next wave hits. Today I can clearly see the reality of the abusive cycle in my childhood, but as a child, I was blind to the pattern of dysfunctional behavior.

I can't imagine the confusion Terri and Lily must feel being shipped off to live with a grandmother in some level of comfort, only to return again and again to live in violence and poverty.

At our house, beans and cornbread are the main food staple. Occasionally we get to eat bologna, but that is rare. And often, we simply go hungry. The stark contrast between Nellie's environment and ours is enormous.

Extended stays at Nellie's require Terri and Lily to repeatedly switch schools throughout the year. No one ever questions why this happens. The disruption to their education is never discussed. We live by an unspoken rule—never question Russell. We live this rule and follow it 100 percent of the time. No exceptions. Questions can be lethal to the asker. This lesson is etched forever in my memory. I can't remember a time when this has not been true for my family. Russell is the dictator with no limits on his power or methods of abuse.

Child Reasoning

Although Lily stated that she wouldn't be returning when she left with Stevie, I do not understand that she is gone for good. Like her trips to Nellie's, I think she is going to be away for a while but will come back. Lily fled in the middle of the night to escape the endless poverty and violence. After that night, Mom never talks to me about Lily again. Two weeks later, Lily reappears at the house, having decided running away from home is a huge mistake. Turns out living with Stevie is as bad as (if not worse than) living at home.

Lily asks Mom, "Can I move back home? I made a mistake by running away, and I am sorry."

Mom replies sternly, "No, you have made your bed. Now you must lie in it." So at age fifteen, Lily has to fend for herself. The fact that she is a minor makes no difference.

Russell is not around when Lily leaves nor is he around when she asks to come back home, so Mom's decision goes unchallenged by him. I have no idea if Russell would have allowed Lily to return home.

It doesn't matter now because Mom's word is final. Lily is gone, and I feel totally and completely alone. I am vulnerable once again. Mom will never allow Lily to move back home.

Even though I am present during this exchange, I do not move or speak. I am frozen. This is the moment that I truly realize that Lily is gone for good and that she will never be coming back home to live. Although I love my mom, she seems on the periphery of my life. She never hits me or calls me names, but she ignores me while Lily openly and continually displays her love for me.

And now Lily is gone.

I am sick with fear and loneliness.

I never share my desperation over Lily's departure with Mom. Russell's chaos and her concern about when is he coming back again consume Mom's attention. Mom remains preoccupied, in a constant state of survival. She has no time to devote to my needs. Surviving—staying alive and keeping Russell happy—devours all her emotional resources.

The psychological needs of her five children must be met through alternative methods or quashed altogether. Fears, feelings, or emotions that have no one to hear them will often be internalized and distorted.

As a child, my need for safety went unmet; needless to say, my emotional needs were neither acknowledged nor addressed. Hearing my siblings and myself described as "accidents" never bothered me as a young girl; however, today, as an adult, I am saddened when I recall my mother's words. I am saddened for the little girl hearing those words and for the mother who felt such a heavy burden. I imagine Mom felt trapped and defined by an inescapable life of poverty and violence. Her attempt to parent five children surely only compounded her feelings of hopelessness and despair.

As an adult, I understand my mother's life was filled with the everyday challenges of trying to survive the poverty, violence, and chaos of our family life. As a young child, I was not aware that an emotional template was being created that would define how I would allow others to treat me as an adult. It would not even register on my radar that this was unacceptable behavior. *Being neglected was normal.*

These childhood experiences were forming my own beliefs about love and relationships and what to expect from others—which was very little, if anything, regarding my needs and wants. It would take many years for me to realize that I needed to think about love differently, including all forms of love: self-love, loving someone else, and how another person loved me.

For the first step in understanding love, I would need to unravel my personal beliefs about love. I would ask myself, "What did it actually mean to love someone?" I had no awareness of self-love, self-care, or what truly healthy love felt, looked, or sounded like, not only for others but also for myself.

I had not developed the self-worth or self-awareness that would have allowed me to grasp the importance of taking care of one's own emotional needs. I didn't know that I had a right to expect any kind of support from others. I had no way of knowing that as a child, I was not taught to love or respect myself.

I did not even know that I deserved to be loved.

As a young girl, I just wanted to hurry up and grow up—to be an adult so I could get out of the chaos. On some level, I knew my family life deviated from the norm. My single goal at this young age was to live a safe life when I got to be an adult. I even created a mental list of things that would make me feel safe. The list included consistently living in the same house, never being evicted, never getting married, never having children, and, most importantly, getting my education.

As an adult, I learned about the predictable rhythm of abusive relationships. The cycle involves the build-up stage, fraught with increasing tension; the explosion stage; and the culmination—the honeymoon stage. Sadly, the vicious cycle repeats itself, with the bookend stages—the build-up and honeymoon stages—growing shorter while the explosion stage increases in duration.

My parent's relationship would follow this classic pattern for the duration of my childhood until their divorce in my early teens. Fear prevented Mom from calling Russell's behavior into question. He had free rein to do whatever he wanted, whenever he wanted.

Questioning Russell meant walking away bruised and scarred. We all learned the lesson well. Never, ever question Russell—about anything. And never talk back in any way that could be perceived as a challenge; you were not allowed to voice any opinion other than complete agreement with what he was saying.

Like a ruthless dictator, there were no consequences for Russell's actions. His family was simply a constant supply of available victims. I learned, like so many others experiencing trauma, to operate in a strict code of silence. After an explosion, when the dust settled, there was no discussion. It becomes just another dirty memory. You're grateful you survived.

Ongoing poverty added another layer to the complexity of living with violence and the threat of violence on a daily basis. Russell would disappear for weeks or months, leaving the family without any financial support. My mother worked hard, attempting to support herself and her five children. But with nothing more than a grade-school education, her earning potential was limited.

In stark contrast, my school life offered an escape from the terror of my home. I enjoyed school and had lots of friends. Intuitively, I knew not to discuss my crazy home life with my teachers or classmates. At school, I acted like everything was normal.

Silence, secrets, and shame comprised my survival tool kit. That moment of Russell appearing in church with the gun taught me the code of silence in public; church members modeled the code of silence as religiously as my family did. Silence was the accepted and expected method of dealing with troubling events in the home or difficult situations in public.

No one ever talked to me about the event with Russell and the gun in church—not Mom, not Russell, not my sister, not any church members. My mother, siblings, and I continued to attend the church. Although church no longer represented a safe place, thankfully, I never felt any judgment from any of the church members because of Russell's intrusion. Church members were simply not skilled or knowledgeable about how to address the situation of an abused woman and her children in the mid 1970s. While I am grateful for their kindness, church did not help me learn to overcome the effects of abuse and trauma.

Shame settled on me like a second skin. Shame became the rigid bars holding me prisoner, unable to ask questions or summon the courage to talk to anyone about the violent environment in which I lived.

The overwhelming feeling of shame ensured my silence about my home life. While the secrecy offered me safety and acceptance in the public arena, the ongoing silence promoted an environment where shame could flourish and take root in my core. As I was growing into adulthood, I began harboring more and more secrets regarding my chaotic family life. With every secret, the shame grew stronger. Each new secret and shameful event only increased the powerful potency of the shame inside me.

3. The Trip

It has been a year since Lily left home. I am accustomed to keeping my thoughts and feelings to myself now and guard my secrets well. Robin, my older sister by two and half years, and I rely on one another for some sense of normalcy.

One sunny afternoon, Mom comes home distraught. "Get in the car! I need to go to Faye's house and make a phone call!" Mom yells at Robin and me.

We are very poor and have never had a phone in the house; we simply can't afford it. So to make phone calls, we have to go to the neighbor's house.

Mom is obviously very upset. The three of us—Mom, Robin, and I—pile into Mom's car. "What's wrong, Mom?" I ask.

"Be quiet!" she snaps back.

I do not ask any more questions. As usual, Mom does not tell us what is going on. We drive to Faye's house, and Mom makes a mysterious phone call. She never talks to Robin or me about why she has to use the phone so urgently. Mom seems anxious and out of sorts for a couple of weeks after the phone call. Russell has not been home for months. I never wonder if the phone call has something to do with Russell. If Russell is gone, that is better than having him at home. I enjoy his absence.

About three weeks after the mysterious phone call, as Robin and I are getting off the school bus, Mom meets us at the front door.

"Girls, get in the car. We are going to Clarksville." This is very unusual. We never take road trips; there is never any money for gas, and I instantly try to figure out what is going on.

Clarksville is an hour and a half away. We do not have any family or friends in Clarksville. I cannot possibly think of any reason why there is such an urgent need to go there.

As ordered by Mom, the three of us tuck into the car and head off for Clarksville. I pray my mom's old car doesn't die and will make the trip. I'm afraid of getting stranded. But after twenty or so minutes on the road, I decide I am going to view this as an adventure. In my mind, I fantasize that we were going out of town to visit our rich uncle who has a swimming pool, swing set, loves his nieces, and can't wait to see Robin and me.

But Mom seems to be getting more upset and apprehensive as we get closer to Clarksville. Worry begins to creep into my mind again—the closer we get, the more it feels like a dark cloud is following us, and I have no idea why.

Clarksville is huge compared to our little one-stoplight town. I look out the car window at the big buildings and watch the traffic drive by when Mom says, "Where is that hospital?"

I feel my stomach knot up, and a shiver shoots down my spine.

"Oh God," I think instantly to myself. "It's Russell. We're going to see Russell." He is the only person in my life who always seems to bring trouble and strife. I do not know what is happening, but I am scared.

Why does Russell have to be in my life? Why can't he just stay away and never come back? I often fantasize about a life without him in it.

A car-horn blast snaps me back to the present. That fantasy is not going to come true today.

Mom drives into the hospital parking lot. The three of us get out of the car and walk toward the hospital entrance. I walk in the rear, slowly dragging myself toward the hospital, fear in my heart. I feel sick to my stomach and afraid that I am I going to get sick and throw up—I am terrified, but I know there is nothing I can say that will stop Mom from making me go inside. If I tell her I am afraid or feel sick, I know she will say, "You have nothing to be afraid of. Don't be a baby."

I know I have no choice but to do as she orders.

I can't imagine if it's Russell, why he would be here at a mental hospital. I wonder why Mom is making Robin and me go with her. I guess I will soon find out.

The three of us walk into the hospital, and Mom tells the receptionist, "We are here to see Russell Lee."

I knew it. I knew it had something to with Russell. This is one time I would have been overjoyed to be wrong.

The hospital's front doors slam shut as we walk in. I feel trapped. My eyes scan the room, looking for a way to escape, but the only exit doors are the ones we came through, and they are now locked. This hospital has locks on the doors. You can't just push the door and leave. You have to ask for permission to be let out. To say I am afraid would be an understatement.

Mom checks in with the receptionist. She says, "Have a seat, and I will let you know when you can go back to see him."

The three of us walk toward the small waiting room. The chairs are dirty, and the windows are fogged with layers of dust and dirt. I cannot wait to get out of this scary place. Wordlessly, we sit on the dingy chairs and wait.

A short time later, the receptionist calls out, "Ms. Lee, you can go back to see Russell Lee now." Mom walks to the receptionist desk. She signs a paper, and she is escorted thought another set of locked doors down a long hallway.

When the door clangs shut, it sends a jolt down my spine. I wonder if Mom will come back. Is she going to be locked up too? Robin and I sit in silence, waiting to hear our next instructions and what we will have to do next. Robin is twelve, and I am ten years old. Even as a ten-year-old, I feel ashamed to be in a mental hospital. However, I am grateful that Russell isn't in a hospital in our little hometown. At least none of my friends will know that I am here.

I hate being related to Russell. Being around him is a cauldron of bruised emotions. I am afraid, ashamed, and embarrassed by him—there is simply nothing about him that I like.

We sit in the waiting room for about half and an hour before Mom comes back into the room and announces, "Okay, Carly, you go next to visit your father. He has asked to see you."

"Are you kidding me?" I say to myself. Doesn't she know how much I despise him? Can't she tell?

Russell is never interested in us. When he does finally come home after one of his extended "out of town" trips, he never wants to see any of us kids. Instead, he is focused on Mom—what has she been doing, what she is planning, who she is talking to.

The hospital rules only allow one visitor at a time, so I have to go by myself back to visit Russell. I am shaking as I walk toward the locked doors that lead to Russell. I know right behind the thick metal door is that long hallway that will lead me to him. The locked door is metal and painted dirty beige. I can still remember the scratches on the paint that expose the shiny metal underneath. The nurse unlocks the door and escorts me through. I can hear the metal clang as the door swings shut—closing out my mother and sister and locking me in with Russell. What if they don't let me out? What if I have to stay locked up her forever with him?

I am terrified but am well trained to keep my mouth shut and say nothing out loud.

The worn linoleum tiled floor is a dirty brown, with gold specks that lost their luster long ago. As the nurse and I walk down the long hall, I can hear the patients screaming behind locked doors. I want to turn and run away, but I do what I am expected to do and follow alongside the nurse.

When we get to Russell's room, it is stark and bare, except for a small worn wooden table beside the bed and a small chair, which sits in the corner. Russell is sitting on the side of his bed. He stands up and steps toward me as if to give me a hug. I shrink away from him, backing up toward the doorway. I try to make myself as small as possible. "I'm going to be sick!" I think.

The nurse turns and leaves the room, leaving me alone with Russell. His full attention is now on me. Usually there have been other people around when I've had to be in his presence, but now it is only Russell and me. I am terrified and disgusted at the same time.

He senses my disgust or maybe my fear. Either way, he steps back and sits down on the bed. He isn't going to hug me—thank God.

I sit down in the chair.

"So how is your Mom doing?"

I respond, "Fine."

"What has she been doing, and where has she been going?"

"Nowhere."

His obsession with Mom is alive and well. He is still consumed with knowing my mother's every move while he's been gone. The truth is, we never have money to go anywhere. We only go to church and back home. But I know better than to say we go to church.

A nurse comes in to give Russell his medicine. He takes the medicine and puts the pills in his mouth. She hands him a small cup of water, which he drinks without comment. "Open your mouth, and raise your tongue," she directs him.

Russell does what she asks. I am amazed that he does what he is told without blowing up. I am terrified that he is going to fly into a rage and start swinging his fists. Even though the nurse doesn't seem afraid—I am. I have never seen Russell take orders from anyone—EVER.

Russell is calm and cooperative, but I know calm and cooperative is not his normal behavior. I know he is acting.

I have seen this act once before. I remember the time the neighbors called the police and asked them to come to our house. Russell had a violent episode, and the neighbors heard the yelling and screaming coming from our house and called the police. Russell answered the door and talked to the police. He acted calm and collected. The police didn't even talk to Mom or anyone of us kids. This was in the mid-1970s, before most law enforcement received sensitivity training on domestic violence. There were no rules or guidelines, and so each situation was handled on a case-by-case basis.

The police never talked with Mom and took Russell at his word that nothing was going on. Russell had lots of experience with perfecting his calm act. But I knew what it was like when the police left, and he no longer had to act calm. I had a front-row seat to the violence he could unleash, and I knew he did not like anyone telling him what to do.

The nurse looks under his tongue—once she feels confident that he has taken his medicine, she leaves the room.

As the door clicks shut, and the nurse disappears, he says, "That dumb idiot. She thinks I am taking my medicine. Let me show you something…"

He reaches into the side of his mouth and pulls two tiny yellow pills from the space between his molars and his jaw.

He laughs. "These idiots think I am taking all their pills. They are so stupid. I am so much smarter than they are. I can fool them about anything that I want to. I am not going to let them mess me up with their pills. I have to play their stupid game to get out of here." With that, he jerks the pillow from his bed and pushes back the pillowcase, spilling several more yellow pills onto the mattress.

He is getting worked up and angry. To calm him down, I say, "It was a clever way to outsmart them by not taking the pills when they thought you were."

Inside I am screaming. Why am I here? Why am I being forced to visit him? Why did Mom make me come here?

Telling the nurse that Russell has not taken his medicine is not an option I even consider. Russell will kill me if I do something like that.

I do what Russell expects me to do—I say nothing. I am a compliant party—*a part I know very well*. Russell knows his secrets are safe with his family—they have always been safe. He has no reason to believe that this will ever change.

"I won't be here long. When I get out, I am going to come home."

I simply sit in silence. The nurse who led me down the hallway to his room comes back into the room and asks, "Is everything okay?"

I look into her face, pleading with my eyes. "Can I go now?" I stand up to leave.

"Come and visit again," he tells me. I never look back.

I walk back down the frightening hallway past all the other patient's rooms. Again I hear the moans, chanting, and discomfort of the other patients. As we get closer to the door that is my escape, we pass a man in wheelchair. As I pass by, he reaches out and grabs my arm. I yank it away and run to the locked door. The nurse touches my shoulder. "Are you okay? Do you need someone to talk to?" I shake my head no but cannot look her in the eye. I am afraid to open my mouth. I don't want to cry. That would get me in trouble with Mom. She would accuse me of "causing trouble." I just want to leave. Now.

I can't remember the drive home. I don't even know if we spoke at all during the car ride. I can't remember Mom ever telling me why Russell was there in that horrible place.

As a young child, I was left to wonder why Russell was in this hospital. Not in my wildest imagination could I have guessed the reason he was placed there.

As a ten-year-old, what I took away from this experience was that Russell always seemed to get his way. Even in a place that had strict rules, Russell didn't have to obey the rules. Instead, Russell played by his own rulebook. As I look back now, I realize that this experience reinforced my belief that bullies always get their way. It isn't true, but in my ten-year-old mind, this was my truth.

At the time, it seemed like Russell was outsmarting them all and doing what he wanted to do.

I did not realize the behaviors that I was developing and reinforcing. I had no way of knowing I was acquiring a well-developed behavior of silence and compliance to avoid violence from bullies. This learning was on the subconscious level, and I would carry these learned lessons into my adulthood.

I was also learning how to tune into a bully's feelings on a subliminal level. This emotional skill would enable me to act quickly when violence erupted. To me, this was the normal way to prepare for and react to potential violence—to be on high alert around high-voltage people and get away fast. I had learned that calls for help or assistance would not be answered, so it was not an option that even came to my mind.

Russell had seared into the very fabric of my soul strict obedience, fear, and the expectation that others would not do anything to help me.

Life was going to offer me many opportunities to learn how to overcome these beliefs.

4. Positive Influences

The visit to Russell at the mental institution produces not a single word of discussion. Mom acts as though it never happened. It feels somewhat surreal to experience something as frightening as visiting Russell in such a terrifying setting, witness his deception with the medical staff, and never discuss it with anyone—ever.

Nine months later, Russell reappears at the house. Suddenly, without warning, my tenuous sense of safety instantly disappears—again. I can only assume that he was released from the hospital and decided to return home. Just like his admittance into the hospital and our bizarre visit, there is no dialogue about his release or return to the house. Russell's stint in the hospital could have been a figment of my imagination, except he clearly had been admitted for some reason. The constant chaos, the continual fear, the clear and present danger confronting all of us becomes a palpable anchor holding the family captive in isolation. Questioning or confronting Russell as usual remains off limits. This episode, like so many others, adds to the growing black hole of dark memories stuffed into the deepest recesses of my psyche and our family history.

The unspoken rules hold firm: no one dares question Russell or mention the hospital visit. The event gets filed as top secret, classified information to be reflected on only within the confines of my own thoughts.

Although we resume the semblance of our "normal" life, Russell continues to dictate daily life for everyone. The long shadow of his intimidation extends into his unexpected absences, never releasing family members from a constant state of alert. The element of surprise serves as his weapon of mass destruction. My mother, siblings, and I live a lopsided life, always slightly off-kilter. Russell comes and goes randomly. Like a bullet that ricochets through a congested room, so Russell careens through my life.

Nearly Nowhere to be Safe
School replaces church as my safe place. Like many other kids, getting up in the morning presents my biggest hurdle with regard to school. But once I'm there, I love school.

I never cause any trouble; no, that might draw attention to myself. I learned early that attracting attention could get you hurt...or killed. Although not discussed, on some level, I know that events at home deviate from the norm. I fear someone might discover the truth surrounding my chaotic and dangerous home life, and I am afraid of what might happen if that is discovered. The deeply established roots of my shame stretch their tentacles into all the free space in my life. Everything revolves around shame—hiding it from others, hiding it from myself, pretending it doesn't exist. Battling constant shame births my coping mechanisms. Shame and fear become the bedrock of my foundation, as hard and unforgiving as any rock formation. They cling to me like the stench of an alarmed skunk's spray.

At school, my safe place, I have a lot of friends, and the teachers like me. I maintain straight As without much effort. Sometimes I spend the night at a friend's house, a welcome relief from my scary home life. But I never return the favor. I would never put my friends in harm's way, nor would I expose my secret crazy home life. None of my siblings had friends stay over either...the risk of exposure looms too large.

We move often, frequently getting evicted for unpaid rent. We somehow always find another place to live—another shack. Broken windows, peeling wallpaper, floors with holes, and water leaks defined the decor. Not shabby chic by a long shot. Too often heat is nonexistent during winter months. Outhouses—modern day port-o-potties—serve as restroom facilities in most of our houses. I don't know anyone else who goes outside to use the bathroom. My desperation to keep my secret from my friends knows no bounds. They simply can't discover how I live.

Adding insult to injury, food is always scarce, and horror of horrors, Russell might show up at any time. I condition myself never to think about having a sleepover; it is not something I dwell on. It's a fact of life I accept. I can never have sleepovers, like some kids with allergies can never have a pet.

A proud and stubborn woman, my mother does not allow even desperate situations to warrant calls for assistance. An eighth-grade education limits her job opportunities and income. With no money forthcoming from Russell, Mom struggles to keep us clothed and fed. Rural towns offer cheaper rent, but job opportunities generally consist of menial work or hard physical labor for low pay. To her credit, my mother takes what she can get to keep us fed, mostly production factory work. Minimum wage fails to provide decent housing or properly feed me and my brother and sisters. Many of my schoolmates are poor, but we represented the poorest of the poor. Wearing brand-name clothing was never an option. Most days, the main concern was getting enough to eat that day.

Because I am hungry much of the time, school lunch is the highlight of my day. My siblings and I always qualify for free lunches. Although no one is wealthy, it doesn't appear that many of my fellow students are on the free-lunch program; most pay something as they go through the lunch line. To their credit, however, none of my classmates make a big deal about it. When any of my peers ask me about something that I feel is a touchy subject, I simply offer them a stony stare in response. The strategy works because often the person asking the question, when faced with a blank firm glare, will simply change the subject. This technique honed my ability to safeguard my secrets.

Ms. Ison, my seventh-grade science teacher, becomes one of my favorite instructors. Her popularity extends to most students. Young and pretty, she relocated from a large metropolitan area to our small town the year before. I love science. Her firm but kind demeanor offers a model for instruction, safety, and approval in one package. Single, she lives alone. I dream of duplicating her success—attaining my independence. My constant, overriding goal to enter adulthood, move far from home, and become self-sufficient focuses my attention and fuels my ambition. Even in grade school, I know I can care for myself better than either of my parents.

One day, Ms. Ison surprises me. "It is such a joy to teach you, Carly."

I think she is just being nice to me because she is nice to all the kids. But it does make me feel good inside.

"I really love science," I respond.

"You are so smart that, who knows, maybe one day you will be the one to discover how to choose the sex of your baby." (In 1979, such talk was usually considered science fiction.)

Wow! I might be an important scientist someday! I smile to myself. Ms. Ison thinks I am smart. Totally good enough for me. School is truly my sole oasis. Surrounded by a sea of chaos, fear, and pain at home, the classroom offers me hope and allows me to dream of a better life as an adult.

I never told anyone about the terrible things that happened in our house. I even kept Ms. Ison's interest and support a secret from Mom. I didn't want Mom to criticize Ms. Ison. This deposit into my self-worth account was tender and fragile, and I wanted to protect it. Deep inside, I was afraid Mom would convince me that Ms. Ison was just being polite, that she didn't really care about me or think I was smart. I couldn't let that happen, so I did what I did best. I went silent.

This self-imposed secrecy and isolation formed a powerful foundation for future abusers, ensuring that perpetrators in my adult life could isolate me emotionally.

The emotional template was set for future compliant victimization.

Once an abuser establishes control, the victim commonly complies with the abuser's demands—to avoid additional wrath or as an attempt to protect others from the abuser's anger. In other words, the victim unknowingly has given all their power to the abuser.

The message embedded in my mother's lack of encouragement and support was that isolation was a way to protect myself. Keeping my mouth shut, and thus maintaining my isolation, was a childhood survival skill that would make me an easy target for any abuser as an adult. Perpetrators simply had to criticize me, shame me, or make me feel guilty or wrong, and I would automatically move into compliance mode. I had honed the art of being the ultimate peacemaker.

Rather than focusing on the negative attack, I locked in on the abuser's perceived goal in an attempt to end the violence.

And the easiest path to reduce the abuser's anger was to agree with him. If he said it was my fault, then I would agree it was my fault. This was the easiest and quickest path to deescalate the situation. It didn't matter if I really thought this or not. The main goal was to get the abuser calmed down and then and only then would I stand a better chance of not getting physically hurt.

Rules, right versus wrong, and injustices were not part of the equation because the abuser always held all the power. Maintaining a stony silence in the face of unjustified criticism was standard operating procedure. My desire to stop the negative attack was stronger than my desire to defend myself or to receive support.

I would "go along" to "get along safely." My choices I knew were to either agree or voice my opinion. It was less painful to just agree.

Another survival skill that had firmly taken hold in my psyche was the development of a controlling and dominating demeanor. While I had no power at home, the example of a powerful enforcer was modeled for me in Russell. I echoed this "enforcing" behavior with my classmates by glaring at them when a touchy subject surfaced. I had learned how to control and dominate simply with my unnerving glare. Although I am not proud that I adopted this role, in therapy as an adult, I realized I used this survival skill to help me cope with my deep shame. As a young child, however, this controlling behavior was operating on an unconscious level. At that tender age, this dangerous coping skill protected me from further damage in my safe place—school.

Even at this early age, I believed that I knew best how to take care of myself. Ms. Ison served as my icon. It would take many years for me to question and wonder if I could relinquish my self-protective habits to achieve my life's dreams.

In the meantime, Ms. Ison's compliments were as precious as gold to me—a real treasure. No matter what happened in the future, I knew that someone important had seen value in me. Many teachers granted these emotional gifts during my middle- and high-school years.

It seems a cruel irony that the very skills that I used as a child to survive would later cultivate the chaos in my adult life that I was so desperate to avoid.

5. Toxic Memories

Time has passed, and I am now thirteen years old. Terri, my oldest sister, who is now twenty years old, has moved out to get married. Both Terri and Lily have daughters of their own. Ernie, my only brother, is now seventeen. He spends most of his time at a friend's house and rarely comes home. He does have a bedroom with some of his stuff here, but he rarely spends the night with us. Ernie is drinking heavily and taking drugs. Looking back, I suspect the alcohol and drugs were his escape.

So for the most of time it is Mom, Robin, and I in our little house that is heated by a wood-burning stove. We do not have air-conditioning either, but the rent is cheap, and there are now fewer mouths to feed, so money isn't as tight. Russell's visits are farther apart, and he seems to stay with us for shorter periods of time. Because of this, a sense of calmness has settled into our lives.

It is summer, and school is out. I have completed the seventh grade and will be going into the eighth grade in the fall. Robin will be a junior in high school, and Ernie will be a senior. It started out a usual hot summer day. Robin and I are home alone while Mom is over at her friend Faye's house.

It has just stopped raining and after being trapped inside all day I want to go out and play. Robin is reading a book and doesn't want to come outside.

I am entertaining myself in the front yard by doing flips when Ernie drives up and pulls into the single-lane driveway.

"Hey, Carly! What's you up to?" he yells.

"Nothing. Where have you been? Are you going to stay awhile?"

"Oh, I don't know. Just wanted to come by and say hello and show you guys the new car I just bought. Go get Mom and Robin." It isn't a new car, but it is a new-to-Ernie purchase.

"Mom is over at Faye's house, and Robin is inside reading," I tell him. I walk over to take a closer look at his car. "Cool car. How do you have the money to buy that?"

"'Cause I am an adult, not a kid like you."

"Ha-ha. So funny," I blurt back at him.

"Ah, I am just kidding. Now don't be mad at me," he replies.

I shrug my shoulders and decide to continue practicing my flips. As I walk back to my shady spot under the maple tree in the front yard, out of the blue, Russell pulls into the driveway. He parks directly behind Ernie's car.

Russell has been gone for several months, and this is the first time he has been at our house on Maple Road. I wonder how he knew how to find us.

"Hey, Weed, how are you doing?" Russell calls me Weed because he says I grow so fast, just like a weed. I always try to avoid speaking directly to Russell. I just shrug my shoulders, as if to say okay.

"Is your Mom home?"

Ernie chimes in. "No, Mom isn't here."

"Where is she?"

"I think she is over at Faye's house," Ernie tells him.

"Where is she, Carly?"

"Faye's."

Satisfied with our answers, Russell turns to Ernie and says, "I see you got yourself a new set of wheels there, son. What kind of engine do you have in that?"

"Let me show you," Ernie says as he pops the hood. Russell and Ernie lean over the engine and begin talking about motors and horsepower while I continue perfecting my flips.

I notice a white car pass our house for a second time. Maple Road is not a high-traffic road, and the same car passing our house twice within a five-minute span is not something that would go unnoticed. The white car slows down to a snail's pace as it makes the second pass. I look at the driver; he is an older man with a head full of white hair, and I do not recognize him. His gaze is fixed on Russell, and his eyes glare with bitterness in Russell's direction.

My heart begins to race!

I look over at Ernie and Russell—they both noticed the car as well. Russell especially has a fierce and angry look on his face. Russell's body is now rigid, and his face is flushed bloodred.

A cold shiver goes down my spine as panic and fear flood my body.

Russell wipes his hands on a handkerchief he's taken from his back pocket. His movements seem deliberate, as if he is preparing himself for what is to come. He starts walking to the end of our driveway, never taking his eyes from the man in the white car as the car just barely inches down the road in front of our house. They seem to be locked together in their own dance—neither willing to break the stare.

Russell's footsteps pick up speed as he gets closer to the end of our driveway and the edge of the street. The white car and its driver have slowly moved beyond our driveway by roughly twenty yards.

Russell's back is to me. His shoulders are stiff and tense—but I manage to relax a little. The white car is now past our house. Surely the white car has left for good. It will be all right—nothing bad can happen now, I tell myself.

But I am wrong. The white car isn't leaving, but instead the driver turns his car around in a neighbor's driveway. He is now headed toward our house again.

I inch up close to the maple tree. I try to hide.

"No good can come of this," I think to myself. The white car ever so slowly approaches our house again.

As it passes our driveway for the third time, Russell is standing at the end of our driveway, right beside the rear of his car. The driver swerves his car into our driveway, toward Russell, who jumps free. The driver rams the rear passenger side of Russell's parked car, where Russell had been standing only moments before.

Oh my God. He has hit Russell's car. This won't be good. My thoughts swirl through my mind as I watch the crisis unfold. Although the white car is moving at a slow speed, the impact is very loud. I can still hear the sound as it vibrates in my ears.

It is as if time is moving through thick syrup. Each moment lingers, and I seem suspended in a dark tension that has me riveted to the spot.

I am thirteen years old, and even at that tender age, I have seen much more than I should have. Even so, none of it has prepared me for what happens next.

After hitting Russell's car, the driver swerves back onto the road, trying to straighten out his car and keep going. I think he knows that hitting that car was a huge mistake. He is desperately trying to get away as fast as he can. Russell takes off on foot in pursuit of the white car. Like a madman, he runs through the front yard. As he passes me, he stops and, with a crazed look in his eye, screams at me, "Get my gun from under my front seat." I can't move; I am frozen with fear!

Now with a deadly stare and in an eerily calm voice, Russell says slowly, carefully, and deliberately, "Carly, go get my gun, or I will kill your mom and sisters."

His eyes are like piercing daggers, and I can feel his rage and hatred. But fear has me frozen. I simply can't speak or move.

It's as though I am watching a movie with me in it. My feet will not budge.

Russell must sense my shock, and he pushes me aside as he runs toward his car to retrieve his gun. I stumble but am able to regain my balance. I remain riveted to my spot, still frozen with fear.

Right past our house, there is a curve in the road and a slight drop off in the curve into a low ditch. After hitting Russell's car, the driver has swerved back and forth across the lanes, and as he got closer to the curve, his wheels dropped off the pavement, and his car went into the curve and then slid into the low ditch.

Russell is now standing at the top of the embankment, above where the white car has gone into the ditch, a loaded .357 in his hand.

The driver is desperate to free his car from the ditch. He presses the gas, but his wheels just keep spinning as the car's motor races. The car is stuck in the wet grass. He can't get his car out of the ditch. There is no way to escape from Russell.

Russell, realizing the white car is stuck, smiles menacingly. You can smell the fear in the air, and it's not just my fear now.

Calm and purposeful, Russell climbs down the embankment and stands beside the driver's door.

I hear the driver yell out and beg Russell, "Please don't kill me! Please don't kill me!"

I think I have to do something. I run toward the white car. I want to plead with Russell not to shoot this man.

Russell stares at the white-headed man and raises his right arm. He points the gun directly at the driver.

And then—the first shot. *Boom.*

I stop, completely still and silent—watching Russell. That is when I hear a second boom. I begin to scream, squeezing my eyes shut, dropping to the ground, and curling into the smallest fetal position I can—I put my hands over my ears. *Boom.*

I continue to scream at the top of my lungs to drown out the gunshots.

I never hear the fourth, fifth or sixth shots—only the screams—my screams.

Finally, nothing but silence.

I look up. Russell is walking toward me—the gun is swinging from his right hand. The driver's front seat is covered in blood. I don't see the white-haired driver, but blood spatter is everywhere. Blood is on the steering wheel, the driver's seat headrest, the interior roof of the car; it's just everywhere. I find out later that the driver's body was slumped over onto the passenger's side of the car.

Russell walks up to me on the road where I am standing. He stares at me.

I do not cry. I do not move. I do not speak.

He says calmly, "You needed to see that. Another lazy stupid idiot is in hell. All worthless people need to go to hell, and now one more is there."

I wonder if Russell is going to kill me. Then I look away because I don't want to look at the gun that Russell will use to kill me.

Then I think, "This can't be real." I must be having another nightmare. I wonder if my screaming will wake Mom up. I know from past experience that if you wake her up she gets mad. But ending this nightmare would be worth having Mom mad at me.

I wonder what I can do to wake myself up.

But this is no nightmare. No. This is real.

Russell gives me instructions. "The neighbors will call the police, and they will be here soon. Carly, don't talk to the police when they get here."

I can't speak. I just look at the monster, Russell.

"I don't want you to talk to the police after they take me away either. If you talk with the police, I will know, and I will come and kill you and your mother and your sisters. It will be just like what you saw me do to that no-good, worthless man today. Do you understand what I am saying to you?"

I stand in silence.

"Now you don't want me to have to kill your mother, do you, Carly?"

I shake my head no, too afraid to speak for fear I might start crying. And afraid if I cry, Russell will kill me right then and there.

Russell accepts my headshake as confirmation. He gives me more instructions. "Have your mother bring you to the jail to see me. And just remember you are not to talk to the police or anyone about any of this. I am going to go around the back of the house and bury the gun. It will make my case easier if they can't find the weapon."

Russell tells Ernie to leave the house and not tell anyone he was here. Ernie complies and gets in his car and leaves.

I don't understand any of this, but it seems really important to Russell that the police not find the murder weapon and that no one talks to the police.

Later, after the trial, I will discover that Russell told the police he had thrown the gun in the pond across the street from our house. I will learn many, many years later why Russell is telling these lies. But at the time, I have no way of understanding why he is setting the scene for the police.

Ernie is gone. Only Robin and I are at the house with Russell. When the police arrive, they immediately arrest Russell. Surprisingly, he offers no resistance.

The police ask me to come over to their car, but I shake my head and refuse to speak—I am not about to speak to the police. I won't even walk off the front porch.

Mom, who is still at Faye's house, hears over the police scanner there has been a shooting on Maple Road. She comes racing home. It is about twenty minutes after the shooting, and Russell has already been taken away by a police car. However, there is a second police car still at the house, and the officer is trying to talk to Robin and me. But I am more afraid of Russell than I am of the police. Russell is the all-powerful one, and I am not going to disobey him by talking to the police. I am not going to be shot, and I am not going to be the reason Russell hurts my mom either.

When Mom arrives at the scene, she sees the police are trying unsuccessfully to question me. But Mom instantly steps in and protects me. "No, you cannot talk to my daughter," she says. Mom turns to me. "Go into the house right now."

I am grateful to be able to leave. I turn and go into the house, and I don't come back outside.

The police finally leave, and Mom comes inside. She never asks me what happened. Although it seems incredible to me now, we never talk about it—not that night or any other night.

Ernie does not return home that night. I am left to sort out my thoughts and feelings about what happened that day on my own.

About a week later, there is a knock on the front door. When Mom opens the door, there are two men in suits waiting on the front stoop.

Hiding in my bedroom, I hear one of the men say, "We haven't been able to locate the gun, and we need to talk to your daughters."

"You cannot talk with either of my daughters," my mom tells the man with finality.

They leave without any further comment. I am terrified that they will come back and make me tell them what happened.

After the murder, Mom forces me to visit Russell in jail. I hate going to see him. Why do I have to go see him? Why does she make me go? These thoughts are never spoken out loud. But Mom repeatedly would say, "You have to love and honor him. It says in the Bible to love and honor your mother and father."

That doesn't make sense to me. Russell has never honored me or my siblings or my mother. Why should I have to honor him? I have never loved Russell, and I certainly don't want to honor him. How can you honor a cold-blooded killer?

At the time, I don't know why Russell insists that I visit him in his jail cell. However, Robin is not required to visit him—only me. I will not learn the truth regarding his motives until nearly thirty years later.

As a thirteen-year-old, being forced to visit Russell in jail after witnessing him murder someone who was unarmed terrifies me. Again, this reinforces to me that Russell is all powerful and can control things, even from his jail cell.

When I do visit Russell, he coaches me on what to say when I am required to testify at his trail. He insists I practice "telling" the jury what a great dad he is and how much I miss him when he is gone.

We repeat the questions and the answers, over and over. Russell wants to make sure that I keep my answers straight. The most important thing I have to say is that I did not see the murder but was inside the house when it happened. This is, of course, a complete lie, but Russell tells me that if I tell the lawyer that I witnessed the murder that I will go to jail—just like him. He tells me that I will go to prison for the rest of my life, and I will die there.

I tell Russell that I wasn't inside the house, that I was outside, and I saw him shoot the man driving the white car. He realizes the threat of jail for me might not be enough to convince me to lie. So he ups the ante, telling me that when he gets out of jail, he will kill my mom and Robin. As usual, this threat works for him, and I fold—and repeat the lie back to Russell: "I was in the house."

During these jailhouse visits with Russell, he always makes fun of the people who are at the jail and the doctors he is required to talk with. He thinks they are all stupid.

Russell brags to me how he can make them think he is crazy when really he isn't. None of this makes any sense to me.

Secretly, I think both of my parents are crazy. Russell is crazy, I think, but I just keep my mouth shut and only say what he wants me to say. I don't want him to get out of jail and hurt me, Mom, or Robin.

When the police arrive after the shooting, Russell willingly admits to killing the man in the white car. He does not try to run away. Quite the contrary, he is calm and collected. He boldly and calmly waits for the police to arrive at the house and arrest him. As a thirteen-year-old, I cannot understand how he can be so calm—but some thirty years later, his "strategy" has become all too clear. For the next year, my fear of Russell intensifies. I see him in jail on a regular basis due to my forced visits, which are enforced by Mom. It is worse seeing him after the murder. It is like I know for sure now what he is truly capable of doing. Now more than ever, I know I do not want anything in my life associated with Russell.

Russell's constant intimidation during these jail visits was wearing on me. I had nightmares about him after each visit, but no amount of persuasion or begging on my part would convince Mom to let me out of those visits. Again, this was reinforcement for the negative value that I placed on myself; my wants, needs, or fears simply did not matter. My voice was never heard—it didn't count. This was my reality, and for me, this was "normal." When I grew up, this erroneous belief had a huge effect on my own adult relationships. It would take a long time for me to abandon my well-developed belief that my needs were not important.

When Russell was arrested, he told the police his name was "Leroy Lee," which of course was not the name he used. His full name was Russell Leroy Lee. Russell had told me during a jail visit that he had given his name as Leroy Lee to help protect his kids. He said that people knew him as Russell, and that by giving the name Leroy, it would be less likely that people would connect him to his family.

I was deeply ashamed of Russell and wanted nothing more than to be disassociated from him. But this made no sense to me.

Looking back, I believe that Russell was concocting his story even then. Russell thought the name Leroy Lee would limit the number of people who would make the connection that he had committed the murder. I believe he thought he could control everything about this investigation and that it would only be a matter of time until he was a free man again.

Russell wanted people to see him in a positive light. He always wanted people to think of him as this great guy who went away to work for his family. He missed the obvious connection that he never brought back any money. Russell was unaware that what a person says often conveys his character to others in ways the speakers are completely unaware of. He believed that he was in control of how others perceived him. But just like all the times before, I never said anything to challenge Russell's reasoning or his version of his story. I don't know if Russell thought up this reason while he sat in jail, but I felt sure he had a different reason for giving the name Leroy besides trying to offer his family protection from public opinion.

Russell was always twisting the facts around or creating an alternative version of a story to make things match his preferred version. An example of this is him saying, "I didn't hit your mother; her bruises are from her falling." To me, this was just another word-twisting game from Russell. However, I did wonder why he gave his name as Leroy. I had never known him to use the name Leroy before.

Because he was so intimidating, people did not speak their minds around him.

His defense-trial strategy was to claim insanity as a defense. He knew firsthand how pleading insanity could help him. I would later learn he had gotten off once before using the insanity plea.

I didn't know it at the time, but the prosecutor was just as determined that Russell would be ruled "competent" to stand trial. The prosecutor went through four psychologists before he found one who would testify against Russell. This fourth psychologist would testify that Russell was "sane" and completely lucid at the time of the murder. While the first three psychologists came to the conclusion that Russell had suffered from temporary insanity during the shooting, the fourth psychologist would file a report indicating that, in his professional opinion, Russell was quite capable of knowing right from wrong and was only trying to fool the system to avoid punishment.

Today I shudder to think what would have happened to me without this fourth psychologist.

Living with Russell and being subjected to his intimidation, conditioned me to cower in the face of a violent, threatening man—even once I became an adult. I would become frozen with fear. Once that happened, I was often willing to do whatever the perpetrator wanted me to do. These feelings of fear arose even when I didn't expect them to. These fear feelings were a very real part of the fabric of who I was. The only way I knew to deal when I was feeling fearful was to try to comply with the bully so the situation would hopefully calm down.

Some professionals have explained this as learned helplessness. For me, I just didn't expect anyone to believe me or to help me. Because I believed that no one would help me (not even my own mother), I stopped asking for help. I never judged anyone for not helping me; I simply accepted the fact that no one would ever be interested in helping the likes of me. *Just as the sky is blue, people will not help you.* I had witnessed enough violence that I had become submissive to my feelings of fear. When I felt fear, I would become compliant.

I learned to survive situations by myself. My own mother knew that Russell had murdered this unarmed man, and yet she was still telling me that I had to love and honor him. She was forcing me to go visit him in the jail. I could not understand why my mother would make me visit him. She had betrayed me. She should never have made me visit Russell. It was as though my feelings were not important—not even worth discussing. I did not yet understand that my life experiences, while I had only lived thirteen years, had already had a profound effect on me.

I was unable to speak of this day until seventeen years later in therapy. I had no skills in setting boundaries and absolutely no understanding about what was acceptable behavior toward me. This lack of emotional understanding and development would seriously impair my ability to recognize and avoid the same patterns in my adult life.

My emotional template that was being developed and reinforced would make it easy for me to be lured in by a bully's sweet façade, only to be torn down with hurtful words and actions when the bully would get angry. But through my adult pain, I would finally be motivated to find another path. The journey would be long and winding, but I would eventually find a healthier emotional path to walk.

6. Mom's New Boyfriend

Multiple drags of the pond by the police never uncover the gun.

I know the gun is not in the pond across the street, but I am not going to speak to the police. Russell's concern over the police finding the firearm causes me to worry about its whereabouts. I know that Russell will be furious if the gun is found. Fear of his anger is the most powerful motivator in my life. To me, his threats have life-or-death consequences.

I ask Ernie, "Do you know where the gun is exactly?"

"You don't need to know. The less you know, the better off you will be. In case the police try to make you answer their questions, it will be better if you don't know exactly where the gun is."

"Will they ever find it?"

"Didn't I just tell you, don't ask any more questions? You don't need to know nothing about any of that," he says.

I never speak of the gun again.

So Russell is now locked away in the local jail. I hate the visits Mom forces me to endure during his localized incarceration while he awaits trial. However, with him being behind bars, the days I don't have to visit him are days when my life did improve. There is tremendous emotional relief because Russell can no longer drop in unexpectedly and rain violence down on us in our home.

My life settles into a new rhythm.

Several weeks after the murder, it feels less likely Russell is going to get out. A couple of months after his arrest, Mom stops going to church. That means that Robin and I don't have to go either. Mom begins hanging out more often with her girlfriend Faye. The two of them start going to the local VFW (Veterans of Foreign Wars) club. The county we live in is dry, so there are no bars or any other place that sells alcohol. The only two clubs are the VFW and the local country club. And the closest we ever get to the country club is driving past it on the road.

When Mom is out during the evening and into the night with her girlfriend, I don't feel scared being home alone with Robin. Robin and I are accustomed to spending a lot of time home alone. Now that there's no threat of Russell dropping in, home life really isn't scary at all. In fact, being alone most of the time is a welcome change from the chaos of when Russell was drifting in and out of the house. The constant state of hyperawareness, waiting for Russell to walk through the door, is over. And it feels like a huge boulder has been lifted from my shoulders.

Ernie continues to stay at his friend's house more often than not. We rarely see him.

As the weeks go by, Mom begins staying out more and more often. I don't mind; she seems happier. I feel better, too, knowing she is finally enjoying herself and having some fun in her life.

In early spring, not quite a year after Russell murdered the white-haired man, my forced visits to Russell at the local jail stop. Mom does not explain why I no longer have to go visit him, and I certainly don't argue with this welcome turn of events. Any questioning would be frowned upon and likely would not have brought any clarity to the situation anyway. Mom as always, is secretive. In this instance, I don't care why. I am elated that I will not have to see Russell each week. However, some hardships remain. We still do not have much food to eat, and the house is cold in winter, but overall life is better than it has ever been.

Spring turns into early summer, and my grade-school days are rapidly coming to an end. As my eighth-grade graduation approaches, I am thankful I don't have to worry about Russell showing up. He is still in jail awaiting trial for the murder. In contrast, I worry about Mom *not* showing up to the celebration.

Mom does not involve herself in my school life. She never attends a single game or practice of the girl's grade-school basketball team for which I play. One of my best friends, Gloria, plays on the team as well. Gloria's parents always make sure I have a way to and from the gym. On game nights, I just spend the night with Gloria. It is simpler that way.

Mom's lack of attendance at my games doesn't embarrass me, but her not attending my grade-school graduation would be humiliating. I don't want my friends to know that even my own mom doesn't think enough of me to go to my gradation.

But I am worrying for nothing. Incredibly, in the same week, Mom attends both Ernie's high-school and my grade-school graduation ceremonies.

I win the eighth-grade science award. I received a small pin with the word *Science* on it. Ms. Ison presents the award to me. I am thrilled!

Gently pinning the award on me, she softly says, "I will miss you, Carly."

I look into her kind and gentle face and feel a sharp pain sear through my heart. Against my will, a tear slowly creeps down my face. I don't cry often, but this pain is real. It is different from the anguish of my home life. I am going to miss the nurturing kindness of my science teacher. I fear I will never meet another person who will believe in me like Ms. Ison does.

Ms. Ison made a critical deposit into my self-worth bank account. Someone I respect and admire thinks *I* am important and enjoys being around me.

With eighth-grade graduation in my rearview mirror, my excitement about beginning high school in the fall gains momentum. I absolutely cannot wait to be an adult. It simply cannot come fast enough for me. I am definitely not going live in chaos. That is my promise to myself.

Robin and I have not yet met any of Mom's boyfriends. Mom never talks about any men and never brings anyone home.

During the summer of 1980, the first housing project in the county opens.

Mom applies, and we are selected to get a two-bedroom apartment. The move both excites and concerns me. The thought of heat in the winter and air conditioning in the summer excites me. However, the possibility of others discovering I live in the housing project causes anxiety. I don't know which is worse: living anonymously in a run-down house with no heat or living more comfortably, albeit publicly, in the housing project. But Mom has made her choice, and late in the summer of 1980, Mom, Robin, and I move into a two-bedroom apartment in the housing project.

Although I am less than thrilled about living in the housing project, I try to remain positive about the move, reminding myself that living near town presents some perks. With our apartment located at the end of Main Street, we will be able to walk to the drugstore and grocery store if needed.

Robin and I share the larger bedroom, and Mom takes the smaller bedroom. Shortly thereafter, Mom asks Robin and me to meet her new boyfriend, Adrian, who lives in an adjoining county.

So on a Friday night, Mom drives the three of us to Pizza Hut in an adjacent town, where we meet Adrian for the first time.

It is a memorable night as we enjoy the rare luxury of eating out. And Adrian seems nice enough—nothing special just ordinary and normal.

Heat will fill our home this winter without having to chop wood or carry coal. No more bathing from a pot of water heated on the stove. Only four years of high school remain before I can leave this town and start my own life as an adult. Things are definitely looking up.

Mom left Russell many times before but always went back to him. This time, however, feels different. She now has Adrian, and Mom has never gotten another boyfriend in all the previous times she left Russell. I am hopeful she will not take Russell back, as he is still sitting awaiting trial for murder. "No," I think. Russell is finally, blissfully, permanently out of our lives.

From my fourteen-year-old perspective, I had witnessed Russell emotionally and physically abuse the entire family. He had never been held accountable for his behavior. Russell had never held a steady job and failed to financially provide for his family. Russell only took from us. Returning from his frequent absences, he would eat what meager food was present in the house. Believing that, at last, Mom would never go back to him was a great feeling.

I never really thought of Adrian as being in my life because Adrian didn't want any young kids. He was interested in Mom, not her kids. I didn't mind if he wasn't interested in me or Robin. I just wanted him to be nice to my mom. Being ignored felt normal to me, and it didn't matter anyway, as Robin and I had each other. That's the way I felt. So I was thankful that Mom had her new boyfriend. His presence gave me some security because it cemented the thought that Russell might at last be permanently out of my life—forever.

Many years would pass before I began to question my ability to know how to have the life of my dreams. As Phillip McGraw states in his book *Self Matters*, "You can't change what you don't acknowledge."

I was unaware of the Family of Origin Work therapy work that would be required to expose my denied and suppressed feelings and patterns of behavior. At this time in my life, I was unaware of my need to release the emotional trauma I had sealed deep inside myself. My current faulty thinking had me thinking that ignoring or silencing the trauma of past, intensely painful emotional experiences would eliminate any impact they might have on me as an adult. At this point in my life, I just believed I needed to grow up so I could make my own decision and choices.

I would learn nothing could be farther from the truth. True healing would mean honoring the feelings attached to those painful experiences. Acting like it never happened was not a way to heal from past hurts.

In the meantime, like a real treasure, Ms. Ison's compliments and attention provided a small gold nugget for me to hang onto. Experiencing her authentic and consistent kindness meant far more to me than the public recognition of winning the science award at my eighth-grade graduation.

Just as I was not aware of the self-imposed isolation that I was perfecting as a child, I was also not aware of the incredible gifts all these teachers were giving me. Their encouragement and belief in me is what I think gave me the strength as an adult to challenge my ingrained childhood survival skills.

The very skills that I used as a child to survive my childhood—don't ask for anything, settle for what you get, don't expect help (emotional, physical, financial or otherwise), and above all else, don't let anyone know if bad things happen to you—would create the very chaos that I so adamantly wanted to avoid in my adult life.

It would take many adult years and a lot of therapy to learn to care for myself well, which for me would include developing skills to find a safe and calm physical environment, communicate my needs in intimate relationships, recognize trustworthy people, be able to open up to trustworthy people, and recognize red flags in other people.

SECTION II

7. Changes

Mom, Robin, and I leave the pizza place. On the way home, Mom asks, "So what did you girls think of Adrian?"

"He's okay," I say.

Mom rarely smiles this much. It feels good to see her so happy. If Adrian makes Mom happy, then he is okay with me.

We have finally escaped Russell's tyranny. Russell has been jailed about fourteen months, and I feel he is finally gone from my life for good. To say that I am ecstatic would be an understatement. I don't believe that Mom would introduce Robin and me to someone she is dating unless there is no hope of Russell returning.

Although Russell is safely locked away awaiting trial, sometimes worry floats into my thoughts. Fear hauntingly reminds me that Russell might get out after the trial. I work hard to keep these thoughts at bay. For now, at least until after the trial, I hold onto the fact that I am outside of Russell's control, and I don't have to visit him anymore. At least while he is in jail. I cling to that safety net. Surely they will never let him out on the street again. For the first time in my life, there is no fear that Russell will show up on the doorstep. I feel free. I am able to relax, to plan a day, to live a peaceful life.

The Trial

Like all chaotic events, we do not discuss the upcoming trial at home. I never mention it. My siblings never mention it. My mother never broaches the subject. The family's strict code of silence remains firmly in place. Russell's incarceration has dramatically reduced any imminent threat of violence, yet we still protect our fear and shame with a heavy cloak of silence. The taboo subject of Russell's legal problems is never to be discussed openly.

Many aspects of life are now better than I can remember them ever being. Mom has secured a steady job at the new sewing factory in town. Her regular paychecks finally provide us with a dependable car and gas money.

Money is not plentiful, but we are no longer cold, hungry, or malnourished. The threat of regular eviction and hurried moves in the middle of the night subside. New clothes or a house phone remain out of reach, but Mom does manage to buy a television set. A wire coat hanger bent into an elliptical shape serves as the antenna. This "fix" provides us with enough reception for a couple of local channels. For the first time in my memory, the electric bill is kept current, and the lights stay on. At last we are warm, dry, fed regularly, and the electricity works. Our new city apartment is in the projects, but for the first time in my life, I have stability and consistency.

I remain embarrassed about living in the projects and do what I can to keep this fact hidden from my friends. I have deep shame about my family's poverty. Living in remote rural areas has kept that embarrassment at arm's length in the past. While this apartment is a safe haven, it also feels confining. I am not used to city living and the enclosure of the walls. My shame is stronger than my desire to go outside, so I stay inside the apartment. Afraid of being "discovered" living in the projects by one of my school friends, my shame and silence keep me locked behind the apartment front door.

Outings are limited to quick walks to the car. Occasionally, when feeling particularly restless, Robin and I will walk across the street to a small fairly secluded public park.

As the weeks roll by, Mom begins to spend more and more time at Adrian's house. Before long, she spends more time at Adrian's than at the apartment, and it might be two or three weeks between her visits to see Robin and me. Her time at home turns from living with us to only occasional visits.

Adrian lives on an eighty-acre farm. I think Mom being in the country is good for her, and it seems to make her happy. I do want her to be happy—she has been miserable for so long with Russell. I really don't even miss her being gone. In the past, when Russell was around, even though she was physically present in the same house with me, she ignored me. So now, her extended disappearances don't change things much for me.

Robin and I watch our two channels of TV, play backgammon, and read. I am counting the days until I am an adult and can escape this town. I dream of living in a big city and having lots of things to do and lots of opportunities.

It is now late August, and school is getting ready to start. I am anxious as I will be starting high school. Mom still living at Adrian's and Robin and I plan to catch the bus on the first day of school on our own. We walk to the entrance of the housing project to wait for the bus. It is a hot August day, and neither of us is sure if we are at the right pickup location for the bus. Nor do we know what time the bus is supposed to pick us up. I am relieved there are no other kids waiting for the bus. I don't know how long we wait, but we finally decide that the bus is not going to come. It is already time for the homeroom bell to ring, and the realization we are going to miss the first day of school settles on us.

Walking back to our apartment, I ask Robin, "What should we do now?"

"I don't know. We need to call the school, but we can't since we don't have a phone."

In 1980, cell phones are years away from full development and mainstream distribution.

The building next to ours houses one-bedroom apartments, occupied mostly by elderly residents. I have an idea. "Why don't we go knock on one of their doors and ask to use their phone?"

"No, they won't let us use their phone. They don't even know us," Robin says.

Knowing that we need to get to school the next day, I decide to seek out a phone by myself. Gathering as much fourteen-year-old confidence as I can muster, I walk over to the next building as Robin heads back to our apartment building. I knock on the door of the first apartment I come to. The TV plays inside, but no one answers my knock. It becomes apparent no one will appear. Determined not to miss another day of school, I refuse to let this rejection deter me from my mission of finding a phone.

I took a deep breath. "You can do this, Carly," I assure myself as I step to the next apartment and knock again on the front door. An elderly lady in a tattered blue nightgown opens the door.

"What do you want?"

I hesitantly respond, "My name is Carly. My sister and I live in the building next door. We don't have a home phone, and I need to call the school and ask why the school bus did not come and pick us up this morning."

"Why on earth have you waited until the first day of school to find out about the school bus?"

I choke back my tears and with a slight tremble in my voice, I reply, "I thought the school had already set it up. I didn't know that we had to do it."

Her wrinkled face relaxes as she replies, "The phone is on the wall over there. I'm Ms. Kerns."

As I walk toward the phone, I reply, "Thank you, Ms. Kerns."

She sits down in her rocking chair, picks up the phone book, and looks for the school's contact information. I dial as she calls the numbers out.

A secretary answers. "Hello! County High School."

Trying to sound very grown up, I say with as much authority as I can muster, "My sister and I live at the new housing project at the end of Main Street, and the bus did not come this morning to pick us up for school."

"I don't handle the bus route. You need to call the bus compound," the secretary barks back to me.

"But who should I call about the bus compound?"

"The bus compound...call the bus compound."

Not to be put off, I ask, "Do you know the phone number?" I am shaking on the inside, but years of practice mean that little disturbance shows on the outside. I hope and pray she does not recognize my fear. My home life has certainly prepared me for abrupt and inconsiderate people, but in this moment, I am determined to figure out why the bus did not come this morning.

She barks out the seven-digit phone number and then promptly hangs up.

Turning to Ms. Kerns, I ask, "Can I make another call to the bus compound?"

"Of course you can, young lady."

Tears are starting to form in my eyes as I quickly look back at the wall. I can deal with the familiarity of meanness, but kindness exposes my fragility.

I take a deep breath, grip the phone with an unsteady hand, and begin dialing the number of the bus compound. Ms. Kerns, noticing my anxiety, asks me, "Why don't you let me try calling."

"Okay." I gratefully hand her the phone.

"Hello, my name is Ms. Kerns, and Carly, the young girl who just called, is here with me. I am assisting her in trying to determine what time the bus should come to pick her and her sister up for school. Both she and her sister will be attending the high school." I stand still, patiently waiting for Ms. Kerns to finish the conversation.

Ms. Kerns responds, "Very well. I will have Carly come back this afternoon at 12:30 p.m." She hangs up the phone and turns to me.

"The secretary is going to look into it and see what the problem is. You will need to call back this afternoon at 12:30."

Relief floods my body. An adult has listened to me and is offering to help. I am very grateful because I don't want to miss any more school days.

"Thank you, Ms. Kerns."

"Now don't be late this afternoon when it's time to call back."

"I promise I won't be late."

Walking back to our apartment, I wonder why Ms. Kern's behavior suddenly changed from cold to nice. She has never met me before today, but I am not about to look a gift horse in the mouth.

Robin and I miss the first day of school, but I am feeling confident about tomorrow. With Ms. Kern's help, I will solve the bus mystery. As the morning progresses, however, doubts begin to take up residence in my thoughts again. What if the school system won't provide bus rides to the poor kids living in the housing project? There is only one high school in the county, so it couldn't be a jurisdiction issue that kept the bus from picking us up.

At that moment, the four miles to the high school could as easily have been a thousand.

At 12:25 p.m., I return to Ms. Kern's apartment. When I knock on the door, she answers immediately.

I call the school again and am told, "Since the housing project had just opened over the summer, no one had thought to set up the school bus route. They are figuring out the pickups and drop-offs and the driver assignment right now. They should know something by 2:30 p.m. You will need to call back later this afternoon."

I nearly collapse with relief. They are going to let us ride the bus to school!

"Thank you for helping me."

"You are very welcome."

I tell Ms. Kerns the good news. She doesn't respond, just smiles at me.

I turn toward her front door to leave.

Ms. Kerns reminds me, "Don't be too late in coming back this afternoon, Carly."

"Okay, Ms. Kerns."

At 2:25 p.m. I appear for the third time that day at Ms. Kern's door. As before, she opens the door right away.

"Hello, it's me again."

Ms. Kerns smiles and says, "Come in. You know where the phone is." I dial the high school again.

The school secretary answers. "Hello! County High School."

"This is Carly, and I am calling about which bus is going to pick up for the new housing project."

"It will be bus 56 and will be there at 6:45 a.m."

"Thank you."

"You're welcome." Click.

Ms. Kerns looks at me and says in a serious tone, "Make sure you catch that bus tomorrow."

"I will. I won't be late either."

"Now you come down and use the phone again if you have any emergencies in the future."

"Yes, Ms. Kerns." I leave to go back to our apartment.

I am proud of myself. Even the adults in the school system hadn't thought of arranging the bus schedule for the housing project. All the other people living there hadn't called or tried to figure out the bus route. Yes, I am feeling very much like an adult. What a wonderful feeling it is to be in control of your own life.

This just makes me feel even more strongly that I can't wait to be an adult.

On the second day of school, the bus stops promptly at 6:45 a.m. Robin and I are the only kids at the pickup. I again feel a sense of relief that no other children are waiting with us.

My relief is very short-lived.

By the third day of school, there are twenty kids in line for the bus.

Like grade school, I love high school, but I despise the bus ride. I especially dread getting on and off the bus. It seems the other kids on the bus don't want "project kids" riding their bus. The bus ride simply adds another layer to the growing pile of internal shame that is my constant companion.

Other than the school bus ride, life is good. Well, good with the exception of my struggle with the decision to play or not to play on the girl's high-school basketball team. Since Mom has not been involved in my basketball games in grade school, I don't expect her to be involved in any activities during my high-school years. I like being involved with school sports and other activities. It gives me something to do, something to look forward to.

In grade school, my friend's parents provided my transportation for games and practices. They were always so nice to me. Playing on the team, however, would now mean I would have to tell my friends I live in the projects. That is the sticking point for me.

As a fourteen-year-old child, I had no way of knowing that suppressed feeling come out sideways in inappropriate ways. In adulthood, these "shoved-down" feelings manifest as codependent behaviors.

In *Making Miracles in Forty Days*, Melody Beattie wrote, "While denial is a survival tool that can save our lives by buying us time to gather our resources and prepare us to face shocking truths, resistance serves no positive purpose. It isn't a survival tool."

Many years later as an adult, deep reflection helped me realize that each family member dealt with the trauma in his or her own way—alone and in silence. How much better, though, might we have all healed had we had the courage and wisdom to speak frankly about our fears and experiences? But that was simply not the way our family dealt with issues or challenges.

Complete denial of my abandonment as a child provided me with coping mechanisms for survival. I can now recognize my denial as an adult, but as a young child and adolescent, my abandonment was completely beyond my comprehension.

As a young child, I was enjoying the new feelings of relief and calm. I was no longer walking around on eggshells in a constant state of high alert while maintaining a perpetual vigil for any indication of another onslaught of Russell spewing violence upon our family.

Mom was spending all her time at Adrian's house, interrupted only by short stops at home to see how Robin and I were doing. This didn't translate as "abandonment" to me at the time. In contrast, I felt grown up for the first time, proud that I was able to get myself to school and take care of my daily needs. Mom leaves us enough money so we could pay our portion of the subsidized rent and buy groceries. Wasn't that enough?

I learned very early on not to expect much (if any) help from the adults in my family. I was grown up now and didn't need Mom's help. That was my truth. This was my reality.

It would take many years of therapy as an adult to become aware of the deep mass of festering, emotional wounds deep inside me. This untreated, internal trauma would continue to unconsciously affect many of my daily choices as an adult. Of course I was not conscious of this until after many, many bad adult choices.

My developing skill set—shame, having no expectations of others, maintaining silence, trusting only myself, and low self-worth—blossomed spectacularly. Like a master chef, I had gathered all the ingredients to complete the recipe for making the perfect victim. For, you see, the perfect victim is always willingly to stay…to give it one more try.

8. Testifying

I acclimate quickly to high school my freshman year. My closest girl-friend, Gloria, wants to try out for the marching band.

"Come on, Carly. Let's try out for flags."

The flag corps, an auxiliary unit for the high-school band, provide visual accompaniment to the band's musical performance. If we make the team, we will perform with the band during competitions and at home football games. During basketball season, we will perform on the drill team.

"I don't know." Thinking about the cost, I hesitate. I know Mom won't have extra money for something so frivolous.

Gloria continues to persuade me to try out. "Don't worry about practice. My mom will come and pick you up. We'll ride together. Come on! It will be a lot of fun."

Gloria thinks my hesitation stems from worries regarding transportation. But I am too embarrassed to share my other concern—the money I would need for uniforms and all the other things the activity would probably require that I don't even know about yet.

However, Gloria's excitement is infectious, and I finally think, Why not? "Okay, I'm in."

"Yeah. Let's make up our routines this weekend."

Creating and practicing routines keeps us busy every day for two weeks.

Try-out day arrives. Excitement and nervousness makes us fidgety and restless. A collection of freshmen girls stands in small groupings in the high-school gym anxiously waiting their turn to try out.

"When they call us, you go first," Gloria says.

"Sure, I'll go first." I am not shy. Practice has etched the routine in my memory. I am ready. My nervousness stems from other sources— what if I make the team? How will I pay for the uniform?

As names are called, each girl performs individually in front of three judges sitting behind a long white table. Girl after girl steps to the center of the gym floor, waits for the music to start, and then completes her routine.

Gloria and I sit patiently awaiting our turns. Five girls later, a judge calls, "Gloria."

Turning to me with a frightened look, Gloria doesn't move or say a word. I stand, walk to the judges' table, and ask, "Gloria and I are together. May I go first?"

Mr. McGaha, the band director, replies, "Sure, is that your music?"

"Yes." I hand him my music and nearly run out to the center of the gym floor. On cue, I perform the routine I know by heart.

Gloria follows me and completes her routine. In her nervousness, she forgets some of the moves. I feel bad for her but reassure her she did a great job. When the last girl finishes, the judges leave the room.

About twenty minutes later, the judges file back into the room. They silently take their seats at the long table.

Mr. McGaha says, "Now all you girls did a great job, but we only have five spots, and there are twelve girls. So if I call out your name, step forward and get the practice schedule."

Mr. McGaha calls the first name. "Carly."

Wow, I made the team! They chose me. Elation shoots through every appendage in my body. The judges actually chose me. This is going to be so much fun. Maybe it will work out after all. I turn to hug Gloria.

Mr. McGaha calls out the second, third, and fourth names…still no Gloria. Fear begins to cloud my thoughts. Oh no, what if Gloria doesn't make the team? But she has to make the team, I silently beg.

The fifth name is "Sue."

Gloria has not made the team. Awkward silence fills the vehicle on the ride home with Gloria and her mom. I don't know what to say. I feel so bad for both of us. I feel certain I won't stay on the team. It has never occurred to me only one of us might make the team.

How can I stay on the team without Gloria?

From a practical standpoint, how will I get to practices and games? Besides, it is too depressing to think about being on the team without my friend.

The next day at school, between classes, I see one of the flag co-captains, Tina. Immediately recognizing her as one of the judges from the day before at tryouts, I walk up to her and say, "Hi, my name is Carly. I made the flag team yesterday, but I've decided that I'm not going to join after all."

She looks at me curiously. I sense her confusion. "Why do you want to quit before you even start?"

"My friend didn't make the team. And besides, I won't have a way to go to practices or the games without her mom to drive."

Tina's look softens. "Well, you are really good, and you shouldn't quit just because your friend didn't make the team."

"Yeah, but we have been friends since sixth grade."

"Well, if you quit, you will never be captain of anything. The choice is yours."

Hmmm. Her words give me pause. I don't want to sit on the sidelines of life. I ask, "What about not having a way to get to practices and the games? Will I get in trouble if I miss any practices or games?"

"Where do you live?"

"On Main Street."

Technically, I do live on Main Street. The housing project is at the end of Main. It is a convenient coincidence that several nice houses, not connected to the projects, also line Main Street but at the opposite end of the street.

Tina responds, "Well, I live right off Main Street, and I can give you a ride when you need one. We will have the same schedule, so it shouldn't be a problem."

"Are you sure it won't be a problem if I ride with you?"

"Nah, it's no problem. It would be a bigger problem if you decided to quit."

"Thanks a lot. I really appreciate it." Excitement once again creeps through me as I contemplate remaining on the team. But dread slithers in at the thought of sharing my decision with Gloria. I really hope she isn't going to be mad at me.

But as it goes, Gloria is angry when I tell her that I'm going to stay on the flag team. She refuses to speak to me for about a month. She even takes great pains to avoid sitting beside me in our shared classes. I feel sad that Gloria didn't make the team, but I can't understand why she should be mad at me just because I wanted to stay on the team. If the roles had been reversed, I would not have been mad at her. Sure, I would have been disappointed I was not chosen, but I wouldn't have taken that disappointment out on her.

It hurts that she doesn't want to be my friend anymore.

Still…being a part of the flag team is a lot of fun. I savor being a part of the group.

On a practical note, the real problem of money for uniforms has to be addressed. I need money for shoes, uniforms, and other things. A lot of small children reside in the housing project. I think that maybe I can earn some money babysitting.

On Friday nights, I perform with the high-school band at football games, but Saturday nights are reserved for babysitting. My busy life leaves me no room to think about a mother who rarely stops by anymore. Besides, Robin and I are inseparable outside of school and my band commitments.

Ernie enters the navy shortly after graduating high school. His visits home on leave are brief and limited.

Robin and I basically share the apartment as two roommates. Despite the fact that we live alone as two teenagers, completely unsupervised, life is good.

The Subpoenas

Or it is good…until Robin and I are served with subpoenas.

Monday arrives like every other Monday. Mondays means a bus ride home; I practice with the band after school on Tuesdays and Thursdays.

It is Monday evening, around 4:30 p.m. The knock at the door jolts Robin and me as we sit at the small kitchen table, completing our homework. Visitors are nonexistent, so a knock at the door isn't necessarily a welcome sign. Robin and I both sit up straight and look at each other with "deer in the headlights" stares. The sheriff's car is visible through the front window. An officer stands at the front door, visible through the peephole. Each beat of my pounding heart feels like a small explosion in my chest. Robin's fear nearly jumps out of her eyes onto me. Whatever lies on the other side of that door, Robin and I will face it together.

We stand side by side, and then Robin puts her hand on the front door and shakily pulls opens the front door.

A sheriff's deputy in full uniform stands in front of us. He clears his throat and asks, "Are you Robin and Carly Lee?"

Robin responds with a noticeable quiver in her voice. "Yes, sir."

"Is your mother home?"

"No, sir. She is not."

"Well, I have three subpoenas here, one for each of you and one for your brother, Ernie Lee. I understand he is in the navy. Is that correct?"

"Yes, sir."

The deputy hands one subpoena to Robin and another to me.

"Just have your mom call the sheriff's office if she has any questions." The murder trial will begin next week. The time to testify has arrived.

The prospect of seeing Russell again fills my thoughts. I am afraid but have no one with whom to discuss my fears. The fear and worry roam wildly around in my head. My conditioning to remain silent holds firm. The apartment is void of any adults anyway. Robin and I never discuss the subpoenas or impending trial.

The next week is a blur. All I can think of is Monday morning and the trial.

Rarely sick, I maintain an excellent attendance record at school. Sunday night, the night before the trial, however, I become violently ill.

Deployed on a ship, Ernie's commitment to the navy supersedes his obligation to the court. He is excused from testifying at the trial. Robin and I, however, do not fare as well. For us, no paths for avoiding testifying appear.

Months have passed since I last saw Russell. The thought of seeing him again ignites the flame of old fears. As the trial has grown closer, and especially since the subpoenas were served, my fears mount. Some are rational, some not. Fearing that one of my friend's parents would be on the jury tops the list. Of course I have never spoken about the murder to any of my friends at school. However, the event was published in the local paper so surely some of my fellow students and their families know. A murder trial makes for big news in such a small town.

I don't remember the trip to the courthouse Monday morning. I can't even say for sure who took us. I imagine it must have been Mom, as we had never discussed the trial with anyone.

In the weeks and months since the murder, the only discussion of the event took place with Russell during my forced visits to him in jail. Those jailhouse conversations took place nearly a year earlier.

Robin and I walk into the small courthouse. As we approach the courtroom doors, I stiffen my shoulders. I am trying to hide my emotions and appear calm. It is all an act, and I am actually terrified.

Benches, chairs, and lots of dark wood fill the large courtroom. Fifteen or twenty people occupy the seats on the open benches behind the tables for the prosecutor and defense attorney. The judge's bench looms high in the front of the room. Dressed in black robes, with a somber expression, the judge appears to disapprove of the entire proceeding.

The jury box is full of jurors. Shame and humiliation settle over me like a dark cloud when I see my former grade-school basketball coach, Danny Smith, sitting in the jury box. As though I am held in a vice, the embarrassment pulverizes me like an old junkyard car being crushed to nothing. I never look again at Mr. Smith throughout the trial—I can't. Mr. Smith will think I am like Russell—a criminal, a maniac.

I listen to the judge and attorneys talking. I don't understand anything they are saying. Fear and humiliation immobilize me. Russell has several times turned around and looked at me and Robin. I look straight at him but try not to show any emotion. Although I am disgusted to see him, I am still terrified of Russell. I would never openly defy him to his face.

When the court clerk calls my name, my legs amazingly function and carry me to front of the room.

Taking my seat on the witness stand requires passing Russell sitting at the defendant's table. The proximity is so close he could reach out and touch me. Thank God he doesn't. I might faint then and there. My eyes remain firmly focused on the floor in front of me as I pass by him.

Once seated on the witness stand, I feel Russell's eyes boring into me, demanding that I acknowledge him. Fear wins—I have never disobeyed Russell. I begrudgingly turn my head to look in his direction.

He mouths, "I love my baby girl."

I want to scream. "LEAVE ME ALONE! DON'T look at me! DON'T speak to me!"

I have not forgotten what Russell wants me to say. When you fear someone as much as I fear Russell, you don't forget or disregard their threats or requests.

The prosecutor, Steve Jackson, smiles, and asks me his first question, "What is your name?"

"My name is Carly, Carly Lee."

"How old are you?"

"I am fourteen years old."

"Who is your father?"

"Russell Lee."

"Is he in this courtroom?"

"Yes."

Mr. Jackson slowly strolls up to the witness stand. With a gentle voice and kind eyes, he looks directly at me and states, "I know this isn't easy, Carly, but I need to ask some questions about the day Russell shot a man on your street in July 1979."

I sit completely still...willing my face to remain expressionless. I had promised myself I would not cry. I will be brave. I will not give Russell the satisfaction of seeing my weakness. I squint my eyes, attempting to keep the tears that are forming from rolling down my face.

"Now Carly, I want you to listen to my question carefully before you answer." I feel my lip begin to quiver, helpless to make it stop. My tears continue to well up in my eyes but thankfully do not spill over.

Mr. Jackson continues. "It is very important that you tell this court everything you know. Were you home the day of the shooting?"

"Yes." Telling the truth is easy.

"Where were you when the shooting started?"

I clench my teeth so hard I think they might crack. I don't want to answer his question. Telling the truth might result in Russell killing Mom or my siblings. I do not want to lie, but Russell is in the courtroom. I feel his stare upon me, and the words he had me practice in my jailhouse visits to him are ringing in my ears.

"I was in the house."

"So you were in the house the entire time."

"Yes."

"So you didn't see or hear anything that day?"

"No."

"Okay, Carly, thank you for coming today."

The prosecutor looks at the judge, "I have no further questions for this witness."

The judge looked at the defense, "Do you have any questions for this witness?"

"No, Your Honor. We have no questions for this witness."

The judge looks over at me and says, "You are free to go, young lady. You may step down."

The entire episode lasts only a few minutes but leaves me trembling. Fear of arrest rages inside of me because I have lied. But telling the truth could result in Russell killing my family or myself. I refuse to look at Russell as I return to the sitting area in the courtroom. Fear and anger form a nauseating ball of anxiety in the pit of my stomach. Disappointment, disgrace, and anger coil like an electric current and surge through me at the realization that I have once again let Russell control me like a helpless, programmed robot.

Shaking, I return to my seat next to Robin. We sit alone. Mom has not accompanied us into the courtroom. A deputy comes over and gently pats me on the shoulder. "You're gonna be okay, young lady." He stands next to me as I sit on the bench, so his gun is about level with my eyes. I squeeze my eyes shut, trying to hold back the tears.

But his kind tone forces the lingering tears in my eyes to spill over and run down my cheeks.

"May I go to the bathroom?" I ask.

"Yes, you can go to the bathroom."

If I am going to have a real cry, so be it—but I will do it alone, in the privacy of the bathroom, not the courtroom.

The Defense

Insanity is Russell's defense. Claiming the locals in town hate him, he pleads temporary insanity as the cause of the murder. Russell never denies that he committed the murder. His defense claims that he isn't legally responsible because he was legally insane at the time of the murder because he was consumed by fear of a local gang.

As usual, there are twelve jurors and one alternate. Before deliberations, the alternate is dismissed. This particular juror will be called back to serve only if one of the original twelve jurors has to leave before a verdict was reached.

Dismissed as the alternate juror, Mr. Smith leaves the courtroom. Relief surges through me. I have always respected my former grade-school coach. The weight of his knowledge that the murderer was my father is nearly unbearable.

The Verdict

The trial only lasts a couple of days. Reaching a verdict does not take long either. Russell is found guilty and sentenced to twenty years in prison for the murder. It isn't life or the death penalty—which I think he deserves—but I am thrilled that he will be locked up and kept away from my family and me for the next two decades. I will be in my early thirties when he gets out. I will be an adult. Finally, I will never have to see him ever again. If Mom tries to force me into visits again, I will just say, "No, you can't make me go see him."

That is the last day I will ever lay eyes on Russell Lee.

WHY DO YOU STAY?

After the trial, I finally felt finished with Russell—forever. At last the chaos would stop, and I could lead a normal life.

As a young child, there was no way for me to know or understand the impact that Russell's behavior and the chaotic environment I lived in would have on my emotional development. This impact to my childhood-development at an emotional level would span decades and heavily influence in a negative way my own choices during my early adult years. But at this time in my life, as a young fourteen-year-old girl, I naïvely thought that with Russell gone, my hardships would disappear as well.

Today, I am appalled my mother allowed her two young daughters, fourteen and sixteen, to attend and testify in their father's murder trial alone. But I didn't question that dynamic at fourteen. I had convinced myself at the time that I could take care of myself—I didn't need help from anyone. I never asked Mom to go with me; neither did Robin. Why? It seemed normal then, but now, as an adult, it seems negligent and cruel parenting.

As Melody Beattie poignantly states in *Making Miracles in Forty Days*, "Feelings that we didn't have the support or ability to deal with when we first encountered them, settle into our bodies." For me, these feelings were shame, embarrassment, fear, and worthlessness. I would carry these emotions into every relationship that I would develop moving forward. They formed the very fabric of my existence without me being aware of it.

Today I understand that I could not have compassion for myself as a young girl. I needed to be tough emotionally. That unyielding, crusty exterior helped me survive. However, as I grew older I believe it also blocked me from developing compassion and openness for others. I didn't think of myself as mean, only as a "no nonsense" person. Sympathy represented a luxury I could not afford. As a child, my inability to develop sympathy for myself created an emotional block for me to develop sympathy for others who didn't get it.

This unrelenting determination and tenaciousness served me well in accomplishing difficult tasks and advancing my career in my early adult life. This robust drive, however, would present problems with ill-chosen romantic partners. I had difficulty giving up on abusive relationships. Instead, I stayed beyond all reasonable expectation, trying in vain to "make it work." In other words, I had developed a very hard head and an unyielding stubborn streak. Needless to say, relinquishing that skill set would not come easily.

9. Solo

I'm a straight-A student, and teachers easily like me. The band community accepts me, and I enjoy the camaraderie I have with members throughout the various sections of the band. Tina, a senior and co-captain of the flag team, enjoys the freedom of a driver's license and her own car. True to her word, she offers me rides to all the ballgames and band practices. On rides home, I accompany her to her house and then walk the few blocks to the housing project. She offers support without asking questions about where I live or anything about my parents. I am thankful that she does not intrude into my privacy...and secrets.

During my freshman year, I become friends with Lucy. A junior, Lucy plays the saxophone in the band. Making casual friends poses no problem for me. Allowing them into the intimate details of my life as a close friend, however, proves problematic. I never completely trust anyone and thus never confide my secrets to friends. Even Gloria, who had been my best friend in grade school, knows none of my deep secrets or the shame I feel regarding my family. Not surprisingly, after the band tryouts near the beginning of freshman year, Gloria and I began to drift apart. I rarely see or talk to her anymore. Our paths seldom cross, and each of us develops a new circle of friends in high school. The majority of my friends now play in the band.

Lucy, my new band friend, witnessed her parents' bitter divorce a few months earlier. It is clear she still feels the sting of that family trauma. Lucy and her mom reside in an upper-middle-class neighborhood not too far from the projects.

Lucy and I share small talk before and after each band practice. One day she asks me if I want a ride home. I refuse—my first instinct is to protect the location of my residence. The shame of poverty runs deep. I fear if Lucy knows I live in the projects, she might not want to be friends with me. Of course, poverty is just the tip of the iceberg. She must never discover the truth about Russell, the violence I've endured, or my living alone with Robin in the apartment. So, no, I definitely did not want her to drive me home to the projects.

As a senior, Robin is busy making plans to move to the big city to attend college immediately following high-school graduation. Her choice of college offers year-round quarterly sessions so Robin will begin classes in June. This means we will not spend the following summer together.

Since it is a two-hour drive from our small town, I know that visits to the large city where Robin is going to attend college will be nonexistent. Dread fills me as my freshman year ends and the time moves closer for Robin to leave. I share her excitement about going to college, but I don't want to be all alone in the apartment. I will miss her desperately. I know we will not see each other often once she leaves because she doesn't have a car and the distance will prevent visits. The lack of a phone in the apartment does not even allow for telephone calls. Overwhelmed by grief and sadness, I shut out all thoughts of her leaving and the dread of living totally alone. These ugly thoughts belong buried and locked away deep in my psyche.

Mom now limits her brief visits to every other Friday—payday. The visits last about fifteen minutes, long enough for her to give me money for rent or electricity. Subsidized by a government program, the low rent allows a little extra for groceries each week.

The arrangement doesn't strike me as odd or unusual. I know that Adrian, Mom's boyfriend, does not want Robin or me hanging around his house, and that doesn't bother me. I want Mom to be happy because she has been through so much. But with Robin's impending departure, thoughts of being all alone begin creeping in more often, and I have no one to help me process these roller-coaster feelings. Band membership provides a great distraction.

The Band

Divided into two units, the band's auxiliary team consists of the flag corps with sixteen girls, and the rifle corps, a group of four girls. The rifle twirlers command center stage when the band performs during football games. Instead of majorettes who twirl batons, our high-school band utilized rifle twirlers. Always pretty girls, the rifle twirlers invariably also hail from well-to-do families.

Imagine my surprise when one of the rifle co-captains, Betsy, approaches me about becoming a rifle twirler. I am stunned. Betsy's dad is an attorney. I wonder if she knows who I really am. I wonder if she knows my father murdered someone. This doesn't make sense. I live in the local housing project. Welfare and food stamps have frequently provided the means for survival for my family. Me—a rifle twirler?

It is a shocker for me to be asked to join this group. I don't come from the right type of family to even think about asking to join their group. I am not even close friends with them. I didn't take ballet or dance classes and have no idea why they would want me to join their group. But I remember what the flag co-captain asked me when I wanted to quit band before I had started: "So you don't want to be co-captain of anything?"

As I stand looking at Betsy, I instantly gave a neutral response. "I'll think about it." My motto is when startled; never tip your hand on what you feel. Think it out before you say anything. That has always been the safest thing for me to do in the past, so the patent response comes out almost without me having to think about it.

I can tell from the look on Betsy's face my response startles and confuses her. This is an elite team, and a spot on the rifle team is a coveted position. She can't understand why I wouldn't jump at the invitation to join her team.

I know that Betsy will never understand my hesitation about joining her team and my internal shame regarding the poverty and abandonment I live with, and I would never share my fears with her. I simply need more time to think this through. Of course I want to be on the team, but there are things I have to consider. I will have to buy more uniforms, and the rifle team members have more expensive uniforms than the flag team. Members of the rifle team also attend a special camp in the summer, and they often have extra practices. How on earth can I pay for it?

Betsy says, "You have two days to let know your decision."

Relief floods over me that she has not rejected me on the spot for not giving her an instant affirmative answer.

I reply, "I'll get back to you by then, I promise." I secretly think I simply must find a way to make this work for me.

Meanwhile my head is spinning with thoughts, worries, and excitement. How will I get to practice? Can I babysit more? Pick up a part-time job after school? I need to do the math to see how much I can possibly make in the working hours that are available to me.

Lucy's first cousin, Paul, also co-captain of the football team, dates one of the other "rifles." So I ask Lucy, "What do you think I should do?"

It never occurs to me to ask Mom what I should do or if she will help me pay for these things. Mom lives a separate life in another county. It feels as if I am no longer a part of her world. Nor she part of mine. If I want to be on this team, I know I will have to figure out finances and transportation on my own.

"Of course you should join the rifle team!" Lucy states the obvious. "Why wouldn't you want to join the rifle team?"

"Well, they seem kind of stuck up." This isn't how I really feel, but it is better than sharing my real concerns with Lucy.

Lucy replied, "You're just afraid."

Just the response I need. Thinking of myself as afraid of anything doesn't sit well with me.

I have started to feel like an adult—and I like it. I just need to work hard, make money, and get out of the poverty and desperation that plagued me as a child. I instinctively knew there are no freebies. I need to create my own opportunities. I never expected that getting to a better life would be easy. I am driven and rigorous in my determination to succeed in life. I made a vow to myself that my childhood would not hold me back.

I have not yet found the route to making much money. I know I need to figure this out quickly if I don't want to lose this chance of being on the rifle team. After thinking on the problem all day, the only answer I can come up with is more babysitting. I calculate the number of nights I can work until rifle-camp money is due. If I can find the customers, I can make enough money. My fourteen-year-old mind succumbs to the confidence of youth. Refusing to consider the things that could go wrong, I focus solely on working and paying for camp.

At the next band practice, I eagerly report to Betsy, "Yes, I would like to join your team."

It is official. Wow. I am going to be a rifle twirler!

My first rifle summer camp is approaching in one month. Time to get those babysitting jobs.

I boldly decide to market directly to all of the mothers who live in the projects. I start at building four—apartments with three and four bedrooms. I figure they will have the most kids. I start knocking on doors.

I build my sales pitch around close proximity. Living in building two, I can be available on very short notice—seven nights a week and twenty-four hours on Saturday and Sunday. Only school and my band schedule limit my babysitting availability. Fortunately, I am an excellent student and never spend much time on studying outside school hours.

To my astonishment and delight, I book a sitting for that very night. As it turns out, babysitting is a booming business in the projects. Before I finish that night of babysitting, I book jobs for the next three nights.

I always watch the children in their apartments. I never complain if the mom returns later than agreed upon, if she wants me to watch additional children, or when someone arrives home drunk and acts mean toward me.

I did learn very quickly as a young girl—you don't stay in the same room as the mother's boyfriend. It can quickly turn into a conversation that you don't want, like being offered a beer, a joint, or a ride somewhere—or worse, if he stands too close to you or wants to hug you. I know that is not the right choice for me. I want to be a twirler in the band, so I don't want any part of those things.

I know it is much safer to stay in the same room as the mom, even if that means following her around from room to room until she and her current love interest leave for the evening.

Two weeks into my babysitting blitz, I have saved about half of what I need to cover the cost of camp. I am so pumped and excited about my financial success and constantly remind myself, I CAN DO THIS! I am doing this—and all by myself.

Camp fees must be paid in two weeks. My determination knows no bounds. Nothing will stand in my way of attending rifle camp. I wish I could get a job making more money, but stores won't hire a fourteen-year-old. With no public bus service available in the small town, transportation remains a persistent problem. Babysitting appears the only option for the moment.

The mothers' boyfriends present the biggest challenge in babysitting. They all know I live in the housing projects, and occasionally they ask about my mom. My routine response is that she is at a friend's. I never offer additional details. If they ask more questions, I just don't answer, and they drop the subject. The questions, however, present more than awkward moments; they increase my sense of shame. They crack open the door for excruciating questions to fill my thoughts: Why isn't Mom ever home? Doesn't she care about me? Their questions expose my vulnerability. They tear at the painful scab protecting my secret: I am not wanted by my own mother. It terrifies me that others might find out that my own mom doesn't want to be around me. If they discover my own mother doesn't want to be around me, maybe they—or their children—shouldn't be around me either. No, Mom's absence must definitely remain a secret. Unlike a message in a bottle, it will not wash up on some shore; rather, like a ship lost at the bottom of the sea, the secret will remain firmly anchored in the deep recesses, decaying where no one will discover it.

I don't remember sleeping in my own apartment during the next two weeks. In between babysitting gigs, I focus on counting my money on trips back to my apartment to take a shower in my own bathroom.

The fees are due in two days, and my stockpile needs an additional forty dollars. A regular customer sends her son to my apartment to ask if I can babysit that night. I usually charge her twenty-five dollars for the night for her two kids. I walk to Janet's apartment and knock on her door.

Janet opens the door in her bra and waves me in. "I've got a hot date tonight with a new guy. Hope you can babysit tonight, Carly?"

I respond, "Yes, I can sit."

"Whew, I was afraid you were already committed to that wild woman over in 7B."

"No, I can keep Sally and Robert for you tonight."

"Oh, you don't mind if Kelly's kids come over too? Kelly is going to meet up with Jackson and me later tonight."

"Well, I am going to have to charge more." My courage surprises even me. I have never asked for more money. My fear of missing rifle camp overshadows my fear that Janet won't hire me for the night if I request more money.

"What? More money? You have never charged more money when I have asked you to keep other kids. You're already here with mine."

"Well, I'm going to have to charge each mom now. It's more kids, so I have to charge more."

Janet shrugs her shoulders. "Okay, I'll let Kelly know that she will owe you twenty-five dollars as well."

"Okay, what time should I be back?"

"Can you be here at 5:45 p.m.?"

"Yep." I walk toward the front door. "I'll see you then."

I have to leave for fear Janet will hear my heart pounding. I am going to make *double* the money tonight. Tonight's earnings seal the deal on rifle camp!

I have done it! Nothing in my young life thus far surpasses this feeling of accomplishment. Finally, I can control my destiny. I am no longer at the mercy of Mom or Russell. I think to myself, "This must be what it is like to be an adult."

I leave for camp a week from tomorrow. Life is good. I have enough time to earn money for snacks to take with me to camp. I continue to smile as I skip back to my apartment.

Then a thought creeps in like a serpent seeking prey. Robin leaves on Sunday to start college. I bite my lip hard. Don't let your mind wander. Don't think about that.

When I collect enough money for camp, I decide that I will ask Lucy if she will drive me to the band room behind the high school to pay for camp. I have already signed Mom's name on the camp release papers, and I will pay my camp dues with cash from babysitting. But my immediate problem is how I am going to get to the band room to catch the bus to camp and then get home when camp is over. Tina with whom I rode during my freshman year is graduating, and I need to find a new ride. I didn't want any of the other rifles knowing where I live. Since I am only fourteen years old, I don't have my license.

I decide to ask Lucy if she will pick me up. Now that school is out, I will have to call Lucy from one of my babysitting gigs to ask her to pick me up. When I call Lucy, I ask her to meet me at the park a few blocks from the projects. This way I can break my secret about living in the projects to her in person.

Feeling as antsy as a cat on a hot tin roof, I anxiously fidget, pushing myself gently back and forth on a swing with my foot in the dirt while I wait for Lucy. I don't wait long before she pulls up in her Camaro. Lucy walks over to where I am swinging and sits on the ground.

I just blurt it out. "I live in the housing project."

Lucy looks blankly at me and says, "So what? My dad divorced my mom and married a girl five years older than me."

We both burst out laughing. Relief floods my body. Now there is at least one other person with whom I no longer have to hide the fact that I live in the projects.

When my laughter subsides, I question Lucy. "So do you think you could take me and pick me up from rifle camp at the high school?"

"You know I will."

Stupid tears well in my eyes and threaten to spill over at her sincere kindness. I am not accustomed to kindness without costs attached. Lucy is indeed a true friend.

My first rifle camp is a blast! I have a natural ability for twirling and learn quickly. It feels like I'm living in another world. The other girls talk about their clothes and, of course, boys. I try to fit in by telling jokes. I think to myself that if I entertain them and they like me, they will not ask questions about my life. No, questions about my life would be awkward and uncomfortable for everyone.

The strategy works. People like to laugh. No one asks me any personal questions, not a single one. And I always ask questions about their lives. So I can keep the focus on them and their lives.

Lucy picks me up and drops me off at my apartment, just as she promised. I'm not ready for Lucy to come into the apartment, so she just drops me off. I walk into the apartment alone.

No one is there. I walk down the hall into the bedroom I share with Robin. There is a letter on my twin bed with my name on the envelope. I know it is from Robin.

I pick up the letter and lie down on the bed. Without opening the letter, sobs wrack my body, leaving me limp. Like a hard punch in the stomach, I can no longer hide from the realization Robin is gone.

I am totally alone.

I finally get the courage to open the letter. I read the first line.

Now don't cry, Carly.

Deep wells of tears flow again. I can't stop.

I cry myself to sleep, the first of many, many nights I will sleep alone in the apartment.

I had silently celebrated my fifteenth birthday at rifle camp without telling anyone. I was too embarrassed to share the day because no one had given me any gifts. I didn't want to explain that my family had no money to give gifts. My well of shame runs deep.

Being asked to join the elite group of rifle twirlers increased my sense of self-worth. Although I felt so very different than the rest of the team because of my family's poverty, a father in prison, living without a parent, and living in the housing projects, I could still participate. I wasn't a complete outsider, but I had a keen awareness that I was very different than the other girls.

Keeping my thoughts and feelings safely locked away without reflection kept me safe and focused on achieving the life I wanted. On the rifle team, I could be any person I chose to be. I could be funny and outgoing or quiet and reserved.

I allowed myself the luxury of one night of crying and self-pity when Robin left. Then I tightly locked those fears and hurts away again. I didn't dare release them again. As John Carnody states in his book *How to Handle Trouble,* "Few things are more debilitating than feeling you are completely alone."

I didn't want anyone to find out I was living completely alone. I didn't want anyone to think I wasn't really good enough to be on the rifle team. And I would offer them no reason to kick me off the team.

I was naïve. I didn't yet know that emotions can't stay locked away. They leak out…at inconvenient and unexpected times, often with inappropriate intensity. This locked compartment would one day burst open. But for now, at fifteen, I believed the sealed container was closed forever; buried and lost in the deepest, darkest recesses of my psyche. They would never be allowed to surface or see the light of day again.

My mother abandoned me, but I couldn't and wouldn't admit that to myself for years to come. It would take many years before arriving at a safe place where this emotional black box could be opened and processed. At fifteen years of age, I was in survival mode. My denial gave me the emotional protection I needed to endure the painful situation alone.

Decades would pass before I would have the awareness and the courage to admit that my past experiences continued to negatively impact my life and my choices as an adult. Awareness could only be ushered in by developing trust in another person who could accompany me down this emotional path, allowing me to face the truth of past hurts.

My emotional-trust muscle was underdeveloped. Life experiences in my family had taught me not to trust others. I carried that learned behavior into adulthood. I didn't realize that lack of trust could lead to a controlling personality.

Avoidance of past hurts doesn't lock them away and prevent further damage. Like draining water, this pain finds cracks and crevices, continually seeping into and eroding decisions and lives. Often times you aren't even aware current conflicts find their origins in a previously inflicted wound.

You cannot heal what you refuse to feel.

10. High-School Years

In the summer between my freshman and sophomore years of high school, Robin moves out to attend college. Now I am the sole occupant of the apartment, its empty hollowness mirroring the growing void inside me. Spending every night with her boyfriend, Mom essentially lives with him now. Her biweekly "drive-bys" to drop off a few dollars are the only interaction I have with her. I assume that continuing this financial responsibility somehow alleviates any remorse or guilt she feels and offers her the illusion that she is still a good and caring "mother."

But here's the really crazy part...I feel happy. Truly happy—perhaps for the first time in my life. Sure, I miss Robin being around, but conscious sadness doesn't permeate my days. I don't dwell on Mom's absence from my life. I am not angry with Mom. I enjoy all the perks of a single adult living alone. Regular rent money prevents me having to move every six months, the electricity remains on without interruption, and best of all, prison bars keep Russell out of my life. For the first time in my life, a sense of calm settles and stays on me for an extended period of time. I can relax. I can breathe easier. The constant eruptions and violence disappear from my life. Even the detested housing project has its bright spot—it provides a safe haven, and the babysitting business is good.

Twirling practice keeps me busy after school. Lucy and I become close friends. She confides more details about her parent's divorce. Her father's affair and continued romance following the divorce with someone only slightly older than her sustain her sense of embarrassment. We have bonded over family-shame issues.

Lucy becomes my one true friend that first summer alone in the apartment. She is my first, and thus far only, close friend. In my world of closely guarded secrets, true, close, intimate friends are a luxury I cannot afford. Most of my secrets remain safely locked away. Lucy, however, has the privileged information of my address. I allow her to pick me up at the housing project instead of meeting her at some generic location.

Lucy doesn't see my housing situation as horrible or odd. Her acceptance of my living in the housing project helps me to accept it as well. We never hang out at my apartment, always preferring to go to her house. Mutual feelings of shame—her dad's affair with a young woman near her age and my family's poverty manifested in my living arrangements—strengthen and seal the bonds of our new friendship. For the first time in my life, I feel I truly have a best friend.

Sophomore year passes without incident. A routine of attending school, band practice, twilling practice, and hanging out with Lucy offer me comfort and a sense of normalcy. I have backed off the cliff edge of the chaos of day-to-day survival.

A member of the honor society at school, I never get into any trouble. I steer clear of anything remotely resembling disorder or danger. Any attention of that sort would expose the conditions of my living alone. I avoid anyone ever having a reason to come to my house or contact my mom. I instinctively know that no adults should know I am living alone. I don't want or need any authority to "look out for me." I don't want to be sent away. I master the art of leaving the false impression that Mom is "out with friends" or busy. Running out the clock until I can leave for college hones my deception skill set. I am ready, or so I think, for life beyond the confines of this small county's boundaries.

Sometime during my sophomore year, Mom's brief visits stop entirely. I am not exactly sure when she stops coming. Extracurricular activity after school or hanging out with Lucy causes me to miss a few of her visits. The lack of a home phone precludes any warning or making advance plans for Mom's drop-in visits. I know, however, the visits have stopped when she no longer leaves rent money.

Babysitting jobs keep a steady stream of funds flowing, and I start paying the rent and my household expenses with my babysitting money. I still babysit every chance I get on the weekends when I am not involved with a band activity.

I am anticipating my sixteenth birthday the following summer, so I start saving for my first car. My dream of owning my own car gets closer with every dollar added to the stash. I will be able to go anywhere, anytime. True freedom. Ensuring I attain that freedom prioritizes every spare penny. I don't buy clothes or makeup like my girlfriends. No way—I am saving for my car and the freedom it will bring.

Band and twirling practice limit my ability to work a more normal schedule at a local gas station or fast-food place. But the babysitting allows late-night work and pays fairly well. In addition, sitting for three or four mothers simultaneously generates more income than minimum wage at a fast-food restaurant.

As I get closer to my sixteenth birthday, my vehicle fund swells to eight hundred dollars. My dream of owning a car will soon be realized.

It's 1982, the summer between my sophomore and junior years. Six hundred dollars makes me the proud owner of my first car. Elation soars through my body!

The age of my "new" car, a 1967 VW Bug, qualifies it for antique plates. Six hundred dollars doesn't buy much, but this mature car starts, and it belongs to me. It's red with a blue hood, so most see an eyesore. However, I see it as a work of art. I sit atop the world! Memories of that VW Bug still coax smiles to my face today.

Holes from rust offer an aged, pockmarked face on the passenger-side floorboard. Light streams through these rusted spots during the day as the pavement rushes by underneath. The gas gauge retired tens of thousands of miles ago, and the driver's side window won't budge from its commitment to its stationary "up" position. These are all insignificant details to me. My baby starts, runs, and belongs to me. Nothing can diminish my delight with my multicolored rust-bucket ticket to freedom.

Because the gas gauge is broken, I am forever running out of gas. I begin carrying a gas can in the car. I start my junior year of high school driving myself to school. My friends joke about my rusted red-and-blue VW Bug, and I just laugh and joke back that they are just jealous. I am proud of my car, and no amount of teasing bothers me. Most of my friends have cars their parents helped them buy. They are much nicer cars than my rusty VW, but I worked and paid for my car, and it feels good. I have wheels. Life is just getting better. I feel like I am on top of the world, and no amount of teasing from my friends is going to make me embarrassed of my rust bucket.

Being an upperclassman ushers in the inevitable dilemma of "boys." I like boys, but unlike most girls, I have no interest in serious dating or eventual marriage. This stance presents challenges. If you aren't going steady with someone, you endure endless solicitations for dates. A steady boyfriend seems safer—and easier. My perfect guy needs to have already graduated from high school. I don't want or need someone constantly around. A boyfriend to escort me to and from class and a constant companion at lunch would feel smothering to me. I need more freedom. A recent high-school graduate, preferably from an adjoining county, would be ideal.

Senior year brings Dalton White into my life. He is two years older than me, and Dalton has already graduated high school. He attended one year of college and decided that college isn't for him. His parents own a successful grocery store in town. Business has declined somewhat after a big chain moved into town, but his parents' store remains profitable. Dalton thinks that since his parents, who never attended college, are successful, college isn't a prerequisite for a successful life.

Dalton's family's financial success and status in our small town do not impress me. But his cool white Camaro and great-looking athletic legs catch and hold my attention. After we are dating a few weeks, Dalton begins picking me up at the apartment. I never invite him to come in. I don't want him to discover that I live alone, nor do I want him to hear the neighbors argue through the paper-thin walls.

Thankfully, he never makes any negative comments about where I live.

Our usual routine is that Dalton picks me up for Friday night football games. Never in my four years with the twirling team and the high-school band did my mother or any of my siblings see me perform during the band performance. I didn't mind, nor did I expect them to take time away from their busy schedules to come to my band performance. I participated in band for me, not for them.

In my last year of high school, Robin graduates with an associate of science in business degree and begins working as a secretary in a large law firm in the city. I am very happy for her, but the lack of phones and vehicles have severely limited our contact during the past couple of years. Letters via US mail are our method of communication.

A few weeks after getting her first job, Robin buys herself a new car. Now she can visit me on holidays and some weekends. On the last home football game of my senior year, Robin surprises me and shows up at the game. She has stopped by Adrian's house and picked up Mom. This is the first time Mom will ever see me perform in the band. It is my last performance. Conflicting emotions vie for my attention. Mom's presence makes me happy, sad, and angry. Why bother coming to see me...now? She hasn't bothered all these years, and now my high-school career is coming to an end. Why now?

Although Robin lives two hours away, through our regular correspondence, she knows more about me than my own mother, who lives in much closer proximity to me. Mom never even signed a report card...she doesn't know I've been on the honor roll all through high school. Why now, Mom? However, I am glad Robin is here. She made the effort to come see me perform, and this makes me feel important. I know Robin loves me.

It would take many years to understand my true emotions concerning Mom. At the time, her abandonment felt more like just being left alone rather than outright neglect and desertion.

As a young teenage girl, I was forced to attend Russell's murder trial alone, to live alone, and to navigate adult interactions alone. I took responsibility for delivering the rent and utility checks on time each month. I bought groceries, organized my own transportation for school activities, and funded all my school needs. While developing self-sufficiency is good, these experiences led me to become an over responsible adult. Being completely responsible for myself at such an early age gave me the false impression that I always had to be responsible—not just for me but for those around me as well.

This mentality set the stage for me to be continually victimized. Perpetrators seek victims who assume full responsibility for anything bad that happens in the relationship. I didn't need to be told it was my fault; I was programmed to automatically believe it was my fault.

My internal drive to achieve a better life kept me on the straight and narrow—a good student, a good team member, and a good friend. I never drank, smoked, took drugs, or cut school.

I wanted a better life. I believed that no one was going to help me. It was totally up to me. I had to work hard and stay out of trouble. Then, and only then, would I be successful. What I didn't yet understand was that hard work did not insulate me from the need to protect myself from predators. At this time in my life, I had not learned emotional protection of any kind. I wasn't even aware it existed.

Soon enough, life would provide me with many opportunities to learn this skill. It would take many hard knocks to teach me how to set healthy boundaries and protect myself.

As a young girl and teenager, my life experiences to this point had created in me a belief system that it was up to me to take care of myself...always. Eventually I would learn that there are people out there—good people—who could be trusted and who could help me. Nancy Groom in her book *From Bondage to Bonding* poignantly states what I could not know yet: "Children's nurturing losses, combined with their own fallen natures, damage their ability to love well." This goes for loving others as well as loving yourself.

11. Name-Calling

During my senior year, Sheri, another twirling friend, makes plans to take some college classes in the spring semester.

"I am going to take English 101 in the spring semester. I will be able to get a jump start on my college courses. You should check with the guidance counselor and see if you have enough credits to graduate by Christmas. I'll bet you do, and then you can take English 101 with me," Sheri said.

"Are you still going to walk in the high-school graduation line in May?"

"Yeah, and I will be the only person with college credit."

"Sounds like a great idea. I'll check it out," I said.

I check with the school counselor, and I do have enough credits to graduate at the end of the fall semester. She also tells me I will need a parent's signature to graduate early because I am not yet eighteen.

A simple signature won't suffice; the school also requires a face-to-face meeting with a parent. I can't just forge Mom's signature this time; I will have to get her to come to school. So the next Saturday, the first Saturday in December, I drive my VW Bug out to Adrian's house to talk with Mom.

Not wanting to discuss it in front of Adrian, I wait for the right opportunity. "It's a un-usually warm December day. I'm going outside to have a cup of coffee. Do you want to join me, Carly?" Mom asks me.

"Yeah, I'll come along."

Walking onto the front porch, I feel the warm sunshine and cool breeze on my face. The blue of the cloudless sky stretches forever. The wind stirs the few remaining dead leaves on the trees. The air smells clean and fresh. I slowly follow behind Mom as she walks to the swing hanging from the big oak tree on the side of the front yard. The spot serves as a gathering place for visitors to sit and pass the time. Grassy fields unfold in every direction.

Mom and I sit on the swing in silence for a few minutes. She finally breaks the silence and asks me, "So how are you, Carly?"

"I'm doing okay. How are you?"

"I haven't been sleeping very well. I think I might be coming down with a cold."

Silence creeps back in. A bird makes a call in the distance.

"It's so peaceful here. I can see why you love it."

"No place is perfect."

I wasn't for sure what she meant by that, but I knew better than to ask any questions. If she wanted me to know, she would keep talking about it. And I didn't want to anger her today of all days, when I needed to ask her to do something for me.

"Well, I hope you get to feeling better soon."

"Well," I think to myself, "it's now or never." I'd better ask her now because I don't want to ask in front of Adrian.

"Uh…I have something I want to ask you."

I look toward her, and she looks back at me without saying a word. Her face is not exactly inviting or encouraging, but I don't have any other options. She is the only person in the world who can do this for me.

"So, Mom, I have been thinking. I would like to go ahead and start college."

Mom looks straight ahead and doesn't utter a word.

"I…have enough credits to graduate at the end of the fall semester, that would be when school lets out in December. So…starting in the spring, I could take English 101 at a local community college. It would help me get a head start on college."

Mom sits silently with her lips pulled into a thin slit—not a good sign. "I just need you to meet with the guidance counselor at school and sign a waiver that says you will allow me to graduate early because I am not eighteen years old yet."

"No."

And just like that, she has made her decision. No explanation, no discussion, just *no*.

"Mom, I just want to get a head start on my college classes. Will you please do this for me?"

"I've given you my answer. No need to ask again." Rising, her exit puts an exclamation point on the negative response as she returns to the house. With her back ramrod straight, she walks briskly back to the house, never looking back. I know that attempting to change her mind will only further deteriorate the situation.

I am furious! She doesn't have the right to make this decision for me! She hasn't made any decisions for me since I've been in high school. I can't understand why she won't do this for me. These thoughts cascade like water crashing over a waterfall in my mind as I remain seated in the swing, stunned by her rejection.

I leave their house and head back to the housing project. I can't wait to turn eighteen and have full legal control of my own decisions.

The next week brings a surprise.

It's Friday night, and I'm in my bedroom at the apartment when I hear the front door open. Startled, I walk into the living room. Who on earth has just walked into the locked apartment?

Mom is standing in the living room.

"Hey, you scared me. What are you doing here?"

"Hi. Just thought I would stop by and see what you were up to." Why is she here? What does she want?

"Is something wrong?" I ask.

"Now why would you ask that? Does there have to be something wrong for me to stop in and see my daughter? I just wanted to see what you were up to? What are your plans for this weekend?"

I don't answer. She won't stay longer than fifteen minutes, and then she will totally forget me. Why take an interest now? After three years of living by myself, why take an interest now?

I have been making adult decisions for myself for three years now. Her "checking up on me" seems ridiculous and absurd.

"The band is performing at halftime at a basketball game."

"Who are you going with?"

"Dalton. He usually comes and picks me up."

"Do you let him pick you up for every ballgame?"

"Why does it matter who takes me to the game? Why are you asking me this now?"

"You are my daughter. Now tell me who are you going with!"

A knock at the front door interrupts the conversation. Mom looks at me and raises an eyebrow. Although I have done nothing wrong, suddenly I feel guilty.

"Who might that be?" Mom inquires.

"It's probably Dalton. Like I said, he is taking me to the game. Let me get the door."

"Hi, Dalton. Come in and meet my mom."

Dalton nods his head in Mom's direction, "Hello, ma'am."

"Mom, this is Dalton, Dalton, this is my mom, Dorothy."

"Hello, Dalton. So you are taking my daughter to the ballgame tonight?" The words feel like judgment as she peers intensely into his eyes as if to see all the sinister motives hidden behind them.

"Yes, ma'am."

"What time are you going to have her home?"

Uh-oh. Standard protocol—I tell everyone, including Dalton, my curfew is 11:00 p.m. This sounds like a reasonable curfew to me. No one knows I live alone, not even Dalton. Fear creeps in as I instantly worry that Mom might bust my cover by revealing that she doesn't live there and certainly has not set a curfew.

"I will have her home by 11:00 p.m. I will drop her off before I drop off Greg."

Mom's eyebrow shoots up again. "And who is Greg?"

"Greg is my older brother. He and his friend Alex are home from college this weekend, and they are going to the game tonight with Carly and me."

Mom's fury and imagination know no bounds when she discovers that Dalton has two other guys waiting in the car. Her penetrating glare turns to me. "You are not leaving this house with three boys."

Shock freezes me in my stance. Dalton looks at me, confused.

Incredible! I am an honor-roll student, in the high school band, paying the rent and electric bill, and solely funding all my high-school activities. I have taken care of myself throughout my entire high-school years. I've never done drugs or alcohol, and yet she treats me this way! She shows up only to embarrass and humiliate me.

She doesn't even know me! My thoughts are running wild. Who does she think she is, talking like this to me in front of Dalton? She hasn't known my whereabouts or activities since she started living at Adrian's house. I can't understand why she is acting this way tonight. Why all of a sudden does it matter to her?

Taking a step toward Dalton, I suggest, "Dalton, will you wait for me outside in the car?"

With relief, he turns without a word and walks out the front door.

I spin around and face Mom with fierce determination. "I am going with Dalton, and you can't stop me." I grab my coat, slamming the door behind me.

Dalton stands beside his car with the passenger door open, ready to facilitate our escape. Halfway to his car, I hear Mom yank open the apartment door and yell, "Get back in the house!"

Without looking back, I keep walking. Mom delivers the fatal blow, hissing, "You are acting like a whore! You can't go with all these men. Get back in this house RIGHT NOW!"

My heart is pounding furiously! Tears well up in my eyes as I climb into the passenger seat. No one says a word as we drive away. When we get to the high school, Greg and Alex fairly jump out of the car while Dalton and I lag behind.

"Are you okay?"

"Yeah, I'm fine. Sorry you had to see that."

"Are you sure you're okay?"

"Yeah, I said I was fine." Please stop talking about it...please.

Thankfully, Dalton does not pursue the conversation. He locks the car, and we head toward the football field. The sting of humiliation leaves a lasting scar, providing Dalton with ammunition to use against me later to further his own agenda.

My mother accusing me of being a whore shocked and hurt me deeply. Nothing was further from the truth, and I couldn't understand why she would humiliate me in front of Dalton, Greg, and Alex. Reflecting on the exchange, I can only surmise that Mom's limited exposure to me during my high-school years kept her from realizing that I was growing up. I was nearly eighteen years old, seventeen and a half to be exact, at the time of this exchange. Mom, however, must have still viewed me as a child. Time had passed, and she had been around me only infrequently, and she must not have been comfortable with the fact that I made adult decisions every day.

In that moment, though, I assumed her projected shame as my own. While consciously I felt I deserved better treatment from even an absentee mother, I still believed life wasn't about getting what you deserved. This episode simply confirmed my belief no one could be trusted and that life was about learning how to dodge emotional bullets and always having your armor on.

My ingrained emotional armor was a mind-set of adopting an accommodating stance, even when I was fully aware that I had not done anything wrong. My learned reaction was to appease the angry person. I dared not openly challenge someone who wanted me to do things their way. So although I did go to the ballgame with Dalton, Greg, and Alex that night, I never challenged Mom either in the moment of her verbal attack or later in her unfair treatment of me in front of Dalton. I rationalized in my mind that it was my fault because I should have known that there was a potential chance of Mom stopping by when Dalton would be there to pick me up. So I should have planned to meet him at his house to avoid a potential chance encounter with my mom.

My mind-set was although my mother was out of line in her behavior, the situation happened because I had failed. I failed to plan better.

It would be decades before I would encounter Nancy, an astonishing attorney whose willingness to stand up for me would begin to pierce the layers of my faulty thinking and help me believe I was worthy of such protection and support.

However, you can't know what you don't know. And I certainly didn't have any idea of how to emotionally protect myself…much less how to protect myself from my own parent.

12. Graduation and Beyond

During my senior year, spring break takes place in the second week in March. Another high-school couple, friends of mine, invite Dalton and me on a trip to Myrtle Beach. Dalton uses the opportunity to press the issue of becoming sexually active. We have never had sex, and I am not sure I am ready. Though curious about sex, I have never actually talked with anyone about it. I know I don't want to get pregnant. I never want any children. Marriage and kids are not part of my life agenda—of that I am certain.

Nevertheless, curiosity wins, and I agree to have sex with Dalton. Planning the night, we prepare for protection to avoid an unwanted pregnancy. Afterward, I wonder what the big fuss was about. I never tell anyone, and life returns to my usual routine after the trip.

My older sisters, Terri and Lily, have both married alcoholics. Each has a daughter. Ernie will be discharged from the navy soon, and Robin continues to work in Nashville. Robin has her own apartment and has begun dating someone.

A few short months are all that separate me from the college life I dream about at the university in the big metropolitan town. The move will be a dream come true for me. I can finally openly admit I am living alone without fear of exposure and one less secret to keep. I won't be different any more than other people my age.

As high-school graduation draws near, I learn that I will graduate third in my class. I'm surprised. I had no previous inkling of my class standing. If I had known, I might have worked harder to be number one or two. I decide to drive out to Adrian's and share the good news with Mom.

Saturday ushers in a bright and cheerful morning. After showering, I begin the nearly hour-long drive to Adrian's house. Driving up the long gravel road to the house, my tires throw up a cloud of dust that leaves a long tail behind me. Conscious, however, of Mom's aversion to the "dustbowl" that seeps through the doors and windows, I slow to a crawl as I get closer to the house. I top the small hill just right before the yard, and the little farmhouse comes into view. I pull into the driveway and park my VW Bug.

Jumping out of the car, I race up the two front steps. Opening the door, I shout, "Hey, Mom, are you here?" She must be; her car is in the driveway.

"Hello, how are you, Carly?"

"I'm great. Guess what? I've got some great news."

"What is it?"

"Well, I found out from school that I am graduating third in my class of 165 students."

"Well, why weren't you first?"

I instantly feel the heat rise in my chest, creeping toward my face. My heart beats faster. Suddenly I don't feel so good. My gaze turns to the floor. Never again will I have the expectation Mom will be proud of me.

In an instant, I travel the painful journey from admirable to unworthy. I do not mention my standing to another person. There is a dinner held for the top ten students of the graduating class, and I do not invite Mom to come. A friend of mine, Megan, is also in the top ten, and I sit with her and her parents. No one at the dinner questions my absent parent.

The graduation ceremony for me is not a joyous occasion. It is just a formality that I have to attend to get my diploma. I do, however, win the trigonometry award. I have kept an A+ grade for my trigonometry classes throughout high school. But this does not feel very significant to me. I am still only third in my graduating class. Criticism has a way of sticking like glue to me.

Now that I am a high-school graduate, it is time to leave babysitting behind. Lily, now an LPN, helps me get a job as a ward clerk in the emergency room at the only hospital in the county.

I plan to work there until I leave in the fall to attend the University of Tennessee.

Working doubles on the weekends helps me get extra weekend pay, and I enjoy adding to my stockpile of savings. Dalton, however, doesn't disguise his displeasure at me working every weekend. No matter. If he wanted to see me, he could do it during the week.

As an ER ward clerk, I ensure the appropriate paperwork is completed during the admittance process. Because the hospital is short on nursing staff, I am left in the emergency room alone my first night. The nurse who is training me says, "We don't get much traffic in the

ER, maybe an occasional kid who is sick or someone with the flu. Just sit back here, and if anyone comes in, just sign them in, take their vital signs, and then call the nursing station."

"Sure, no problem," I reply.

The first night passes without incident. I fill the time reading magazines. The second night proves much different.

It's a nice June evening, and the weather is warm. A drunken man startles me when he staggers through the sliding ER doors. Clutching a light jacket, he shouts, "I've been shot." I stare silently as he opens his jacket and blood spills across the counter, seeming to stretch its sticky fingers toward me.

Horrified, intense fear floods my body, holding me hostage in its unrelenting grip.

He has been shot in the chest, and he keeps touching the bullet holes as if he is trying to see if they are real.

In a weak voice, I finally say, "Don't put your fingers in the holes."

I then realize that he is trying to stop the bleeding by putting his finger first in one bullet hole, then the next. Lurching around the counter, he grabs me. "You have to help me."

I freeze, unsure what to do next. I stretch and grab the phone. I buzz the nurses' station with a shaking hand and squeak out, "Please, someone come down here. There is a man who has been shot, and blood is everywhere!"

Working that night, Lily soon learns of my dilemma. She and several other staff people come running down the hallway into the ER. Only one surgeon in the county has experience with gunshot wounds. I am ordered to call him immediately. Surgery will most definitely be required to remove the bullets from this man's chest.

The surgeon arrives about forty-five minutes later and immediately disappears into the operating room with the patient and several nurses. The drama has extended well past the end of my shift. As I reflect later on the event, my reaction to his appearance in the ER surprises me. I am accustomed to living through trauma. Why did this event trouble me so deeply?

I return for my next shift the following day. I am told that the shooting victim will make a full recovery. I tell myself that I shouldn't be so sensitive and need to grow thicker skin. I have seen worse than this. I can't let tough situations get the best of me. I need to act like an adult. I never see him again.

After the excitement of my second night, all is calm in the ER for the remainder of the summer.

As the warm summer days are going to end soon, I am anxious and ready to begin my college experience. I am planning on rooming with a high-school friend, Megan, in the college dorm. We signed up months ago to share a dorm room. Now there are only three more weeks, and we are going to make the two-hour drive to the large metropolitan town that to us is the BIG CITY. Soon we will begin our college adventure.

Dalton, however, does not share my enthusiasm. Having graduated high school three years previously, he watched friends' romances end when one partner left for college. Since college isn't for Dalton, he makes it clear he thinks it isn't for me either. Although Mom had not supported my early high-school graduation, she always stressed education. "Get your education. It is the only thing no one can take away from you." Recognizing the truth of her words, I knew I wanted a college education. Of this I was 100 percent sure.

Mom was the oldest of three children in her family and had two younger brothers. When her mother died unexpectedly, she was forced to quit school in the seventh grade to care for her younger siblings. When her father remarried a couple of years later and she could have returned to school, she found her classmates had moved on without her. She did go back and get her eighth-grade diploma, but because she was two years older than her classmates now, she did not want to attend high school. I can only presume that this experience formed the foundation for her insistence that her kids complete their education. She knew the difficulty of returning after an interruption in school attendance and wanted more opportunities for her children than she had experienced.

Attempting to reassure Dalton, I say, "I am going to the University of Tennessee, but I still want to keep dating. Just because some of our friends broke up when one went away to college doesn't mean we will break up."

"That sounds like an empty promise," he grumbles.

I don't know what the future holds for me, but I know attending college is in my future. I don't want to commit to anything but school for the next four years, but I also don't have the heart or guts to break up with Dalton.

Employing Mom's tactic, I don't respond to Dalton's statement or question. I am simply not going to promise something that I have no intention of doing.

A few days later during a date, Dalton asks me to marry him. I am very shocked. I have no intention of marrying him.

"No, I am going away to college, and it doesn't make any sense for us to get married."

"But...you slept with me."

I don't say anything. I feel the pierce of his words as though he has plunged a knife into me. The pastor's words ring in my ears: "Save yourself for your husband." Mom's voice echoed the pastor's. "If you don't save yourself for your husband, when you marry, your husband will know you have slept with someone else, and he will never trust you. You will suffer in your marriage."

Seizing my silence as an opportunity to convince me, Dalton continues. "If you don't marry me, I will tell everyone that you slept with me. Everyone will think you are a whore, just like your own mother called you." Familiar shame engulfs me.

Tears begin to flow silently down my face. The depth of my shame and sorrow breaks me, cleanly and easily, like dried firewood twigs. With one bad decision, I feel I have ruined my life. What can I do? Dalton starts the car and continues to drive down to the lake's edge. He stops the car just short of the water. Turning to look at me, he asks, "Will you go for a walk with me?" I can't get out of the car. I feel like dying.

As I sit in silence, Dalton senses that he is breaking me down because I am no longer saying no. He continues with his plan. "We can get married, and you can still go to college. Just go to the local community college."

My head is throbbing. I cannot think or focus. Dalton repeats himself. "If you don't marry me, what will everyone think of you? What with your mother accusing you of being a whore."

Agreeing to marry Dalton seems the only way to avoid further shame being heaped on me. So after a couple of days, I finally agree to marry him. We decide that we will marry in December after the fall semester has ended.

I tell Megan I will not be going to the University of Tennessee but instead, the local community college. She says, "Carly, we have been planning this all year. Why are you backing out now? Are you pregnant?"

I just say, "No, of course not."

I don't think she believes me, but I know time will tell that I am not pregnant. I simply cannot and will not tell anyone the truth about why I am marrying Dalton. The shame is too deep, and silence is the preferred path for me, even if it means ruining my own life.

I tell Robin mid-August that I am engaged and going to marry Dalton in December. "Why? Why would you do that?" Robin demands.

Robin knows I don't love Dalton. But I cannot tell her the real reason because of my intense shame. Robin doesn't speak to me for two months. I never tell her Dalton has blackmailed me into marriage, threatening to expose our premarital sex.

When Robin finally begins speaking to me again in September, still angry, she grudgingly agrees to be my maid of honor. My good friend, Megan, my would-be roommate at UT, is my sole bridesmaid.

There are no smiling faces in wedding pictures. My "big day" is not a joyful occasion for me, my family, or my friends.

Looking back, it is difficult to understand how I could have been so naïve to allow myself to be blackmailed into getting married. Shame had been such a close companion and powerful influencer for most if not all of my life. If only I would have had the courage to share the truth with Robin, Lily, or Megan, I have come to believe they would have offered the support necessary for me to ignore Dalton's threat and pursue my journey to UT. Unfortunately, in my life up to that point, I did not have enough experiences to understand that not all people will judge me so harshly, but instead support me when I had made a wrong choice.

Maybe it was the type of shaming—being called a whore earlier by my own mother and then being accused of potentially being a whore by Dalton—that made me feel such intense shame.

Regardless of the why, I was used to dealing with shame. This was not a new experience to me. For me, the only way I knew how to deal was to go silent on the subject. At least then it's still secret, and in my mind, the being secret keeps the shame away from prying eyes and ears.

After all I had been through so far in my life, I was not about to be publicly shamed by letting everyone I knew find out that I had slept with Dalton.

I didn't realize that by hiding my shame I was letting someone else take my power away from me. This experience would lay the groundwork for Dalton to manipulate me. For once people learn they can manipulate you, it's not about IF but WHEN—because they WILL manipulate you when it serves their purposes. Manipulators know they have to let you win sometimes to keep you off balance. But on the decisions important to them, they seem to always to get their way.

So at that point, Dalton might have found a way to manipulate me by getting me to marry him, but he would not win his war against my continued education. For some reason, this was one item on which I simply refused to budge. It was simply not an option for me to give up on my dream of attending college. Dalton must have sensed this, because as long as I agreed to marry him, he would not contest my desire to attend college...at least for the time being.

Section III

13. Marriage

After marrying Dalton, I keep busy with work at the hospital on the weekends and attending classes at the local community college during the week. Transitioning into married life, I wouldn't describe myself as deliriously happy, but the daily chaos and constant uncertainty of my childhood years begins to recede into my past.

Part of my weekday routine includes stopping at the post office after class to collect the mail. This small gesture helps me feel in control of a small part of my life. It harkens back to those days at the projects when I stood in line to pay the utility bill. On this particular day, three envelopes greet me as I open the box. Stacked neatly on top, an official-looking envelope addressed to Mr. and Mrs. Dalton White grabs my attention.

Feeling my throat close up, the despised tears well up in my eyes and start spilling down my face. I don't exist anymore. My name isn't even on the envelope. Seeing "Mrs. White" on the envelope seals the loss of my identity, my freedom, and my ability to control my destiny. I feel an overwhelming and desperate sense of loss. Walking despondently back to my car, my marriage weighs heavily on me as a terrible mistake. As though blinded and unsure which way to turn, I take a tentative step in the dark woods of my bleak situation only to discover I'm sunk to my ankles in mucky quicksand, now unable to change course.

Some bright spots in my marriage offer solace. Dalton's parents, Nolen and Jean, accept me, unconditionally and without question. I quickly grow to love Nolen and Jean, not only in-laws but also actual parents in many ways.

In our first year of marriage, Dalton works at a local chain grocery store. However, growing up watching his parents operate their own grocery store, he has similar dreams. He doesn't like working for someone else. He begins to talk about how great it would be to open our own grocery store. I don't want any part of it—not my idea, not my dream. You can have that dream, but it's not mine.

Though (or maybe because) he was successful in roping me into marriage, I refuse to allow him to coerce me into working in a grocery store alongside him every day.

Dalton's parents think Dalton's idea is a splendid plan for our financial future. Offering seed money for the venture, Nolen rationalizes a personal loan from them, saying the bank would be using his savings at the bank to fund a loan to us anyway. Nolen's argument seems simple: "Why pay the bank the higher interest rate, when you could just pay Jean and me the higher interest rate?"

"I think that is a good idea, Dad."

"I think Dalton and I need to talk this over," I respond.

"What is there to talk about, Carly? We already know this is what we want to do, right?"

It is a generous offer from Nolen and Jean. My concerns center on Dalton's commitment to the long hours and sacrifices I know it will take to build the business. I'm not convinced Dalton is willing to work that hard.

He currently works in the butcher shop of a local chain grocery store. But he only works three days a week. Dalton doesn't exactly display great ambition—truth be told, he doesn't display any ambition.

But I feel backed into a corner with no one else seeing my point of view. So this is the infamous moment, the moment I capitulate.

Relinquishing my hopes and dreams of true independence and free-dom, I concede and allow Dalton to override my opposition. In a final, feeble effort to cling to my dreams, I offer a meager challenge in my hesitation.

"Well, I just want to make sure that this is what Dalton wants to do."

"I know this is what I want to do," Dalton states firmly.

"Okay, if that's what you want to do. I'll sign the papers for a loan from your parents."

Once home, I let Dalton know in no uncertain terms that my agreement does not entail "running" the store. This is his dream, so operating the store is his job. As long as he understands that, I will sign the loan papers.

"I will only sign these papers if you agree to run and manage the store. I don't want to have anything to do with it."

"Of course, I am going to run the store," he barks, irritated I would question the decision. We borrow the money from Nolen and Jean.

Having grown up around the sport, Dalton is an avid golfer. His parents are long-standing members of the country club, which they joined before Dalton's birth. Nolen and Jean continue the tradition, presenting us with a membership to the country club as a wedding present.

I am somewhat concerned that Dalton will not give up his free time to actually run the store. But I have made my position clear; I will not work in the store.

We open the store in February 1986. It is a specialty meat store with a glass front. So we choose a location near a busy intersection. Several employees conduct the day-to-day work. As the weeks roll into months, Dalton begins spending more and more time on the golf course. He increasingly relinquishes decisions to the employees—choices he, as the owner, should be making. Business begins to suffer.

About nine months later, Nolen approaches me.

"Carly, you know it isn't good that neither you nor Dalton spend enough time in the store managing it. As owners, one of you needs to be in the store to ensure that things are being done the way they should be and that no one steals from you."

"I know. But I can't make Dalton go to the store more."

"Are you going to school for something in business?"

"I am undecided on my major."

"Wouldn't it be great for you to have some business experience by working in the store keeping the books?"

If Dalton were asking, my answer would be a resounding "No." But I respect Nolen. I don't want to disappoint him. I reluctantly set aside my dreams to help Nolen secure a future for his son.

"Well, I guess I could help out a couple of days a week." I don't look at him. I don't know if Nolen is looking at me. I don't know if he sees the disappointment in my face or recognizes the resignation in my voice. If so, he does not acknowledge or question me about it.

I cannot sustain working at the hospital and the store while also attending school. Something must be sacrificed; quitting school is not an option. Submitting my notice at the hospital, I start working in the grocery store. Within a few weeks, my work schedule grows from "just a couple of days" to full time at the store.

Refusing to totally give up on my dreams, I stubbornly continue attending classes.

My feelings about the store and my relationship with Dalton see-saw back and forth, keeping me unbalanced. As my work at the store increases, Dalton's commitment to it decreases. The more I learn and invest my time and energies into the business, the less he seems to care about the store.

I work every day in the store, except Sundays when we are closed. Somehow I manage to keep up with my schoolwork. My mother's words ring unceasingly in my ears: "You've got to get an education, Carly…that's the only thing they can't take away from you."

I am frustrated, but I don't yet see Dalton is taking advantage of me. My overdeveloped sense of responsibility will not allow me to leave the store duties undone. It never occurs to me that my doing both his job and mine weakens us both.

Dalton and I constantly argue over school. I finish my second year of college and receive an associate degree in arts and science. I make plans to continue on in pursuit of a bachelor's degree.

"Why do you want to go to school? We have a business, and you don't need a degree."

"I'm getting my degree."

In the fall of 1986, I begin classes at the UT. It is a two-hour drive each way, and I make the round-trip drive three times a week. I work in the store the days I don't go to school.

The traveling, working, and arguing take their toll. I drop out during the spring semester of my junior year of college.

Over the summer, I decide to go back to UT and take Tuesday and Thursday classes. I will ask Robin if I can stay with her on Tuesday and Wednesday nights; I will drive back home after class on Thursday. Robin has her own apartment, and I'm sure she won't mind letting me stay with her. Maybe then I will have more time to study, and I will only have the long drive once a week.

Anticipating Dalton's irritation with my decision, I strive for creative ways to break the news to him. I have made up my mind, and I will not give in, no matter what it costs me. I tell myself that I have supported him by agreeing to sign the loan papers for the store and then agreeing to work in the store.

Sunday afternoon presents the best time to approach him. He will be in a good mood after golfing all weekend. I faithfully rehearse my script repeatedly in my mind. I am ready to make a stand for what I want. I anxiously await his return home.

The tapping of his golf spikes on the front porch announces his return.

"Hello, Dalton."

"Hello. What's for dinner?"

"Well, I wanted to talk to you before we eat."

"Yeah, what's up?"

"I…I was thinking that I would register for college at UT and start in the fall. I could take Tuesday and Thursday classes and stay with Robin on Tuesday and Wednesday nights. I could use those nights to study."

"Why do you keep bringing up going to school? I thought you were done with that."

"I am going to finish school, and I can't work every day that I'm not in school, drive two hours, come home, and argue with you all the time. If I go to UT and take Tuesday-Thursday classes and stay with Robin, I won't have as much driving time. I will also have time to study."

"Well, I don't want you to go."

"I'm going. If you don't like it, then I will just move there and stay gone all week."

"Are you threatening me?" His tone, however, reflects more anxiety than anger.

"I'm going back to college, whether you like it or not. I am going to major in accounting." My decision is nonnegotiable, and he looks squarely at me.

"What if I say no, you can't?"

"It's not your decision to make. I can either stay there Tuesday through Thursday or just move there altogether."

"Okay…how long is it gonna take for you to get a bachelor's degree?"

"I'm not sure. I will need to talk with the counselors." Oh, my God. He's actually giving in. I'm going to be able to go back to college.

I start UT in the fall. For the first time, I am able to explore the big city without the pressure of rushing home, preparing a meal, and making sure everything runs like clockwork in the house—even if is only for two weeknights every week.

I love school and my newfound freedom; home life, however, is a different story. My relationship with Dalton grows progressively darker and more confrontational. His frustration turns into physical violence. Smacking me becomes more frequent when I say something he doesn't like. I instinctively return to familiar behavior. Like an abused animal, I shrink into the silence and safety of my internal world. I rationalize the situation, telling myself that it could be worse. At least there are no stitches or broken bones. Childhood taught me if you don't have to go to the hospital to get stitches, it's really not that bad. By comparison, Dalton's verbal and physical abuse seems minor. I don't actually even consider it abusive. More like he is just mean and not nice.

However, into my second semester at UT, Dalton's violence escalates. He begins throwing things at me. The slightest imagined transgression triggers his anger. As I return each Thursday night, he picks a fight as soon as I walk through the front door. These disruptions keep me from focusing on my homework. When I realize it is a ploy to keep me upset and unable to focus on schoolwork, I stop speaking to him. It is better to just listen and absorb his frustration. I can do my homework after he tires of the argument.

I witnessed this pattern of behavior in my mother's responses to Russell over and over again during my childhood…the silence, the unwillingness to engage, the retreat of the soul.

I had always believed that I would have to work harder than others to achieve the same success. I intuitively knew the truth of John Carnody's statement in *How To Handle Trouble*: "If we have not grown up in a secure family, protected by love and a minimal prosperity, we have begun life with a solid strike against us."

Even though I went to college, worked at the store, and took care of the house and meals—while Dalton worked part time and golfed full time—I didn't see this as unfair. The distribution of work and fun between us was "normal" based on the models I had witnessed.

The only thing that I knew with certainty was that I wanted to go to college. I would do whatever it took to stay in college and get a degree. I expected to have to work hard to achieve this goal. This, coupled with my overdeveloped sense of responsibility and my low self-worth, meant I voluntarily shouldered the bulk of the work and did not complain. After all, I was getting to go to college.

14. More Violence

After a year at UT, I decide to stop working in the store. I cannot identify a specific event that triggers my decision; I simply decide I'm done with the store. I don't discuss the decision or concerns with anyone. Talking about my problems with another human is the last thing I want to do. I keep my own counsel, and like the old saying goes, "He who keeps his own counsel has a fool for a client."

Sunday afternoon arrives as a perfect fall day. The crisp air invites the drying leaves to a final dance as they descend gracefully from their branches to the ground. It is a great day, and this is the day I am going to take back a small slice of my freedom. Today I will tell Dalton that I am no longer going work in the store.

He has been playing golf with his buddies all afternoon. If he has had a good day on the golf course, which I hope he has, it will be easier for me to break the news to him. I hear the screen door open.

Dalton strides into the living room, dropping his gear on the floor.

"We need to talk," I tell him.

Mimicking a newscaster opening the nightly news with a tragic world event, Dalton announces in a serious and somber tone, "I lost today." Moving on to other news, he continues. "I'm tired and hungry. I don't want to talk about anything. I just want to get something to eat."

"I'm sorry you lost, but this is important. It can't wait."

"Sure, it can."

"No, it can't. I've decided that I am not going to work in the store anymore."

The statement momentarily jars Dalton out of his morose thoughts. "You can't just quit! You can't do that to me."

"Call it what you want, Dalton, but I never agreed to work in the store. You were the one who wanted to open a store, not me. I'm not working there anymore."

"Who will run the store?"

"You wanted a store; I guess you have to run it."

He momentarily looks away and swings his head up and looks right at me. "We'll sell the store then."

"That's fine with me. I don't care what you do. I'm just letting you know that starting next month, I won't be working there anymore."

The afternoon progresses better than I expected. The following week, Dalton meets with his dad. They decide the best option is to have Jean, Dalton's mother, fill in the gap until Nolen and Dalton can find a buyer. Looking back, I realize that Dalton's expectation I would fill in the gaps in his work ethic was not that different from his father's expectations of Jean.

We sell the store for a profit. After paying off the loan from Dalton's parents, a sizeable amount of money remains. Never having taken ownership of the store, I feel I am not entitled to any of the money from its sale, even though I committed to the financial liability on the loan papers.

I continue my studies at UT while Dalton decides he wants to be a farmer. Flush with cash, he begins looking for a plot of land.

I spent most of my childhood in rural areas so I like the idea of living on the land. I am not sure Dalton will make any better a farmer than he has a grocer, but we have the money to pay cash for a farm, and so I go along with the idea.

We buy a small farm at an estate auction and get such a good deal; we are able to pay cash for the place. I think it is a wise financial investment, and even if Dalton doesn't work as a farmer, at least we aren't going to lose money on the place because we have paid under market value at the estate sale.

Not working in the store gives me valuable time to work on my studies. Dalton doesn't like or understand my devotion to school. On some level, I am sure that he feels threatened by it.

I am now able to study on the weekends. It is a Saturday, and I have been studying for a difficult test next week. The house is quiet. Croaking frogs in the surrounding woods keep me company. I don't realize how late it is when I hear Dalton arrive home. For some reason on this particular night, his temper flares when he discovers I still have my nose stuck in a book.

Exasperated at the constant harangue about school, I respond, "This is a broken record. It's useless to have this argument. I am not quitting school."

This is a familiar dialogue, and I fear a long argument. Tonight, however, is different. Before the last syllable leaves my lips, Dalton leaps across the living room. His face contorted with fury, he strikes, hitting me hard in the jaw. My knees buckle under the intense pain. Shards of light flash in front of me like fireworks exploding. I grab the edge of the coffee table to break my fall.

I plummet to the floor, wedged between the coffee table and the couch. Instinct tears through my body, urging me to flee, but Dalton holds me down. As I look up, his heavy farm boots fill my weak gaze and limit my view. It takes a minute to register that the groans I hear belong to me.

Crawling across the living room floor, I look desperately for anywhere to hide. Like a cat playing with prey, Dalton stealthily follows me. Touching his foot to the side of my head, he presses my face hard against the cold, unforgiving floor. "Stay there," he growls. Removing his foot from my head, he kicks me three or four more times. I nearly lose consciousness.

My lungs burn, my head is throbbing, and while I can no longer feel the pain, I began choking. I can't get my breath. Something about my gasping for air breaks through the fury of his assault, and he stops kicking me.

"Are you all right?" he snaps.

"Something is wrong. It hurts when I breathe," I whisper.

"Well you aren't bleeding, so you must be all right."

"How could you have let this happen to you again, Carly? How could you have been so stupid?" It never occurs to me to blame anyone for my situation but me. Oh God, I am living my mom's life. My husband has beaten me and probably broken my ribs, and yet I am the one who feels humiliated. I am the one who must bear the shame.

The fight stops, and I get up and sit on the couch gasping for air. I am in full-on survival mode. Instead of calling 911 or the police, I start being solicitous of Dalton.

I'm sorry, Dalton. I shouldn't have provoked you like that." As I hear the words come out of my mouth, I think of my mother that night on the road saying, "I'm sorry, Russell. I didn't mean to make you mad."

Dalton sees no need to go to the hospital, suggesting instead that I see a campus doctor when I return to school.

"When you go to school, why don't you go see a doctor on the campus? No one will find out if you go to a doctor up there." His logic is for his own protection. He does not want anyone in town telling his parents about any broken ribs.

To avoid making Dalton angry, I agree to go along with his suggestion. A few days later, the campus doctor informs me that I have two broken ribs. Responding to questioning about what happened, I limit the story to falling on an end table. I don't think the doctor believes me, but he doesn't pursue the line of questioning. He wraps my chest and stomach and tells me to get some rest.

Between having my ribs broken and the day-to-day stress of our broken relationship coupled with the pressure of school, I fall into a deep depression. I drop out of school.

Things ease up a little after I drop out of school. Dalton starts talking about having children. I know that I never want to have children. The more he talks about it, the more convinced I am of not having children. I have been taking the pill, but I also add an IUD for extra protection. Not having children is one accident I am 100 percent confident that I know how to prevent. I don't care what Dalton says or does. This one thing is in my control and not his.

I need something to do. It is time to find a job. I begin searching for an accounting job in our small, one-stoplight county. My application at the local sewing factory results in a job offer in the accounting department. With precious few office jobs in the county, I should feel elation at being selected for the coveted position. Instead, I watch my dreams slipping through my fingers like water swirling down the drain.

A few weeks into my new job, I drive the familiar path to work mindlessly listening to the radio, oblivious to the heavy clouds hanging thick and full of moisture in the air. Suddenly my car loses traction with the pavement, and it begins to hydroplane. My vehicle slams into a pickup truck head-on at forty-five miles per hour.

My right foot is crushed because it was on the gas pedal, and I didn't have enough time to react to apply the brakes. My foot is mangled in the car wreckage, and I have to be pried out of the car by the Jaws of Life. I was wearing my seat belt, and due to the force of impact, the seat belt locked, and my upper body was thrust forward. My left collarbone is broken during the accident.

At first I am told that I might not ever walk again. But after having surgery and wearing a cast for six months, I am able to walk.

The particular spot where I wrecked had a slight dip in the road, and it held standing water. There have been many accidents at this location and mine is just the latest one.

A couple of months after my wreck, another girl wrecks on another rainy day in the exact same location. Only she isn't wearing a seat belt. She is thrown through the windshield onto the hood of her car. She dies at the scene of the accident.

Of course the whole town is upset at this tragic accident. Her death at the same spot as my accident is emotionally overwhelming for me. I feel this could have easily been me and that somehow I have cheated death.

I think of all the things that I dreamed of doing when I was younger. And now I can't do any of those things because I am married. And I am married to someone whom I had never loved. I hate my life. I don't think I ever hated my life before this point.

In the fog of this depression, I decide to leave Dalton as soon as the doctor clears me to drive a car. When the day comes and I tell Dalton I am leaving him, he immediately employs guilt tactics. They worked before, why not again? "You would be lying to God if you left me. You promised me and God for better or worse."

This religious argument no longer has the emotional power to keep me from leaving. I leave the house on a Friday evening. But the next four weeks, Dalton is constantly calling me and accusing me of lying to God by leaving him.

The emotional guilt I feel is very powerful. So I go back to Dalton. The undeniable mistake of going back settles on me within a few hours of my return to our home. I vow to myself I will not leave him again until I know no amount of pleading, shaming, or manipulating will make me stay with him.

One year later, I leave Dalton for the second time—for good. Feeling guilty and ashamed for having "lied to God," I pack only my clothes into the "work" car we use to run errands and refuse to take any money. It helps to ease my conscience knowing that I didn't take any of the money we earned when we sold the store.

To Dalton's credit, he makes a small attempt to get me to take some money, but it was never about money for me. No amount of money is worth my freedom.

"No, you keep it all." Forgoing my share of our assets serves as my apology—my payment—my punishment—for breaking my promise to Dalton and to God.

For many years, I had a saying about how people respond to self-improvement. Getting better is like jumping off a building. Some people will figure things out on the way down, and some have to hit the ground before they can start all over. At that time in my life, I was careening down the side of the building, waiting to meet the sidewalk head on. It never occurred to me in those days to grab an awning and save myself the devastating trip to the bottom.

Dean Martin, the actor, once said, "You can't fall off the floor." I couldn't get a clean start without hitting the ground.

Leaving everything behind was a defining moment for me. Removing all options sometimes opens up new vistas, and this time, options I had never known existed presented themselves. The day I left Dalton the second time, I knew I was free. I felt I could finally have the life I had dreamed of. I felt like the world was my oyster.

It never occurred to me that I could put myself first, that I had the freedom to decide on a plan of action a path of my own choosing without having to appease someone else's needs first. I had always believed that I could only do what I wanted for me after I had met the needs of everyone else first. My life, I believed, was to be worked into my spare time. I had relegated my life to leftovers. I was unaware that I lacked the ability to put my needs first. Without realizing it, I was creating the "perfect victim."

Little did I know that the next perpetrator was only days away from entering my new life.

15. New Town, New Perp

The grip and influence of religion holds a powerful sway over my beliefs and thinking. My mother, a Jehovah's Witness, drills in me certain moral imperatives. She lives out a prime example: once you marry, you stay married…no matter what. Her adherence to such dogma robs her, my siblings, and me of a peaceful and safe home life. Those same bug-a-boos continue to wreak havoc with my mind. It's not right to divorce anyone. I married him until death do us part. I took an oath.

Breaking the rule of no premarital sex set the stage for Dalton to blackmail me into marriage. Before God and many witnesses, I promised to stay with Dalton for life...for better or for worse. Obligation, not love, motivated me to keep that promise for five and a half years.

Although I have experienced much sadness and hardship in my young life, at twenty-three, I still feel young enough to recover. Surely life still holds some fun for me. I stand confident, ready to reclaim my life.

I feel buoyant with freedom following the divorce. I decide that what I never speak of, to anyone, can never affect me. What's in the past remains buried. I move on...but have I?

The first step in my moving-on and forgetting-the-past process involves moving to Nashville. I want to live in a big town with total strangers. No one in Nashville knows my family history...my secrets... except my sister, of course. A novice at recovery, I believe a change in geography will precipitate a change in my emotional health. Being innocent, I remain unaware of the fact that "geography only changes geography" and not your emotional knowledge.

Dalton refuses to sign the divorce papers, so I file a no-contest divorce. The divorce will be final in six months with or without his signature. So in this waiting period, I start my new single life.

I land my first job interview for an accounting clerk position at a major hotel chain. With over a hundred employees and eight full-time people in accounting, the environment is busy and vibrant. The hotel catering department manages parties on a continual basis. I make friends with several of the staff members, and five or six nights a week after work, we go out. Not one of my new friends knows I've been married. I want people to believe that my life until now has been simple and boring. This perception keeps uncomfortable questions at bay. And I have plenty of experience at keeping secrets.

Occasionally a question arises about my parents. I tell everyone that my father died (he is still in prison and dead to me), and that my mother lives out of town now that she is remarried.

My second week in Nashville, a work night, I'm on my way to meet some of my coworkers for a drink. The warm April air caresses my face and gently lifts my hair as the evening breeze drifts through the car window. The spring evening tempts everyone to taste the sweet promise of the onset of summer.

I pull to a stoplight, waiting for the green glow to indicate my turn. A Mustang convertible pulls alongside me. The guy on passenger side greets me with a wicked smile. "Hey, my friend thinks you are cute," he says as he nods his head toward the driver. "Can he buy you a drink?"

I roll my eyes, turn my head to the front again, and proceed to roll up the car window. "Nervy," I think. "I don't even know them… city guys sure are rude."

The traffic light in the turning lane turns green; the Mustang pulls away. A minute later, my light turns green, and I drive straight ahead toward a hip little bar called the Alley Cat. Located in one of the oldest neighborhoods in town, the pub is housed in a remodeled hundred-year-old building. The ground floor even has a tournament-sized sand volleyball court.

Walking into the Alley Cat, I don't see my coworker, so I find a seat at the bar and order a drink. About ten minutes later, guess who appears. Yep. In walk Mustang guys. They spot me at the bar alone and saunter over. The driver of the car claims the barstool beside me.

He is a plain-looking guy of medium height, broad without being fat, with reddish hair. "This is fate. We are meant to be together. By the way, my name is Jamie. Can I buy you a drink?" I don't think so…Jamie.

With as much sarcasm and derision as I can muster, I state the obvious with some embellishment. "Well, I already have a drink, and I am waiting on my girlfriend. If she doesn't show up, I'm leaving. So… no, you can't buy me a drink."

In 1990, there are no cell phones. I cannot contact my friend to see how long she will be delayed or if she is coming at all. But I have no intention of letting any man do *anything* for me, and that includes buying me a drink. Letting a guy buy me a drink equates to agreeing to be friends, and I want no part of that.

Thirty minutes later, I decide my friend is not coming. Jamie tries to talk me into giving him my phone number, but I refuse. There is absolutely no way I am going to get locked into another relationship. I'm not playing hard to get. I simply don't want any romantic involvement. Not with Jamie. Not with any guy.

After the conversation in the bar, Jamie keeps showing up in my life. If I go to the Alley Cat, he is there. If I go to another bar, he shows up there too. Over the next several weeks, I see him a couple of times a week on average. He doesn't have my phone number, we never go out "together," and I never let him buy me a drink.

Several months later, returning to the office following lunch with a coworker, one of the girls at the front desk stops me short as I walk into the office suite. "Carly, you got the weirdest phone call while you were at lunch. A man who said he was your husband called, and he wants to know when you will be back."

My surroundings start spinning. The view around me begins to blur. I don't say a word, but the look on my face betrays me, disclosing my secret.

In shock, Jewels exclaims, "Oh, my God! You *are* married!"

Embarrassed and humiliated, my carefully guarded secret now feels like tabloid news. Jewels will not stop talking, unable to conceal her amazement. "And all this time we thought you were just a simple country bumpkin! What else are you not telling us?"

I silently look at her, my face expressionless.

The agony persists. "I can't believe you didn't tell anybody you were married. Why didn't you tell anyone?"

In a flat voice, I weakly explain, "We're separated and getting a divorce."

"Hey, Carly, what else aren't you telling us?"

A jittery, forced laugh erupts from the depths of my being, sounding more like the cry of a wounded animal. "That's all. There is nothing else."

Recovering from the shock of being outed, a wave of relief washes over me, cleansing some of the shame. I don't have to pretend anymore. I can evict the obnoxious worry worm from the dark recesses of my mind; I don't need to be concerned about being found out anymore. My coworkers now view me as a woman of mystery. It all works.

$\mathcal{Q}$

My ability to view my marriage as *mine*, seeing my part without blaming others, proved critical to my being able to move forward into the next chapter of my life with a positive outlook. I never expected anything to be easy for me; I never expected help from anyone.

I have continually felt, however, that I should have known more and subsequently made better decisions at any one particular point in time of my life. My persistent problem was the absence of healthy adults—even just one—to turn to for advice or guidance when I needed help. With no parents or trusted, extended family members to turn to, I was left to make my own decisions with unhealthy, limited life experiences as my guide.

My unwillingness to seek guidance or counsel from others outside my family limited my ability to choose wisely. My intense shame surrounding my childhood and failed marriage prevented me from trusting or approaching anyone. I had learned to be totally self-sufficient, beginning with my earliest childhood memories. I was many years away from recognizing my need for help and the guidance offered by safe, healthy, caring people. I didn't have any awareness yet of the existence of safe people.

In my naïvety, once again, life was on the upswing. Life was definitely better than my childhood years living with Russell and Mom, better even than my calmer high-school years living alone, and absolutely much better than life with Dalton.

My tenets for life held firm. Never get married (my blackmail marriage to Dalton didn't really count in my book), never have children, and get your education. These were the keys to a great life. If I just stuck to these rules, a GREAT life would surely follow. I unconsciously dragged all the emotional baggage, triggers, and hindrances from my traumatic early years into adulthood. I was completely unaware of the chokehold influence that these experiences would exert, keeping me from achieving the stable and secure life I so desperately wanted.

I thought I was on top of the world and starting my grand experiment. I had no idea in reality I was "fresh pickins" for the next bully. And I had already met this bully; his name was Jamie.

Section IV

NAÏVE ADULT

16. Freedom but New Deceit

Sandwiched in the center of all us kids, the ultimate middle child, Lily stands five feet six inches tall, with soft, light-brown hair. She has a temperament matching her physical attractiveness, and I do not remember a single instance of Lily raising her voice. After marrying Stevie—her escape route from our traumatic home—Lily discovers he is an alcoholic. Refusing to seek help, Stevie's ongoing physical abuse finally wears Lily down. Eleven painful years and two children later, Lily reaches her breaking point and ends her marriage to Stevie. She moves to Nashville with her children in pursuit of better employment opportunities about two years prior to my own divorce.

When I leave Dalton for good, I move to Nashville and move in with Lily. Although I do not have children, Lily and I share other commonalities. Chief among these is the trauma of physical violence experienced in our marriages; we do not judge one another. We understand and share the pain and shame of the mistake of staying married to abusive men.

My sister Robin also lives in Nashville; however, we aren't close. I keenly feel Robin's judgment, especially regarding my marriage to Dalton, which she deemed a mistake from the very beginning. I never talk to her about my fears or failed marriage for fear of a sermon on the mistakes that I have made. Robin does not experience violence in her marriage, and she could simply not understand what Lily or I have gone through. Robin is focusing on wanting to have children, a path that I would never consider for myself.

For three months, Lily and I share a modest house with her two children. When the lease ends, we move to a larger split-level house.

I occupy the lower level, and Lily and her kids inhabit the upper level. We share the two-car garage, living room, kitchen, and laundry room. I have the luxury of my own bathroom. Lily and I get along well, and I am happy. I love my job, and I have lots of new friends. Yes, life is definitely good.

The accounting work at the hotel provides a welcome challenge. A fifty- to sixty-hour workweek seems like a normal schedule to me. I don't mind the long hours; my new life continues to thrill me.

In June 1990, I am promoted to assistant controller. My hard work is starting to pay off. My past begins to fade. The painful memories begin to lose their intensity like fading photographs. On October 25, 1990, my marriage to Dalton officially ends. What many experience as a dreadful or tragic day, I celebrate as the happiest day of my life thus far. I consciously think, "I am over-the-moon happy." I left Dalton emotionally long before I left him physically.

Lily joins me in celebrating my official status as a single woman. To honor the occasion, I buy a pair of divorce earrings—nothing like a little bling to mark a grand occasion.

I continue going out for drinks several nights during the week while maintaining a sixty-hour workweek. Emerging into the full bloom of young adulthood, I fully exploit the advantages of my youthfulness. Several months pass. I continue to see Jamie two or three times a week in the bars. I repeatedly refuse his continual requests for my phone number. I am only home long enough to fall exhausted on the bed and sleep. It feels much safer to keep people, especially men, at a considerable distance outside the boundaries of my inner circle.

Jamie owns a small local landscaping company. Although cell phones remain several years away as a common accessory, Jamie has a car phone mounted on the console of his car. He gives me the number. A few more weeks pass. Jamie's persistence pays off. I finally relent and give him my work number. He immediately begins calling me at work. Always witty and upbeat, he makes it a habit to try to discover my work group's extracurricular plans. Maintaining my comfort with secrets and ensuring my continued freedom, I don't always tell him where we are going. However, finding me doesn't prove too difficult because we limit our usual haunts to two or three neighborhood bars.

I am in a particularly good mood one evening. My new life feels solid. I feel safe. As usual, Jamie appears at the bar. We have several drinks. In the wee hours of the morning, the bartender yells, "Last call."

Jamie optimistically offers, "Let's get one for the road."

"Why don't we not...but you can come back to my house, and we can have one there."

Jamie's surprise is almost comical. He recovers quickly and nonchalantly responds, "Yeah, that sounds like a good idea."

On the drive home, I wonder if my impulsive decision is a mistake. If he comes on too strong, I can quit seeing him, I think. Jamie, however, maintains his funny and charming persona. We are intimate that night.

The evening isn't forced. I am intentional in my desire to be intimate with someone after Dalton. I want to prove to myself I can sleep with a man without a lifelong commitment. I have to know that I can sleep with a man without marrying him.

That night changes our relationship. Seeing me out at bars, Jamie now remains close by my side throughout the evening, almost, but not quite, hovering. Sometimes I invite him to leave with me; other times I don't. He doesn't push too hard to go home with me but let's me know he is disappointed when he doesn't receive an invite to spend the night with me.

I feel I have total control of my life. My biggest mistake in life thus far—admittedly, a massive one—was marrying Dalton. I feel that I have learned a major lesson from that experience. I am not going to repeat that mistake ever again. Success means not making the same mistake twice. Surely everyone makes mistakes.

I think that successful people in life distinguish themselves by not blaming others and humbly learning from their mistakes. Quite simply, successful individuals refuse to repeat the *same* mistakes.

I certainly don't want a solo relationship with anyone. The irregularity of the relationship with Jamie meets my needs perfectly. Our relationship does not in any way strike me as odd or unusual. Jamie introduces me to his friends who accompany him to the bars. I, in turn, introduce Jamie to all my hotel friends. I only see Jamie in the bars and nightclubs, and that suits the demands of my hectic work schedule beautifully. A bonus is that our limited contact also allows me to keep the relationship on a surface level. This keeps any expectations for extended commitment off the radar. No worries here. I am a young adult enjoying a carefree life. Nothing appears out of the ordinary. We're just two adults with a mutual attraction, having a good time.

Four days before my first Christmas in Nashville, Sue—my boss, the hotel controller—calls me into her office. "Carly, do you think you could go to Colorado and work as the acting controller while Renee is out on maternity leave?"

Six months pregnant, Renee, the controller at the Colorado hotel, must spend the remainder of her pregnancy on bed rest. Shocked and elated that management has chosen me as the interim replacement, I seize the opportunity.

"Yes! I'll go. I can stay as long as you need me there."

"Great, you leave tomorrow morning."

I'm flying for the first time in my life, and my company is paying for it. I'm a bona fide business traveler!

I love Colorado, the fancy hotel, and my new office. The hotel is a ski-in/ski-out hotel located in beautiful Beaver Creek. I get to stay in one of the hotel suites while I am working here. I enjoy a beautiful "residence"; the hotel benefits from my twenty-four-seven availability as an employee. I meet people from all over the world. I learn to ski!

To say I feel like I have landed in a dream would be an understatement.

The hotel is willing to pay my flight home every other weekend. However, flying back and forth from Nashville to Colorado means I will spend most of my weekends in airports as there is not a direct flight and the layovers will consume my weekend time.

I inquire if the company will alternately fly someone out to visit me. Sue informs me, "That shouldn't be a problem. The cost to the hotel is the same either way."

"Okay, I'll work out the flight arrangements with purchasing."

I have not limited my romantic interests to Jamie in Nashville. I "date" several other people casually. Dave is probably my favorite casual male date. He works for one of the hotel's vendors. I instantly liked him when I first met him. He came to the accounting department to get a copy of an invoice for his company, and from the beginning, he made a point of trying to find a reason to talk to me. I could tell he wanted to ask me out, but he is very shy.

I feel relaxed and at ease with Dave. He is funny and calm and laughs easily. Not exactly handsome, he offers comfort and safety. His calm, reassuring demeanor is his most attractive quality. Dave claims the title of becoming my first male visitor from Nashville. We have a great time skiing and dining. I never sleep with him. It just doesn't seem relevant.

Several weeks pass. I decide to invite Jamie to come to Colorado for a visit. It is February, prime skiing season, but a slow time of the year for landscapers. I know Jamie will not be busy until the weather breaks in the spring. I call him at work and invite him to come out to Colorado.

"I can't come, Carly."

I immediately assume the issue is money.

"Oh, no, you don't have to worry. It won't cost you anything. My company will pay the airfare, and you can stay with me so you won't have to pay for a room either." Silence. A full minute passes. Wow. Really? Surely he doesn't think I'm asking for a bigger commitment. It's just a visit.

"No, I can't come." A long pause. "I'm married. I have two kids."

Wow! I didn't see that coming. Shock nearly cuts off my oxygen supply. I've known him for eight months, and *I had no idea* he is married. How can he be married and consistently be at the bars three or four nights a week?

"Why didn't you tell me?" I ask, appalled.

"Because you wouldn't have spoken to me if you had known." He is stating the obvious.

"How long have you been married?"

"Ten years."

"Well, have a nice life." I slam the phone down.

Oh my God! My horror at discovering I have been dating a married man is exponentially compounded by the fact I've slept with him. I feel incredibly dumb. Why didn't any of Jamie's friends tell me he is married? He has two kids! How could I be so stupid?

In a small town, you could no more hide the fact that you were married than you could hide the fact that you were breathing. I remembered hearing the old men that invariably gathered in the diner say, "You have to be careful about the big town. People aren't always who you think they are." For the first time, I understood what this saying meant.

Reflecting on the situation today, it amazes me I wasn't mad at Jamie for lying to me. Instead, I directed my anger at myself for being so gullible. I assumed all responsibility for his infidelity. My desire to keep others at arm's length provided Jamie with the perfect opportunity to engage in an illicit affair. I offered myself as the perfect playmate. I had not suspected for one second that he was married.

It never occurred to me at the time to place the blame, shame, or anger on Jamie. It never entered my consciousness that Jamie—the one with all the pertinent knowledge—was the one at fault. Rather, I immediately internalized all the blame and shame of sleeping with a married man. *I* should have known better. Of course *I* should have known to ask him if he was married.

As a child, I observed Mom accept full responsibility countless times for the abuse Russell heaped on her and his children. It was *always* her fault. This stance became a part of my DNA. It wasn't Jamie's fault he had lied about being a married man. No, instead it was *my* fault for not seeing the obvious signs, for not suspecting, for not being more alert. I bore sole responsibility for his egregious behavior.

Today, I know that Jamie's lies belong solely to him. At that time, however, I had no conscious awareness I was assuming responsibility for his behavior. I was a naïve victim, unknowingly snagged and trapped in his web of lies.

True to my nature, I didn't talk about the disaster to anyone. I just kept busy and worked harder than ever. It helped to keep my mind distracted. I was a full-fledged workaholic, and the company loved the work I was doing. Working hard is a great attribute for anyone to have. But working hard at your job will not help you change your behavior or thinking skills. It might keep your thoughts at bay, but this was just a coping mechanism, much like alcohol can be used as a coping mechanism. My underlying self-blaming and willingness to accept all the responsibility for all that went wrong never even hit my conscientious as an underlying issue that I needed to deal with.

I remained unaware that there was any need whatsoever to address the underlying issue of my self-blame, which was driving me to accept all responsibility for the situation. As Wayne Dyer has stated, "You can't solve a problem with the same mind that created it."

An out-of-control work schedule provided me with distraction and partial relief from the condemning judgment I placed on myself.

17. New Normal

As March forces winter to recede, my temporary stint out west ends. Declining a permanent position in Colorado, I return to Nashville and the familiar comfort and safety of my old job as assistant controller.

My adult experiences with men thus far have been less than what I would classify as successful. I feel more strongly than ever my best plan of action is to stay away from men. I vow not to get involved with another one. Jamie and Dalton have taught me charm, humor, and great legs do not outweigh or diminish abuse and deceit. No, I have learned my lesson. Men cannot be trusted.

As time passes, I fall back into my old extracurricular patterns. I once again regularly meet my friends after work at our usual neighborhood watering holes. Having a drink at the Alley Cat one evening, I look up to see Jamie walking briskly toward me.

Bluntly and forcefully, he adopts an offensive stance. "Well, you know we were bound to run into one another at some point. You don't have to like me, but let's act like adults."

"Just because we are going to run into each doesn't mean that I want to socialize. I can act like an adult, but you are a loser."

Fumbling, he effortlessly switches to a defensive posture. "I'm unhappy. I stay married because I don't want to leave my kids."

I walk away. What else is there to say? Over the next several weeks, I continue to go out, and Jamie continues to show up. Each time I run into him, the tragedy of his story line increases: He's trapped in a loveless marriage. He is sacrificing himself and his own happiness "for the kids." Sadly, he convinces me of his selfless heroism.

"I am hardly ever home. We only stay married because we can't afford to divorce." What wife would willingly allow her husband to go out all the time? He convinces me that it's a marriage in name only. I start seeing Jamie again, now with the full knowledge that he is a married man.

The lease on my and Lily's shared house ends soon. Lily does not want to continue to rent. She wants to purchase her own home. I understand but am not ready to be a homeowner again just yet. We decide to pursue separate housing when the lease ends.

Sharing a house with Lily eased my transition to Nashville after the divorce from Dalton. I have enjoyed living with Lily, and it is cost-effective, but I am ready for my own place, a space that I can call mine. I decide to move to an old area of town that showcases beautiful, historic homes, many which are over one hundred years old. Single-family dwellings in the early 1900s housed multiple generations. Many of these grand homes have been converted into condos and apartments. It's a desirable location, where young professionals flock, and it's close to restaurants, bars, tattoo parlors, and shops. Offering a Bohemian flair, the neighborhood also offers a short commute to my work downtown.

I lease a small, one-bedroom apartment; it's simple, small, and utilitarian. My private apartment is in a converted triplex.

No pictures, mementos, or plants adorn the cozy space. Essentials such as dishes and flatware, a queen-size bed with a dresser and side table, and plenty of mouthwash and hair-care products in the bathroom identify occupancy in the small apartment. The lack of personal memorabilia, however, borders on starkness. The apartment is sterile, and no one could identify it as belonging to me. It's a place to hide from the world—to cocoon—but never meant to be shared with friends or family.

About a year after I move into my apartment, Jamie calls me one evening. "Hey, Carly. Can I come over tonight?"

"I guess. What time will you get here?"

"Around six."

"Okay, I'll see you then."

Ten minutes before six, the heavy knock on the door startles me. Jamie typically doesn't knock when he knows that I am expecting him. He also knows I rarely lock the door. Childhood lessons have taught me that the scariest people are those you live with, not some unknown burglar. I do not worry about intruders bothering me. Being the sole occupant in my apartment means I am safe.

Jamie has a deep scowl above his brow. "Are you okay?" I tentatively ask.

"I've gotta tell you something."

"Okay." I sit on the couch. Jamie crosses the room to the window seat. He directs his brooding gaze out the window, lost in thought. Finally, he turns to me, his penetrating look firmly in place.

I wait, saying nothing.

Flatly, almost without emotion, he finally states, "I am getting a divorce."

"What? When did you decide this?"

"It's been a long time coming. There is no reason I should stay married."

"We need to quit dating for a year. I don't want to be the reason you get a divorce."

"You aren't the reason we are getting a divorce, and it's stupid for us to quit dating now. We'll be able to go out anytime now, and I can go anywhere you want to go."

"After being in a miserable marriage, don't you want to date other girls for a while? I don't want to be your rebound person."

"I just want to be with you." He moves to sit beside me, and I see his eyes glisten with moisture before he rests his head on my shoulder. "Don't you want to be with me?"

"Of course I do. I'm just confused."

"Well, we can see each other all the time now."

I never wondered about or dreamed of being able to see Jamie more frequently. Although I'm grateful I will no longer be involved with a married man (technically speaking), I am not sure I want a bigger commitment. The thought of being with him all the time is unnerving.

Jamie's divorce is finalized quickly, and we begin openly dating. I meet Jamie's two children, Jason and Allison. I fall hard and quick for Allison. She is seven years old and is a bundle of nonstop, fun energy.

However, my relationship with Jamie is not progressing nearly as well. We fight all the time. Jamie's jealousy emerges from out of nowhere and spirals rapidly. He was never jealous before.

It's our first night out on a real date; Jamie is taking me to dinner. The waiter, young and attractive, arrives for our drink order.

"What can I get you guys to drink?"

"I'll have a Long Island iced tea," I respond with a smile.

"A beer."

Receiving our drinks, I smile again and say, "Thank you."

Jamie's anger flares. Snarling, he accuses, "Well, go ahead and flirt with him right in front of me."

Embarrassed and humiliated, I do not react. Intently observing the pattern of the napkin on my lap, I feel the fingers of my old familiar companion clamp onto me like a vice as shame washes over me. Clearly uncomfortable, the waiter ignores Jamie's comment, instead asking, "Are you ready to order?"

"You go ahead. I need a minute to decide." Jamie gives no response.

I look up and smile at the waiter, my small apology for Jamie's bad behavior. I have no idea what I want to order. Upset and anxious, I am no longer hungry. In an effort to break the awkward silence, I ask the waiter, "What would you recommend?"

Jamie screams, "Well, why don't you just f—— him right here? You are acting like a whore."

I feel the heat crawl from the base of my neck and journey up my face. I can offer no excuse for Jamie's insane behavior. I rise without saying a word and quickly walk out of the restaurant. Having met Jamie at the restaurant, thankfully, I have my car here and can drive myself home.

Alone in the safety of my apartment, hurt and confusion erupt as the flood of tears refuses further containment. What am I doing? Why did he act that way?

Jamie calls repeatedly, leaving multiple messages on my answering machine. "I am so sorry, Carly. Please pick up the phone."

Jamie's phone messages tell the sad tale of his wife cheating on him first—thus, his fear that I, too, will be unfaithful to him. Understandable, I think, but I remain unmoved. The phone continues to ring periodically throughout the night. His monologues fail to sway me. I don't care. He embarrassed me publicly, and there is no excuse for his crazy behavior. I can't let that go.

A knock on the door the following evening sends me to the peephole. I cannot imagine Jamie has the nerve to come to my apartment.

"Go away. I don't want to see you," I bark out loudly enough so he can hear me through the door.

"I will stay here until you open this door."

Fearful the neighbors will see him standing outside my door, I relent, open the door, and allow Jamie to step inside. It never occurs to me to call the police.

Jamie keeps apologizing, intense and insistent that I forgive him. "The way you were looking at the waiter made me think that you wanted to be with him."

"Crazy, he is crazy," I think, but I keep the thought to myself.

"You are from the country, and you don't understand all the signals that you are sending."

My nightmarish childhood and single living arrangements as an adolescent solidify my belief I am different from others. Jamie's comment confirms my insecurity about my own gut feelings. The accusation hits pay dirt. I wonder, "Could he be right? Am I unconsciously giving off signals to other guys? Can Jamie's behavior be my fault?"

I remain silent and give no response to Jamie's pleading. He takes this a cue to continue. Like a skilled politician, Jamie stays on message. "You give mixed signals to the waiter," he accuses.

Having no baseline against which to evaluate my own behavior, I accept Jamie's explanation for his inexcusable behavior. Jamie is not responsible for his own anger—I am. My anger persists for a few days. Jamie's pushy and persistent badgering, however, convinces me to forgive his misinterpretation of *my* behavior and take him back. Foolishly, I do.

I fall back into my old patterns. Instead of confronting Jamie about his unacceptable behavior, I adjust my own behavior. When we go out, if we have a male waiter, I give my drink and dinner order to Jamie, who then relays it to the waiter.

Unaware I am giving up pieces of myself, I feel like such a slight alteration to my behavior can avoid a repeat of the embarrassing incident with the waiter. And isn't a relationship supposed to be about give and take? I shouldn't also expect to get my way.

Jamie's custody agreement means he gets his children every Wednesday and every other weekend. The bar scene naturally comes to a close for us. Ready to give up the hectic pace of constant nightlife, I enjoy having Jamie's kids around. We settle into a couple's life. I play house and dedicate energy to building a good relationship with Jamie's kids. I am oblivious to Jamie's increasingly dangerous, controlling behavior.

Jamie's parents are divorced. After meeting and talking with both of them, I begin to suspect that Jamie has a criminal record. Comments at family gatherings continue to fuel this suspicion.

After my experience with Russell, I realize I need to know if Jamie has a criminal record, so I go downtown to the courthouse and look up his record. There are several drunk-driving arrests and an assault charge. I am shocked and decide to break it off. He is not the person I thought he was.

I break the news in a phone call. "I don't want to see you anymore."

"What are you talking about? Why don't you want to see me?"

"I know about your criminal record."

"Who told you?"

"I looked it up myself."

"You did what? What gives you the right to go snooping around in my business? Who do you think you are? How could you do that?"

"It is public record, and I have a right to know these things if we are going to date."

"You are sneaking behind my back! Only a no-good loser would go behind someone's back and do something so low."

"I have the right to look at your record. I need to know what kind of person you are.

"You don't have the right to go behind my back. There's something wrong with you! I don't know if I want to keep seeing you. I don't know if I can ever trust you again."

"I am trustworthy. I am not the one with the criminal record."

"You are not a person to be trusted. You went behind someone's back. You should be ashamed of yourself."

Like a skilled athlete shifting effortlessly from defense to offense, Jamie shifts the focus of the argument from his criminal record to my integrity. Suddenly, I feel compelled to defend *my* actions.

The issue is no longer his criminal record, but my lack of trustworthiness. Realizing his anger is increasing with every syllable uttered, I seek the quickest escape route. "I need to go. Please don't call me again."

Jamie does not call. No flowers, no long-winded phone-message pleas, no phone calls at work, no unexpected knocks on my door.

I made the right choice.

Then, at the end of the first week, I receive a phone call from Allison. I don't have caller ID, so I didn't know it was Allison calling until I answer the phone.

"Hi, Carly."

"Oh. Hello, Allison."

"How are you?"

"I'm fine, sweetie. How are you doing?"

"I'm good. I miss you. I was wondering if I can come over to your apartment and spend the night with you?"

I love Allison. We took walks together and fished for minnows in the stream. Since Jamie and I began dating openly, I have attended all of her ballgames.

"Of course you can, Allison." Warmth seeps through my every appendage at the knowledge Allison still wants to see me.

She is calling from her dad's house, so Allison gives the phone to Jamie, and we discuss when he can drop her off. He does not mention seeing me or ask how I am, and I am relieved that he only wants to discuss Allison.

On Saturday morning, as agreed, Allison rings my doorbell at 10:00 a.m. Saturday is going to be an all-girl day. I have lots of fun things planned for us to do. The plan is for Jamie to pick Allison up at noon on Sunday.

However, on Sunday morning at 11:00 a.m., there is a knock at the door.

"Hmm…who on earth can that be?" I wonder. I look through the peephole and see Jamie standing in the hallway.

I open the front door and don't say a word.

"Hello, Carly."

"Hello. Why didn't you call first?" He waits for me to invite him in.

"I had a change in schedule at the last minute." He walks past me into the apartment. Allison walks out of the bedroom and sees her dad.

"Oh, Dad, I had the best time ever!" she gushes. "We went to the movies, and I got a candy bar and popcorn."

"I'm glad you had fun, sweetie. Why don't you ask Carly if she wants to come to our house for dinner tonight?"

"Please, oh, please come over for dinner! Please say yes!"

Looking into Allison's pleading eyes, I don't have the heart to dampen her childish anticipation. "Yes, I'll come over—but just for dinner."

Jamie adopts an apologetic and sweet demeanor as bait. I bite, and Jamie reels me in like a gullible fish…again.

The cycle repeats itself, beginning with an increasing number of arguments. Jamie doesn't like my job. I work too many hours. He complains that I don't have enough time for him and the kids. I adjust my behavior. I quit my job and secure another position with fewer demands and less pay. For me, less pay is worth fewer fights with Jamie.

But Jamie's criticism doesn't stop. I don't wear the right clothes. I don't say the right things. I don't talk to the right people. According to Jamie, I don't do anything right. I continue to adjust. I learn what triggers him. I stop calling my friends. Like dripping water changing even the hardest surfaces over time, Jamie slowly and increasingly isolates me. Within months, none of my friends remain on speaking terms with Jamie.

My sister Robin doesn't meet or know about Jamie until we are openly dating. Robin makes no attempt to disguise her dislike of Jamie. The feeling is mutual. They can't stand each other.

Lily doesn't like Jamie either but for my sake tolerates him. Lily wants to support me. If I want to be with Jamie, she will support that decision.

Our arguments increase until it seems like that is all that exists in the relationship. I'm tired of fighting all the time. I tell Jamie with resignation, "I don't think we should continue seeing each other because all we do is argue."

"We only argue because you have your own place. If we lived together, I would know where you are, and you would know where I am. Then we wouldn't fight."

I remain guarded, not convinced living together will change the relationship. Jamie's insistence once again weakens my resolve to end the relationship. But his relentless persuasion finally wears me down, and I consent. "Okay, I'll move in with you, and we will see if this is going to work."

Seeing Allison on a regular basis is the one bright spot about living with Jamie. I am not close to his son, Jason, but I have grown to love Allison just like a daughter.

Surprisingly, the new living arrangements seem to improve my and Jamie's relationship. We have been living together about eight months when Jamie starts talking about building a house together. He envisions an extravagant house, but I desire something much simpler.

The prospect of remodeling an older home intrigues me. Jamie rejects that idea. Too much work. He wants to build a new house. We discuss it often but cannot agree on a location or price range.

Fear of returning to poverty lurks like a predator on the fringes of my thoughts. I don't want a large house payment, preferring something smaller that allows me to live well within my means. Jamie won't hear of it. He wants something fancy, something to impress his friends and family.

Being self-employed as the sole owner of his garden center, Jamie does not have the income to qualify for a mortgage payment. Jamie can't qualify for the loan without my income. Jamie's cooperativeness increases significantly.

On several occasions, Jamie asks me to marry him. My response never varies. *No.* I don't want to get married. I don't want to marry anyone. I don't share with him, and I don't trust him. Not financially. Not otherwise. Loving someone is not the same as trusting them.

Predictably, I keep my own counsel, not once sharing my dilemmas with coworkers, friends, colleagues, or family members. I console myself with the fact that my adult life is far better than my childhood.

Today, I easily recognize my faulty thinking. At the time, I truly felt that my life—although not exactly what I had planned—wasn't bad.

At times, Jamie was actually charming and funny—when he wasn't being manipulative and mean. Although I wasn't sure where or how Jamie might fit into my life on a long-term basis, I had no such reluctance where Allison was concerned. I loved her as though she were my own child.

Upon reflection, Jamie's manipulation now seems painfully obvious. But during this time in my life, all my thoughts were filtered through my toxic, internal shame. These intense feelings influenced decisions that were not in my own best interests. These shamed-based decisions, however, helped me to continue to hide the craziness of my home environment from others and thus avoid their judgments.

Fear of embarrassment and harsh judgment from others silenced me, keeping me from sharing my situation with anyone. My own behaviors reinforced Jamie's efforts to isolate me, keeping me locked in my toxic-thinking cycle. Same thinking; same results. Strife and arguing were my normal baseline.

18. Illness

Jamie's persistence in trying to convince me to build a house with him knows no bounds. His relentless requests, while failing to convince me it will be a wise commitment or sound financial decision, begin to wear me down.

A savvy businessman, Jamie operates a successful business. Yet memories of watching him use less-than-ethical practices to cheat his clients raise suspicions he may try such tactics on me. I don't want to be his next financial victim. I do not want the stress of maintaining constant vigilance, carefully watching every detail and purchase required to build a house. Observing Jamie utilize his street smarts on several occasions makes me nervous that I will become the source of his next windfall.

Jamie oozes enthusiasm as he excitedly tells me about ten acres one of his landscaping clients has for sale. Although it's been landlocked for several years, the owner has recently purchased a stretch of land leading to the plot that can serve as the driveway to the property. Straddling two counties, the acreage is located in Davidson County, our county of residence, while the driveway is located in adjacent Sumner County.

Other than a possible conversation starter, I see no issues with this interesting quirk. Unbeknownst to me, the county of record for the property—and driveway—will prove a menacing problem for me in the years to come.

Since access to the property has been limited for nearly twenty years, cedar trees and dense underbrush dominate the landscape. Now that it is no longer landlocked, the owner wants to sell the property quickly and has reduced the price to about one-third of the cost of comparable land. Jamie and I agree we can clear the land, selling the wood to offset the cost of logging the area.

Together, we purchase the land.

I meet Jamie's dad, Alan, about four months after Jamie and I start openly dating. In the process of getting a divorce from his fourth wife, Alan is pursuing his latest love interest, a woman named Misty. Never lacking female company, Alan enjoys plenty of live-in girlfriends between marriages. Clearly, his father's serial relationships bother Jamie. He frequently comments to me that he doesn't want to be like his dad by introducing multiple women into his kids' lives.

Claiming physical abuse, Alan's latest wife has a protective order issued against him. The first time I meet Jamie's mom, Betty, who was Alan's first wife, she flatly informs me Alan is extremely physically abusive. Betty does not hesitate to share graphic stories about the abuse she and her children endured under the monstrous reign of Alan. Even twenty-five years after her divorce from Alan, Betty is still very bitter.

I believe Betty, but I refuse to blame or judge Jamie for his dad's abusive behavior. I know only too well the pain and helplessness of having an abusive parent. I certainly don't want anyone to judge me because of my parent's bad deeds. The information actually pushes me in the direction of having more understanding for Jamie. This information helps me to overlook some of Jamie's infractions because I understand the difficulty of growing up with an abusive parent.

I don't like Alan. I never tell that to Jamie. Regardless of what Alan has done, he is Jamie's father. Their family drama is none of my business. But it does explain some of Jamie's erratic behavior.

The business office for Alan's small fence company sits adjacent to Misty's place of employment. A mutual acquaintance introduced Misty, a recent widow, to Alan after his recent divorce from wife number four.

Lonely following her husband's death, Misty succumbs to Alan's practiced charm. She relishes the newfound attention.

Meeting Misty for the first time over dinner with Jamie and Alan, I find her full of life and an easy conversationalist. She is authentic and immediate, and I trust our new friendship. Crossing the street en route to the restaurant, I offer Misty a thinly veiled caution. "Don't ever let Alan change you. You are so full of life; just don't let him change you."

Misty laughs. "Oh no, Alan will never change me. I am too independent to allow that."

Developing the self-awareness that I am beginning to alter my own behavior to avoid fights with Jamie, I want to warn good-hearted Misty not to do the same. Misty and I will revisit this conversation years later, reflecting on advice I so easily gave but was unwilling to follow myself. Unfortunately, Misty will also confess years later that she would not have believed it possible she would change so much to avoid fights with such an abusive partner. You make slight changes over the course of the many arguments, and after many months, you don't even recognize yourself.

I am excited to spend more time with Misty during a vacation the four of us plan. Alan and Jamie take the lead in finalizing plans for a Michigan fishing trip for the four of us. Alan's verbal abuse toward Misty, however, casts a sickening pall over the adventure from the beginning of the trip. Misty can do nothing right in Alan's mind. Alan is in full-on attack mode. I realize the sordid tales of Alan's abuse of his family have not been embellished. He is the ruthless monster others describe. I feel deep, compelling compassion for Misty and wonder if I can help her in any way.

Jamie's efforts to calm Alan only exacerbate the situation. Jamie finally backs off, taking cover and staying as far away from Alan as possible.

Arriving in Michigan in the safety of my and Jamie's room, I optimistically venture, "I hope a good night's rest will help him calm down. Is Alan usually like this?"

Jamie offers a softer, concerned underside. "It's not uncommon for him to get this way. Misty doesn't deserve this, and I hope for her sake that he calms down. Maybe then we can all enjoy ourselves."

A charter boat will take us out fishing on Lake Michigan both early morning and late afternoon for the next two days. Worrying about Misty, I do not sleep well and wake exhausted the following morning. I don't want to go fishing. "I don't want to go out this morning," I inform Jamie. "I'm going to sleep in. I'll join you guys for the afternoon trip."

"No. I want you to go. We didn't drive all this way for you to sleep in a hotel room."

More than sleep, I want to avoid Alan, but I also don't want a fight with Jamie, so I comply. "Okay, give me a half hour, and I'll get ready."

Alan's wrath shows no sign of slowing. To emphasize his misery, he openly complains to the boat captain about Misty. His behavior embarrasses all of us, even Jamie.

Back in our room after the morning fishing trip, Jamie confesses, "I want you to let me know if I ever act like Dad." This is music to my ears, and Jamie continues. "The way Dad is acting is horrible, and I know I can be like him sometimes. I know you are a good person. You can teach me to be a good person."

"Of course I'll help you."

"I promise, when we get back to Tennessee, I will never be mean to you ever again, Carly."

I believe watching his dad's cruelty toward Misty has taught Jamie a hard lesson. Jamie's discomfort is real; he doesn't want to be lumped into the same category as Alan.

Alan's mean-spirited and inhumane behavior overshadows the entire trip. Back home, Jamie reminds me of my promise. "You will help me to be a kinder person, won't you?"

"Yes, I can do that," I lovingly agree.

Jamie reveals a previously hidden part of himself with such openness, sensitivity, and humility. It seems clear this experience pierces a core part of him. When he exposes such vulnerability, Jamie convinces me he really wants to change his own behavior.

My fears vanish. I firmly believe all of our problems are fixable. For the first time in our relationship, Jamie readily admits and accepts responsibility for his bad treatment of me. Of course I will help him in any way possible. He tells me again he recognizes that I am a good person. He pleads with me to teach him to be a good person too, a better partner and father. My heart swells with hope at this positive turn of events.

Returning from the Michigan trip, Jamie and I turn our attention to tackling our overgrown property. We accomplish much of the work ourselves, hiring outside help only to remove the larger trees and chip the limbs piled in teepee mounds throughout the clearing. We can do this. We can build a house together. If things don't work out, we can always sell the property. Clearing the plot will only increase the value of the land.

Our new property becomes my oasis. Continuing to work very long hours as an accounting recruiter, I love coming to our patch of land and working on clearing it. It grounds me, giving me a sense of stability I've never before known. I thrill at the wind whistling through the canopy of trees above. Feeling a million miles away from civilization, I am still relatively close to shopping centers and restaurants. My personal sanctuary...at least that's what I think at this time.

Now married to Adrian, Mom still lives on his farm in rural Tennessee. Before I head out to the land to continue working on clearing it, I call Mom to see how she is doing.

Adrian answers the phone. "Hello."

"Hi, Adrian. How are you doing?"

"Oh, I'm fine. How is everything in Nashville?"

"Good, just working on clearing the land. Is Mom there?"

"Yeah, let me get her for you."

A few moments later Adrian's voice comes over the phone line again. "Your mom says she isn't feeling well and doesn't feel like coming to the phone. She is resting on the couch."

Strange. Although she wasn't the most attentive mother when I was growing up, Mom looks forward to my calls and always seems pleased when I call. I know that Mom faces her own struggles with Adrian and isn't completely happy in her marriage. Unwittingly, the thought flashes through my mind: Has he hurt her?

"Is she all right? How long has she been sick?"

"Oh, she has been tired a lot lately."

"I guess I need to come and see her. Tell her I will come down tomorrow."

"Okay, I know she will be glad to see you. Take care."

"Okay, bye."

Leaving work early the next day, I make the two-hour trek down to see her. When I arrive, Mom emerges slowly from her bedroom, walking tentatively into the living room. Her sweat pants look dingy and rumpled as though she has slept in them for days. Her tired, life-less stance shocks me. Her color looks dull. Although never a large woman, she appears thinner than when I last saw her.

"Mom, are you okay?" I ask in alarm.

"I'm okay, I guess, just feeling really tired. I went to the doctor last week, and he wants to run some tests. He supposed to give me the results when I see him next week."

"I'm going with you."

"Okay, Carly, that will be fine."

The following week I again make the two-hour drive to Mom's house to accompany her to the doctor.

Mom doesn't bother with chitchat on the ride to the doctor. Conserving her energy, she remains quiet, apparently lost in thought, looking out the car window at the cornfields and modest houses lin-ing the road.

The physician runs a small practice located in the center of town. As a general practitioner, he sees a little bit of everything. Sitting ner-vously in the waiting room, I fight back worry that Mom's cancer from a few years ago has returned. The doctors assured us at the time that they had gotten it all when they removed the colon cancer six years earlier.

They had been so confident about the operation that Mom's sur-gery had not been followed with any chemotherapy. She had been clean for the past six years. The silence between Mom and me as we sit in the small waiting room is deafening. Keeping our fears, our anxieties, our pain locked in our own thoughts, we do not engage in any discussion. About anything. No, we maintain the family tradition of solitary isolation.

Mom's name is called to go back to a room to wait for the doctor. We both get up and walk toward the nurse. The nurse leads us down the hallway to the last room on the left. Smiling gently, the nurse pushes open the door, directing us inside the room. "Now just go in here, and the doctor will be in shortly to see you, Ms. Colin."

The room is clinically stark and clean, and Mom gingerly climbs onto the examining table. The stiff paper crinkles as she adjusts her position. Leaning forward, she places her hands on her knees; her heard droops dejectedly. At a total loss, I do not know what to say. I painfully realize that I have never known how to talk to my mother about anything that really matters. Important topics are a deep gulf between us we have never been able to successfully navigate.

The elderly doc appears at the door, his shiny bald head and potbelly exuding country-doctor friendliness. He hesitates in the doorway, as if momentarily contemplating an escape. Sucking in a deep breath, he enters the room and firmly closes the door behind him. Looking at the floor, he greets Mom. "Hello, Ms. Colin. How are you feeling today?" My heart aches as I watch Mom valiantly strive to see his expression, searching his face for answers.

"I'm still tired all the time. Did you find out anything from the test you ran on me?"

Finally, he looks into her eyes, but says nothing.

"Well, spit it out. What is wrong with me?" Mom demands.

"You have a tumor in your colon, and it has spread to your liver."

"What does that mean exactly?" I ask quickly.

"It's cancer."

"How far along is it?" I implore, pleading with my eyes for a more optimistic response.

"It is stage four," the doctor responds.

Still not comprehending, I push further. "How many stages are there?"

"Four."

Mom stands up, her look of determination locked firmly in place. "Let's go."

"Mom, we can't go. We need to ask some more questions."

Mom squares her thin shoulders, rising to her full height. "You can stay and talk, but I am leaving. I don't need to hear anymore." She walks out of the room.

I remain, asking the question that quashes all other questions. "How long do you think my mom has to live?"

"Probably two months at the most."

Two months! My mom will be dead in two months...this can't be true; this just can't be happening. These horrendous thoughts sear through my mind, shattering any ability to hear any other information the doctor presents.

I don't remember driving Mom home or the ride back to Nashville. I call Lily as soon as I get home. Lily is a nurse. She will be able to help me understand what is wrong with Mom. "Lily will know what to do," I think.

The thought of my mother dying devastates me. The finality of never truly having a mother begins to pierce my consciousness.

Jamie's attempt at compassion is a cold dose of harsh reality. "Well, she is dying. There is nothing you can do. People lose their parents every day. Just deal with it."

I return to my familiar pattern. I keep my thoughts and fears to myself. I silently suffer the vortex of swirling emotions inside me. I once again become my own island. I am alone. I will have to deal with this in isolation...just as I have done with all the other struggles and crises in my life.

I realize today Jamie offered support only if he felt there was something in it for him. At the time, however, I could not see this clearly. I had grown up with people who wouldn't or couldn't meet my emotional needs. Jamie's inability to help me through the crisis of my mom's terminal illness seemed normal to me at the time. Therefore, I accepted his callousness without question. Who was I to ask for his time and sympathy? Wasn't he busy enough with his business and his kids? I felt I didn't have any right to burden him with my emotional neediness.

It wasn't an issue of feeling like I wasn't deserving of sympathy; quite simply I didn't realize what I was experiencing with Jamie was not acceptable. My internal compass could not gauge the difference between acceptable and unacceptable behavior. My behavior gauge maxed out just measuring physical violence. If someone wasn't hitting you, things were probably in the normal range.

I vowed to myself that I'd be stronger emotionally. I told myself I didn't need Jamie for any emotional support. I didn't need anyone. I could handle the challenges of my sisters and brother arguing over Mom's care. I didn't need to bother Jamie. Not only did I not need emotional support, I could also carry a full load at work, keep the house, be present for Jamie's kids, and help take care of my mother.

I was superwoman—I just didn't have the great outfit! There was no room for vulnerability in my character. Being vulnerable invited danger.

I was unaware that to be healthy, I would need emotional healing for the very old wounds inside of me. It would be a few years before I would learn to discern and identify safe people (therapists, fellow Al-Anon members, etc.), open up emotionally, and learn to rely on trustworthy people. Quite simply, in order to heal my emotional wounds, I would have to learn how to be vulnerable to safe people.

It would not happen anytime soon. For me to want to change my current life, for me to acquire the drive to change myself, things would need to get really bad. And in changing myself, I would then change my life.

And believe me…I had no way of knowing just how much worse things were going to get.

19. Remorse and Apology

Mom decides to get a second opinion. She eventually sees four doctors before finding one willing to treat her advanced-stage cancer with chemotherapy. Mom steels herself for the fight of her life.

The first few months of treatment, Mom chooses to stay at her home and only travels back and forth to Nashville for medical appointments. Unable to tolerate the chemo very well, she is admitted to the hospital several times for inpatient stays due to complications from the treatment. Since I am the only sibling without children, it is easier for me to stay overnight with her during these hospital stints. Because Ernie lives out of town, he is unable to help with Mom's daily care.

Caring for Mom limits the time I have available to help Jamie with his kids. He resents my time commitment to her. We begin arguing regularly. Jamie complains I am spending too much time with Mom and can't cook, clean, and help take care of his kids when they come to our house.

My siblings cannot agree on Mom's care plan. The five of us siblings have many arguments about the best approach to ensure she receives the best care possible. However, Adrian doesn't want to be involved in any of Mom's health-care decisions or accept any responsibility for her daily care.

Seven months after Mom's initial diagnosis, Jamie and I finish clearing the land. He is anxious to begin building. I want the house but have serious concerns about becoming more deeply intertwined financially with Jamie. Witnessing some of Jamie's dubious business dealings, I don't want to be his next victim. I can't afford to invest my money in the house only to be cheated out of it. So I am hesitant to sign the construction loan papers. And we only seem to arguing more and more.

Jamie is leaving his half of the house to his children. The information provides a convenient ruse to explain my reluctance to commit to the loan to build a house. I tell Jamie I am fearful if something happens to him, I will then jointly own a house with his two children, and his ex-wife will be able to make decisions on their behalf. As usual, his response is swift. "We need to go to my lawyer friend. I used him on a previous business deal. He is a good guy. We will have a partnership agreement drawn up between us."

"How will that protect us?" I ask.

"The partnership agreement will spell it all out. We will own and pay for the property and maintenance of the property fifty-fifty. We will carry life insurance on each other to pay off our respective half in the event either of us dies. We will have two policies, one for you and one for me. You will be the beneficiary of my policy, and I will be the beneficiary on yours. The insurance money will be used to buy out the half interest in the house from the other heirs. The surviving person would then solely own the entire house. The heirs still get their financial portion as well. This agreement will protect each of us from having to financially deal with the other person's family."

I have very little experience with attorneys. The only attorney I ever hired was for my divorce from Dalton. It never occurs to me that I should get a separate opinion to protect my own interests. Instead, I naïvely believe this legal contract will protect me financially.

"Okay, I'll sign the agreement," I say, not realizing that this very agreement will be the very thing that Jamie will later use against me.

Andy Wilson, Jamie's attorney friend, draws up our partnership agreement.

It is 1995. Russell has been incarcerated for sixteen years. With a twenty-year sentence, I know he will be released no later than 1999. Four short years away.

I am torn about telling Jamie about Russell before building the house.

Although dead to me, Russell is still very much alive, sitting in a Tennessee prison cell. I have no idea if he will cause me problems once released from prison. My fear of Russell reappearing continues, rumbling in the recesses of my mind like distant thunder warning of an oncoming storm. The shame I carry associated with Russell maintains its powerful grip in my life.

Telling Jamie about Russell weighs heavy on my heart.

Mom's deteriorating condition only adds to my stress level. I am not sleeping or eating well. Sibling arguments over Mom's care reach crisis level.

Being a caregiver for Mom is time consuming. But I have to give her all I can. I believe I would not have survived Russell without her. She has been a good parent. I promise myself I will tell Jamie about Russell before signing the partnership agreement. I will tell him by the end of the week. At least I'll know one way or the other. If Jamie doesn't want to build the house with me after finding out about Russell, we can both walk away before we are in too deep.

I just hope Jamie understands why I am so committed to helping with Mom's care and why I never told him about Russell. It isn't like I have been keeping a secret from Jamie. I have not told anyone about Russell since moving to Nashville.

I ask Jamie to ride out to the property with me. As we pull up the driveway, my stomach starts cramping, coiling like an internal enemy about to strike. Decision time. It is now or never.

The sun shines brightly in a cloudless blue sky as Jamie pulls his truck into the clearing.

"I think we should have the house face east so we can see the sun come up from the deck," he says.

Getting out of the vehicle, I walk over to some logs stacked from the previous weekend's cutting and ask Jamie, "Will you sit with me? I need to tell you something."

He senses that something is wrong. His response reveals that he suspects I am still hesitant to begin building the house. Taking the offense, he pursues his usual argument. "If we have our own home, we will finally be happy."

"I need to tell you about my father."

Surprised, he sits down beside me on the log. "I thought you said he was dead."

"Well, he is dead to me, emotionally dead. But he is not physically dead," I state flatly.

"What do you mean he isn't physically dead? Where is he?"

"In prison. He murdered a man when I was very young and was sentenced to twenty years."

"Why didn't you tell me before now? Why have you been lying to me all this time?" I can hear the anger in his voice.

Shame creeps in like smoke finding every crack and crevice to choke off any life. Desperate, I seek refuge and oxygen longing for Jamie's understanding and acceptance. "I didn't want anyone to know about him. I haven't seen him since I testified at his trial a decade and half ago. I was fourteen years old and he is not a part of my life and I consider him dead to me. But I felt you should know before we build a house together. I don't know when he gets out if he will try to look me up or not and I didn't want you to be surprised if he shows up on our doorstep in five years."

"You shouldn't have kept it a secret from me. Are you keeping other secrets from me?"

Ouch! It feels like a knife is stuck in my chest. Breathing becomes harder. How can he not understand that this is hard for me? I just concentrate on my next breath. "No."

"Well, I forgive you for not telling me sooner, but don't ever lie to me again, and I mean ever," Jamie says.

With Jamie being appeased for the moment, relief flows through me. I no longer have to feel guilty for keeping Russell secret. I am grateful Jamie doesn't make a big deal out of my father being a murderer. I doubt that everyone would have been that understanding. I agree to apply for the house loan the following week.

The following week, we sign the contract with the builder. Building plans begin in earnest. The day arrives to pour the foundation, along with torrential rain. The builder calls Jamie from the site with bad news. Soggy and saturated ground postpones pouring the foundation, and the forecast has nothing but rain in store for the next two weeks.

The month-long delay has made Jamie angry. He calls the builder. "Listen, it has been over a month since we signed the contract, and you said you could have this built in eight months. This isn't going to happen if you don't get started. You need to pour the foundation now."

"The ground has to be dry before we pour the foundation. I would like nothing more than to get started, but I can't control the weather. The foundation will just have to wait."

Jamie's foul mood persists right along with the inclement weather. The same week Jamie makes the angry call to the builder, Mom is hospitalized again. I stay the night with her in the hospital. My absence only serves to compound Jamie's already high level of frustration. I take work clothes with me, intending to shower in Mom's hospital room and go straight to work. I also don't want to run into Jamie at the house the next morning. He calls me early the following morning on my cell phone.

I answer apprehensively. "Hello."

"There isn't anything to eat here in this house!" Jamie screeches.

Sitting in Mom's hospital room, I don't want her to know that he is yelling at me. My mask falls effortlessly into place, revealing nothing. My silence infuriates Jamie, but I refuse to respond.

"Can you hear me?" He hurls the words through the phone line.

"Yes," I say calmly and softly.

"Are you going to bring some groceries here today or not?"

I continue as though nothing is amiss. "I don't know if I will have time. If Mom is discharged, I may need to drive her to Robin's house. I won't know until the doctor comes in and gives us the test results."

"Well, I don't care what you have to do. You better get some groceries in this house." *Click.* Jamie hangs up without waiting for my response.

My mind feels like jelly. Partially relieved that Jamie's abrupt end to the conversation absolves me from responding further, I also fight the urge to burst into tears. Why can't he understand how hard this is for me? Why can't he just go get groceries?

As I leave the hospital, I wonder what I am doing. I have heard that you shouldn't make long-term decisions in times of crisis. Mom's cancer certainly constitutes a crisis for me. I want to break up with Jamie but don't have the emotional energy to leave him. Maybe Jamie is right, and I'm not carrying my load. I have not been helping him and his kids nearly as much since my mother has been sick. Maybe I am wrong. I feel conflicted. Am I being too emotionally needy, or is Jamie out of line? I know I feel lonely and unsupported, but I'm unsure if my feelings are the CORRECT way to feel.

Mom doesn't get released from the hospital, so I don't go home after work.

Jamie calls that evening while I'm at the hospital. "Why aren't you home?"

"Mom wasn't released. I had to come back to the hospital to spend the night with her."

The name-calling begins. Filthy, disgusting language that would make anyone hearing it feel dirty. I listen without offering any response.

Jamie finally asks, "Are you listening to me?"

"Yes."

Jamie continues his abusive tirade. "You better come home tonight, you stupid lying b———."

I try rationalizing. "What are you talking about? I haven't lied to you."

"You lied about your father being dead. You are nothing but a liar and a cheat."

"What do you mean a cheat?" I ask incredulously, clinging to rational thought in an attempt to keep my head from spinning.

"You're a liar and a cheater. You've dated a married man. I can't trust you for anything."

"I haven't dated a married man."

Jamie says, "You dated me, and I was married. You will lie about anything. I can't trust you in anything."

What? Shock keeps me silent. Rational discourse is clearly not an option. I know stating the obvious—that Jamie is the one who initially hid the fact that he was married—will only fuel his anger.

Reiterating his earlier directive, Jamie orders, "You better be home tonight, and I want you to make sure we have something to eat at the house."

Oh my God. The last thing in the world I want to do is go home and be with that jerk. Early life lessons had taught me, however, that doing what I am told is the quickest path to appeasing my tormentor. Winston Churchill's wise counsel would have served me better. "You can't appease an alligator."

I pick up dinner on my way home. I won't make the mistake of coming home without something to eat. When I get home, the house is silent. Jamie is gone.

Exhausted from constantly interrupted sleep at the hospital, my goal is to take a quick shower, catch a nap, and return to the hospital before Jamie gets home.

After showering, I decide that peace and quiet is more valuable than a nap, so I head back to the hospital. I leave the food and a note for Jamie. It will have to be enough for tonight.

My life becomes a blur of rushed showers after work, quick naps, and nightly vigils over Mom. The scenario plays out repetitively over the next year during Mom's multiple stints of in-hospital stays and complications from the chemo treatments.

Allison again emerges as the bright spot in my and Jamie's relationship. Bubbly and fun loving, she is full of life. Jamie and I get her a Dalmatian puppy. She names him Nickels. Unfortunately Nickels gets sick and dies at five months. Jamie and I decide to get another Dalmatian. After discussing it further, we take the plunge and decide to get two.

Responding to an advertisement, Jamie and I go to see a new litter. I want littermates. Jamie wants a male and female. Fine by me. There are eight puppies in the litter—four females, four males. Jamie picks one of each sex.

Having purchasing the puppies in Indian, we decide to name them Indy (for the male) and Anna (for the female). Instantaneous, unadulterated true love.

We take Indy and Anna with us when we go to pick up Allison at her mother's house. Allison comes running out of the house as we pull into the driveway. She comes to my side of the truck. I have Anna in my lap.

Opening the door, Allison squeals with delight. "Oh, look! She is so cute. Please let me hold her."

"Be careful with her. She is just a baby." Allison kisses Anna and cuddles her close. Jamie, who has Indy tucked under his jacket, hands the second puppy to me.

Allison starts jumping up and down. "Oh, oh, oh! There are two."

"Can I hold both of them?"

"Sure, sweetie, but be careful."

"Oh, thank you, thank you, thank you. I love them, and I love you."

It feels good to have Indy and Anna. I love them, and they love me back. Our love is not complicated, unlike my relationships with humans. Although we purchased the dogs for Allison, they provide a great source of comfort for me as well.

Mom has surpassed the doctor's original prediction of two months to live by far. It has been fourteen months since the doctor gave us his prediction of two months to live. But recently Mom's condition is worsening significantly. Traveling to Nashville for doctor visits becomes too much. She decides to temporarily move to Nashville. With her four daughters in Nashville, it will be easier for us to care for her locally.

My sister Robin is a stay-at-home mom with two small boys. Mom decides to stay with Robin, and Robin and I become Mom's primary caregivers.

With a terminal diagnosis, hospice is enlisted to assist with Mom's care. For the first time in her life, she gets counseling on a regular basis. Now bedridden, she startles me one afternoon with an unusual request. "Carly, come over here. I want to talk with you." Curious, I scoot my chair closer to her bed. She reaches for my hand. Thin blue veins reveal her fragility through paper-thin skin.

"Carly, I am sorry that I left you alone at the apartment when you were young." I let go of her hand.

"You don't have to apologize. There is nothing to apologize for."

"Carly, listen to me. I am sorry. It wasn't right."

"Mom, it doesn't matter." I can't accept an apology when one isn't needed. She never brings it up again. Days later she slips into a coma.

Mom doesn't want to die in a hospital, so it has been planned that she will remain at Robin's house. Hospice advises us that she will pass within twenty-four hours. She doesn't.

Robin and I begin giving her water with a medicine dropper. Caring for her around the clock is emotionally and physically exhausting.

I stay overnight with Mom, waking to administer her medication, and Robin takes care of her during the day while I go to work.

One night at Robin's, my cell phone dies, and Jamie can't reach me. Furious, he calls Robin's home line. Robin answers and brings the portable phone into Mom's bedroom. "Jamie is on the phone," she states with no further comment.

As I put the phone to my ear, I can hear him screaming, "We don't have any toilet paper in this house!"

He continues ranting about everything that is wrong with me. After several minutes, I hear a *click* on the line. Jamie, however, doesn't break stride in his verbal assault. Robin's voice comes on the line. "I'm sorry, Carly. I didn't realize you were still on the phone." She hangs up her extension.

Realizing that Robin has heard him, Jamie becomes further enraged. Looking for an escape, I simply say, "I need to go." I am in emotional overload. It is embarrassing that anyone, much less Robin, heard Jamie verbally abuse me. My relationship with Jamie cloaks me in a shroud of shame and humiliation.

Robin appears in Mom's bedroom about thirty minutes later. "Are you okay?"

"Sure, I'm fine."

"I am sorry. I didn't know you were still on the phone."

"No problem." At that moment, I know with certainty I have to deal with my relationship with Jamie once caring for Mom is no longer my top priority. My shame is unbearable.

I couldn't know what I didn't know.

I didn't know at the time that Jamie's behavior was completely unacceptable. I realize now that I was navigating Jamie's emotional land mines.

Today, I recognize Jamie's behavior as toxic. Jamie's goal was to pick a fight with me. There was nothing I could have done to prevent or alter his agenda.

I was unaware that my internal barometer for my emotional well being was out of balance. Because my internal compass for respect and boundaries was not in proper alignment, I allowed others to treat me badly and unfairly without realizing that I was giving my power away. I compartmentalized intense emotions I was not equipped to process. Instead I sealed them off, slamming the lid shut.

Incredible as it may seem, I also did not have a conscious awareness of any links among Jamie's verbal assaults. Viewing Jamie's outbursts as individual, separate incidents, I never saw the underlying pattern of behavior. The totality of his abusive behavior remained outside my awareness.

My gauge for what to expect from a partner was completely off balance. Growing up with no parental attention to my needs, Jamie's lack of attention to my well-being didn't seem abnormal to me. I can't stress this enough. As crazy as it sounds today, and even typing these words it seems ridiculous, at that time in my life, I didn't understand that Jamie's verbal assaults were abusive.

During my childhood and adolescence, I had learned that the aggressor calls all the shots. Only after ensuring the aggressor's needs were met could I then attend to my own. If my needs conflicted with the aggressor's, then my needs became irrelevant and immediately became a lower priority. Appeasing the aggressor kept me safe. This false belief was ingrained in me.

Today it also saddens me that I could not hear Mom's apology for abandoning me as a young teen. My belief at the time when she offered me her apology was there was no need for an apology. From my perspective, the housing project provided a roof over my head and kept eviction at bay. Abandonment was simply not a term that I would have ever used to describe my experiences.

For me to understand why Mom was apologizing, I would have had to *feel* my abandonment issues. I still had a few years before I would be emotionally ready to experience these intense emotions and feelings. I was blind to the driving influence these abandonment issues exerted in my current life choices.

"You can't heal what you won't feel" described me perfectly.

I had not yet reached my emotional bottom. I would experience significantly more pain before recognizing the need to look deep inside myself to understand my internal influencing factors. My life would hit new lows before I became willing to consider the possibility that I needed to change my thinking. Only in understanding myself and why I made the choices I was making would I be able to begin to make better choices. As a child, I longed for a secure and safe environment. As an adult, I seemed to always end up in the same chaotic, difficult situations I sought so desperately to avoid.

I would keep doing what I was doing until the "pain of the same" became greater than the "pain of change"—then, and only then, would I change.

Unfortunately, I had a very high threshold for pain.

20. Endings

My continual refusals of Jamie's marriage proposals infuriated him. Nothing could convince me to forge that bond with him. I had witnessed his mean streak more than once, and something inside of me would not give on this point; besides, I had no desire to marry him— or anyone else for that matter, ever again. My rejections of his regular marriage overtures constitute a source of continued irritation for Jamie.

Switching tactics, Jamie begins pressuring me to have a child with him. No, I don't think so. I rationalize that he already has two kids, and another child will only complicate things. Jamie isn't as persistent about having a child as wanting to get married. I don't think he really wants more kids; I sense he just wants to limit my freedom. Having a child would accomplish that goal.

Jamie constantly tests my boundaries and persists in attempting to gain more control over me. Clever, he cloaks his suggestions as helping me out. In his latest "offer," he tries to convince me to sign my car over to him. "Since I have fleet insurance on all my company vehicles, I could save you money on your auto insurance. It would still be your car, but you would just need to sign it over to me. In my name, it will qualify for the fleet insurance."

"No. Absolutely not. I will not sign my car over to you."

"You are just stupid if you don't want to save money."

Jamie is a smart guy. He'll understand logic. "My insurance is not that expensive; I am not going to put my car in your name." He rejects logic. Signing my vehicle over to him becomes a perpetual topic for argument.

His tactics for trying to gain control over me knows no bounds.

To keep the construction bank loan low, Jamie and I agree to pay cash for several items during the construction of the house, splitting these costs fifty-fifty. To keep things simple, we create a joint construction account. Since I am still heavily involved in Mom's ongoing care, I turn management of the account over to Jamie to pay the builder and various subcontractors as needed. Since Jamie deals with the contractor, he notifies me of the amount I need to deposit into the construction account when it is time to pay for items such as carpeting, kitchen cabinets, or lighting fixtures. Jamie has full control over the construction account.

It is time to buy kitchen cabinets. One of Jamie's enormous group of friends is going to install them and has gotten us a great deal on some high-end cabinets. Jamie gives me what he says is the total cost and asks me to deposit half of that into the construction account.

"Okay. Did your friend give us an invoice?"

"He didn't, but I will get one."

"Okay, when you get it, put it in our construction invoice file. I'll put the money in the account by the end of the week."

I never question Jamie on the cost of construction items. I trust his business experience to get us the best price. I am absolutely confident that he will not pay more than necessary. Unfortunately, I also never question Jamie's reconciliation of our construction account. Jamie shows me invoices for the construction charges we are paying out of pocket. I trust we are paying equal amounts for the various items.

In the spring of 1996, about eighteen months since we found out about Mom's cancer, she quietly slips into a coma. I care for Mom at night at Robin's house—turning her regularly to avoid bedsores and administering pain medication. My bed is a small cot in her bedroom. Fear limits my sleep; I am terrified that she will die while I am sleeping. Mom has expressed a fear of dying alone, and I didn't want to be asleep when she died.

Shocking everyone, including her doctors and hospice staff, her coma persists for weeks. Incredibly, she clings to life without food and only drops of water from the pink sponges on sticks we use to regularly swab her mouth. Only her shallow breathing confirms the faintest glimmer of life.

In the darkness, I listen intently for the next breath. Sometimes her breathing stops. My breathing stops too—a mix of sympathy and apprehension. There it is again. The faintest of breaths. I breathe again too.

May 24, 1996. It's early, not yet 7:00 a.m. I'm going to lie down for just a few more minutes. Robin will take over at 7:30 a.m. so I can get ready for work. I take one last glance at Mom to ensure she is still breathing, and I turn away from her bed, facing the wall on my small cot. Exhausted from lack of sleep over the last several weeks, I immediately fall asleep.

I wake fifteen minutes later, and the absolute stillness in the room instantaneously jars me out of my grogginess. My heart pounds as I sit up quickly to peer at Mom's chest to check her breathing. Nothing. She is completely still. Mom is gone.

I feel an overwhelming, unbearable sense of loss. Never—not even living alone in the housing project—have I felt so completely alone and isolated. I have a cruel partner and no children of my own.

I feel like no one in the world really loves me. In this terrible time, I feel completely alone.

The tragedy is Mom began showing me love during the two years following her terminal diagnosis. She wanted to be with me. She finally had time for me—and now she is gone. Forever.

The Funeral

The prearrangements for Mom's funeral reflect her cryptic style—simple, quick, inexpensive. No embalming and viewing of the body was to be for immediate family only. Closed-casket visitation in her hometown with burial in a small cemetery in central Tennessee, beside her parents were the arrangements that had already been pre-planned.

Jamie and I drive to the family viewing and public visitation. My ex-husband, Dalton, and his mother, Jean, attend. Surprised, I haven't seen Jean since my divorce from Dalton six years earlier. Jean and I hug each other.

"It is so good to see you, Carly. Not under these circumstances, but it is good to see you. How are you?"

"It is good to see you, too. I am okay, I guess. How are you?"

"I am doing okay. You know I will always love you. I still think of you like a daughter."

Jean's words of affection comfort me. Having just lost my mother, I am feeling lonely and unimportant. Dalton also expresses his sympathy for my loss. "Hello, Carly. Sorry about your loss."

"Thank you." There is not a chance I will hug Dalton, but I appreciate the thoughtful gesture he made by coming.

"So how have you been?" Dalton asks.

"Busy—working and taking care of Mom. What about you?"

"It's the same old same old around here. Do you like living in the city?"

"I love it." It's an odd question and a conversation I'm not willing to pursue.

Jean says, "We heard the announcement on the radio about your mother's passing and wanted to come by to offer our condolences."

"It is very nice of you. Thanks for coming."

Dalton leans toward me as if to ask a secret. "Do you have any children?"

I step backward. "No, I never had any kids." This conversation needs to stop. If Jamie sees me, I know he will be furious that I am even speaking to Dalton. I really have nothing to say to Dalton anyway. "If you will excuse me, I need to go find Lily. Thanks for coming." Circumstances require no further explanation.

"Well, you should stop by and see me sometime. Or call. I still have the same phone number. Do you remember our phone number?"

"Yeah, I remember it. I'm pretty busy. You guys take care." Right. When pigs fly. I quickly walk away but not before Jamie reenters the room and sees me talking with Dalton and Jean.

As expected, Jamie is furious. Incredible as it seems, I am grieving the loss of my mother while worrying Jamie will be mad because my ex-husband—who knew my mom—shows up to express his condolences. I don't want to fight with Jamie. Even more importantly, I don't want him to make a scene. Not here. Not in front of all these people. Not in front of my family.

I need space away from Jamie to think straight. With my emotions in a constant state of alert throughout Mom's illness, compounded by Jamie's constant barrage of angry words toward me, I feel confused and disoriented. I decide to take some time off work to figure out my life's direction as soon as we get back to Nashville.

The house is nearly finished. Leaving Jamie before the house is completed would be a nightmare. It will be easier to split the investment with the house completed.

We bury Mom the following morning. Adrian drives Mom's car behind the hearse. Jamie pulls in behind Adrian. My siblings file in behind us in their vehicles for the funeral procession.

Mom discovered a few months before her death that Adrian was having an affair. She never confronted him. She simply didn't have the energy. She made me promise, however, that I would not let him keep her car. She didn't want the other woman driving her one prized possession. I gave her my word. I am determined that Adrian will not get to keep her car.

While driving to the gravesite, I notice that Adrian has already put a Masonic sticker on Mom's rear bumper. He is already trying to take over her belongings.

Uncle Al, Mom's brother, invites everyone to his house following the burial. Although we haven't spent much time with them because of Russell, I enjoy Mom's birth family. Uncle Al is my favorite relative. He is kind and gentle, and he always seems genuinely happy to see us. He insists his nieces and nephew come to his house following the graveside service.

Al shares how the Davis family, Mom's family, has a reunion every Labor Day weekend. He extends the invitation to us. "All of you kids should come down this year and get to know your family down here."

Ernie jumps in. "I will come if somebody else will promise to come."

I agree. "I'll come."

So Ernie and I make plans to meet at Uncle Al's house on Labor Day weekend for the annual Davis family reunion.

On the drive back to Nashville, Jamie and I stop to have dinner. Jamie excitedly talks nonstop about purchasing furniture and moving into the house. "When we get moved in, I want to throw a housewarming party."

"My mom just died. I don't want to have a party."

"You knew she was dying. You've known for a long time she was going to die. She's dead; now you just need to get over it."

In stony silence, I bleakly ponder the rest of my life. My entire life, I've anxiously anticipated turning thirty. I don't know why, but somehow thirty seems a magical age to me. I am twenty-nine years old. The magic is due to arrive in a few short weeks. Except now thirty is looking more mythical than enchanting.

I have all the components I think are necessary to have a good life. Education, a great job, no kids, single (or at least not married), and soon, I will be the coowner of a beautiful house. Happiness, however, remains elusive.

I begin to realize that my formula for the good life needs some revision. Something is missing.

I intuitively know I need some space from Jamie—some peace—to think about what I need to do next.

Mom's death was very difficult on multiple levels. Although I knew Mom was sick and dying, I was not prepared for the overwhelming feelings of vulnerability and isolation her death brought. Any hope for unconditional love vanished along with her passing. I shut everyone out. My refusal to talk to anyone about my feelings only isolated me further.

My siblings knew only what I told them. Although they probably had suspicions about how Jamie treated me, I never confirmed their assumptions. Any occasional tentative questioning from them was countered with silence or vague responses.

On reflection, perhaps I thought that if I didn't talk about my abusive relationship with Jamie, then it wasn't really happening. At a minimum, I rationalized it wasn't as bad as I thought it was.

Although I relinquished some of my power to Jamie—as with the construction account and by appeasing his anger by putting his needs before my own—I never gave him complete control over me. I maintained my own bank account and my own car, and I always supported myself. These acts of independence gave me the illusion I was in control of my life. I believed this fierce independence separated me from other domestic-violence victims. I wasn't like them. I was different. I could leave anytime I wanted. No, I was definitely not like them in any way.

Unfortunately, more often than not, I convinced myself that this was true.

21. Moving In

Jamie and I schedule the final walk-through of the house with the builder the week following Mom's funeral. Everything appears in order. We schedule the closing on the house with the bank. While getting ready for the move, I begin packing. I am hopeful after the move, I will find some quiet time to myself to sort out my thoughts and decide what I want to do with my life.

Jamie tells me that his friend Jack will help with the move. Jamie met Jack through a mutual friend a few months earlier. They quickly found common ground over their passion for deer hunting.

I met Jack a few weeks earlier at Jamie's office while doing some of Jamie's accounting work. Jack is recently divorced with sole custody of his two children. Kim, Jack's ex-wife, has little to no contact with her children. With the miserable role models I have experienced, I find it difficult to comprehend how a father would or could raise his children alone.

Jack helps us move into the new house the following week. Knowing moving day can often be problematic, I am pleasantly surprised everything goes smoothly. There are no major problems, not even a minor hiccup. During our first night in the house, Jamie proudly announces, "I want to start planning our housewarming party. We can invite everyone and show off our new place."

Just three short weeks ago, I buried my mother. I need to make some major life decisions. I do not want a party. I want some safe, quiet time to myself. "You know I told you, I don't want to have a housewarming party. I need time to process everything that has happened with Mom." She has not even been gone a whole month, and I've had no time to grieve.

"You had almost two years to get ready for her to die. I don't want to be around someone who mopes around all the time. We are going to have a party to show off our new house."

Part of me feels guilty. Jamie has a right to be happy and excited about our big, new, beautiful house. By far the nicest house either of us has ever lived in, it is our dream home. I just need a little time to recover from my roller-coaster life the last couple of years. I wonder if Jamie is just being selfish by trying to force me back into a social life, or am I being selfish by refusing not to participate. But he convinces me entertaining is the "right attitude" to adopt.

Every new weekend brings a new cookout. It doesn't stop with the just the one new house party. It's an every-weekend event. And it's my job to make sure all the necessary supplies are stocked for a successful cookout: food, drinks, ice, condiments, napkins, skewers…the list never ends. Jamie reigns over the grill, cooking the meat. All other preparations fall to me, including clean up. Jamie thinks the distribution of responsibilities is fair. End of discussion.

I am exhausted keeping up; I just want some time alone. Finally, after two months of endless weekend parties, I make up my mind. I tell Jamie, "I don't want anyone over on the upcoming Fourth of July weekend."

"Listen, you can't just decide that on your own. This is my house too," he says.

"You are right, it is your house. If you want to have a party, then you plan everything and do all the cleanup. I don't want to be involved," I firmly reply.

We argue intensely, and he won't back down from hosting a Fourth of July party.

Fine. I eventually cave under his unrelenting pressure. It feels like an official festival. The party lasts three *long* days. Some people stay over Saturday night; Jamie mixes our guests Bloody Marys for breakfast Sunday morning. The partying and drinking continue throughout the weekend into the holiday on Monday afternoon, long after I have left to go to work.

A few days later, I decide I must confront Jamie about his partying. I cannot put it off any longer. I will talk to him tonight.

I leave work early arriving home about 4:00 p.m. I nervously wait for Jamie to arrive. As he is self-employed, he can come and go as he pleases. I don't know what time he will be home, but I am determined to have a discussion with him tonight. Darkness is settling in as I see the headlights from his truck flash through the trees, announcing his arrival. Sitting on the deck, I stretch my head backward, looking toward the star-filled sky, take a deep breath to gather my courage, and coach myself: "You can do this." I remind myself nothing will change if I don't address my concerns. I have not worked this hard to be miserable in my own house. I desperately want Jamie to understand I need some time and space to grieve. I feel empty. I feel hollow.

Gravel crunches under the tires as Jamie pulls his truck up beside the house. The door slams, alerting me he has exited the vehicle. My heart begins to race as he walks around the corner toward the deck steps. I am always uncomfortable asking for something that I know he will not agree with. I brace myself for a fight.

He slumps down in a lawn chair beside me.

"Hello. How was your day?" I can do this, I repeat to the committee in my head.

"Long. I had a late appointment tonight, but I think the job will be a good one if I get it."

"That's good." Long pause. "Jamie...I need to talk to you about something."

"Oh shit! I can hear that tone. Wait. I need to go get a beer first," he says as he rises and walks toward the kitchen.

I wait while he gets a cold one. Looking again for courage and wisdom in the sky, I send up a silent plea to whoever is up there or listening to give me the strength and courage to have this conversation. Suddenly the allure of the gorgeous night sky and chirping crickets seeps into my conscious awareness. I feel gratitude well up inside me for the chorus of nocturnal life around me under the star-studded blanket spread above me. It is truly a beautiful night. Pondering the sparkling stars, I reconsider my conversation plans. Do I really want to ruin the evening by broaching the problem of hosting continual parties?

Jamie returns to his chair, refreshment in hand.

I can do this. I need more nights...no, I need some weekends... to be like tonight. "Well, I don't want you to get mad, and I hope you understand. I don't want to continue having parties *every* weekend. I need some time alone. I need time to process Mom's death. I need time to grieve her."

"Well that is just about the stupidest thing I have ever heard. We already settled this. I am not going to let you hold me back from having fun in my life."

"I am not trying to hold you back from having fun, but I don't want to have people over every weekend anymore. It's just too hard on me," I explain.

"Well, if people come over, it is your responsibility to act like a hostess and have food here for them," he commands.

If I am anything, I am responsible. Of course I will do my part. "I will make sure there are drinks and food in the house to grill, but I won't be joining in the parties," I respond, standing my ground.

"Well, we'll see about that!" he spouts back.

The magic of the evening evaporates. Suddenly it just seems dark. Tired and frustrated, I go to bed.

I diligently ensure sufficient food and drinks are stocked for Jamie's continued weekend parties. Jamie never offers me reimbursement for the food or liquor. In his mind, maintaining adequate supplies is my sole responsibility. I am not ready to wrestle with him on that topic. I focus my energy on achieving some peace and quiet, and for now, that is me not being present during the parties.

The arrangement works the first couple of weekends. Then Jamie decides that he wants me to participate in the festivities. As the next weekend is rapidly approaching, he forms his strategy. When I arrive home Thursday evening, Jamie greets me from the couch. "Come in here and sit with me." I settle down beside him. "Carly, I need you to know that I am embarrassed because you are not at the parties when our friends come over. You need to be downstairs when people come over and not hide in your office or the bedroom."

Really? Again? "Jamie, we have gone over this. I need some time to be alone."

"Alone? You can be alone every weeknight. I want to live and have some fun," he continues.

"Okay. You have fun. I am not stopping you. I just don't want to be around people all the time. The weekends are the only time I can gather my thoughts. I know you don't understand, but I just can't participate in round-the-clock weekend parties," I contend.

"It's embarrassing for you not to be around. People ask questions," he says.

"Tell them I am grieving my mother's death."

"Come on now, we all knew she was dying. You have had time to get over her dying. I am sick of you using that for an excuse," he gripes.

Continuing to defend my perspective would be an exercise in futility. He would not understand. "I am not going to participate in weekend parties right now. I don't want to."

I just need to set a firm boundary, knowing that he will not, or cannot, be supportive of my needs. Jamie can't make me attend his parties. The possibility of a breakup fails to persuade me.

Seeing my resolve and being unable to persuade me to join in his parties, Jamie begins going out every weekend, arriving home in the wee hours of the morning—always drunk. Some nights he doesn't come home at all. Regardless of when he returns, the stench of liquor accompanies him.

I am not sure if Jamie is having an affair. I don't think I really care. What I do recognize is the same behavior he displayed when I first met him; he is out several nights a week into the early hours of the morning.

In addition to the stress of dealing with Jamie, I serve as executor of Mom's will. Following her wishes for the distribution of her meager belongings, I attempt to get her car back from Adrian. Adrian, however, is contesting Mom's will. I don't care. I will keep my promise to my mother. I will not let Adrian's "other woman" get Mom's car. I can't let that happen. I promised Mom.

It takes a few weeks, but I win the battle with Adrian. The process entails strife, turmoil, and ultimately lawyers. I feel compelled to inform Adrian of my unwavering commitment to keep my promise to my mother, a desire that she clearly spells out in her will.

He answers the phone. "Hello."

"Hello, Adrian. This is Carly. Listen very carefully to what I have to say. I am the last person in the world you want to mess with over Mom's car. I will get her car one way or the other." Dead silence. "Remember how crazy Russell was? Well…his blood runs in my veins. Make no mistake about it; you will *never* drive my mother's car."

I wait for a response from Adrian. Silence.

"If I have to come down there and set the car on fire, I will. But I might decide to hotwire it instead and drive it into your house. So think very carefully about how you choose to respond to my attorney's request to honor Mom's wishes and turn the car over to me. I am not afraid of you or of prison. I made a promise to Mom to not let you keep that car. Trust me, you will not keep that car."

More silence.

"This isn't a threat. It's a promise." I pause. Seconds tick by slowly. "What else do you want, Carly?" Adrian asks.

"My attorney will send you the list of items spelled out in Mom's will."

"Well, I will wait for this letter."

I resist slamming the phone back into the receiver.

My attorney sends Adrian a letter requesting the car and Mom's meager personal belongings.

There is no counteroffer or further attempt to negotiate. Adrian agrees that the vehicle and personal effects can be retrieved. A date is set for pick-up.

On the prearranged date, I rent a U-Haul. Ernie and I make the trip to Adrian's to retrieve Mom's car and personal effects. The day is warm. It reminds me of sitting on the swing out in the yard drinking coffee with mom on my occasional visits.

As I pull the U-Haul into the driveway, we see Mom's car parked in front of the old barn. Black trash bags are stacked in the rear seat and under the barn's lean-to. Mom's personal belongings are haphazardly stuffed inside the trash bags. I start to cry. How can he be so disrespectful?

Ernie and I load the trash bags into the U-Haul. As I look around the farm for the last time, I say a silent thank you to whoever might be listening. "Thank you for letting me get Mom's car."

I have kept my promise to my mother.

Robin needs a car. Since she and I had been Mom's main caregivers, giving the vehicle to Robin seems like the right thing to do. Doing this gives me some peace because I feel Mom would approve.

The good feeling is quickly overshadowed by the ever-widening chasm between me and Jamie. The intensity and frequency of his verbal assaults escalates. It's early August. Thursday night, heading into the weekend, Jamie optimistically suggests, "We haven't had a cookout in over a month; let's have one this weekend."

"No. I don't feel like company," I reply.

"Well, I am not living with someone who acts like they are dead all the time. You are an emotional wreck. It's probably because you are an alcoholic," he says with venom in his voice.

What is he talking about? I hardly ever drink alcohol. Sure, I drank moderately in my early days after arriving in Nashville. Having experienced true freedom as a young adult for the first time in my life, I sowed some wild oats. A year and half of drinking every weekend, however, became tiresome. Jamie knows that. Since moving in with him, I have consumed very little alcohol. Why on earth is Jamie accusing *me* of being an alcoholic?

"You can't hide the fact you're a drunk! Everyone knows it. Just because you won't join in the party, it doesn't stop people from knowing the truth about you. You are only fooling yourself if you think people don't know you are an alcoholic," he ruthlessly charges.

Alone, I call Lily. "Hey, Lily. I need to ask you a question. Jamie is accusing me of being an alcoholic. Why on earth would he say that about me?"

She responds instantly. "Well, he can't admit that he is an alcoholic, so he is going to accuse you of being one. When you won't drink with him, it makes him mad."

"But alcohol doesn't rule his life. He does work some days, and he doesn't drink every single day," I respond.

"It doesn't matter that he works some. He is still an alcoholic. There are different kinds of alcoholics."

Hmm…I define an alcoholic as someone who drinks every single day beginning as soon as his or her feet hit the floor in the morning. People like my two oldest siblings' spouses. Jamie doesn't do that. Although Jamie drinks excessively, he also works occasionally.

Could Lily be right? Could Jamie be an alcoholic? What does it mean to be an alcoholic? Would alcoholism explain his erratic behavior? What impact would his being an alcoholic have on our relationship? I wonder.

Nearly twenty years later, I realize that Jamie never registered, nor did he ever acknowledge, my need to grieve and mourn the loss of my mother. His indifference to my emotional pain devalued me as a human being. My family history of unmet emotional needs created the internal dialogue that made me question my right to even request the emotional space needed to grieve the loss of my mother. My behavior was, after all, affecting Jamie. He didn't deserve that—did he?

I was being trampled emotionally. Today, I recognize Jamie's behavior as completely out of line and selfish. Manipulative people don't feel concern for others. Jamie was completely controlled by his own desires, and he had no interest in hearing how I felt. I realize now that my need to grieve was a *normal* reaction to my mother's death.

Although unable to protect myself, I did not hesitate in adopting a firm stance for others. I never wavered in my promise to Mom.

Under no circumstances would I have allowed Adrian to keep her car. Somehow, being able to stand up for others, in this case Mom, made me feel like I wasn't being run over in my own relationship.

Prevailing in carrying out Mom's wishes simply made me feel good about not only my promise to her but my ability to take a stand. It was a win for fairness. I believe Mom recognized my internal strength before her death, and therefore, she asked me rather than one of my siblings to get the car from Adrian.

I knew I had a can-do attitude, but I was unaware that I somehow couldn't use this internal strength for my own personal benefit. I was unsure if I even had the *right* to have any wants or needs. If I experienced a need or want that someone said I shouldn't be feeling—it would immediately make me question if I even had a right to feel that way.

My self-worth was nearly nonexistent.

This self-doubt prevented me from protecting myself both physically and emotionally from the abusive behavior of others. Although I was completely self-sufficient and self-reliant, I failed miserably at protecting myself emotionally or financially from Jamie. I was completely blind to others' manipulation. Self-doubt about my value served as the lock holding me hostage to my abuser's demands.

While I was quite capable of vehemently fighting Adrian's selfish behavior, I doubted my own sanity when I questioned similar behavior in Jamie.

I failed to recognize Jamie's behavior as that of a raging alcoholic. I was trying to rationalize Jamie's behavior without recognizing that his erratic moods kept me in a state of confusion. Jamie's constant swings of temperament, alternating between pleasantness and extreme demands, kept me off balance. My relationship with Jamie did not involve any give and take. Any rapport consisted of a one-sided conversation—with him voicing his thoughts, opinions, and expectations and my subsequent compliance to keep the peace. I never considered how Jamie's self-absorption had shrunk his sensitivity to others.

The ongoing chaos kept me in a state of confusion. Forever trying to understand Jamie's point of view and to avoid fighting, I continued to try to reason through an unreasonable situation. I didn't realize that I was simply spinning my wheels, digging myself in deeper.

22. Patterns

Jamie continues to stay out drinking several nights a week, arriving home in the early morning hours or later the following day. Friday morning of the Labor Day weekend dawns bright and cheerful. I plan to meet Ernie in Tennessee to attend Mom's family's annual reunion. I look forward to seeing Uncle Al again. I also want to visit Mom's gravesite.

Arriving home from work around six in the evening, I find the house empty. I assume that Jamie is out drinking, getting a head start on the long weekend. We are now barely speaking, acting more like roommates who rarely see each other.

I plan an early night in order to get plenty of rest in preparation for the drive to Tennessee the following morning. I go to bed around eight thirty and fall asleep almost immediately. Emotional exhaustion keeps me in a perpetual state of tiredness.

Located on the first floor, the master bedroom sits close to the back entry to the house. A hallway connects into the kitchen. Jamie's fumbling attempt to unlock the back door wakes me. A glance at the clock tells me it is 2:00 a.m. After several minutes of jangling keys, some cursing, followed by more jangling keys, I hear the door open. The strong smell of alcohol quickly flows down the hallway into the bedroom. I am disgusted, with Jamie and myself. How could I have been so blind? Why didn't I recognize he is an alcoholic before getting financially involved with him? Jamie staggers down the hallway, stumbling into the bedroom. I lie perfectly still on my side of the bed, pretending to be asleep. I don't want any interaction with him. Jamie gets in bed, rolls over to my side, and slurs out, "I want to talk to you."

"You are drunk, and I am not talking to you while you are drunk," I reply angrily.

Jamie stumbles over his words again. "Nooo, we have to talk. I...I want to talk now."

Filled with contempt for him, I can't bear the thought of sleeping in the same bed together. I get up, grabbing my pillow. "You are nothing but a drunk, and I don't want anything to do with you," I say as I stalk out of the bedroom.

I walk into the living room and sit on the couch. I will catch a couple more hours of sleep on the sofa before heading to Tennessee. Jamie, however, remains intent on talking and follows me into the living room.

My words upset him. I am glad. He should be upset. He has certainly upset me repeatedly the past few weeks.

Jamie plants himself in the living room, swaying like a giant tree in the wind. "Don't say that. Don't say that you don't want anything to do with me. Please don't say that," he begs.

I am so angry. I want him to hurt like he has hurt me. My contempt knows no bounds. "I don't want anything to do with you. You are nothing but an alcoholic, and I am leaving you."

Jamie again begs, "Don't say that! You can't leave me!"

What part of this doesn't he understand? I repeat my conviction. "I am leaving you. I don't want anything to do with you."

Like deadly lightening, he strikes without warning. Lunging, Jamie grabs me by my hair, pulling me to him. With tightly clenched fists, he pummels my head with repeated blows. The first hit is a hard undercut to my jaw. I stagger backward, falling onto the couch. Jamie immediately jumps on top of me, pinning me down. Continuing his assault, he delivers blow after blow after blow, concentrating his hits on my head. I instinctively attempt to protect my head with my arms, but like a skilled boxer, he easily makes continued contact with my face.

I slide off the couch onto the floor. There is no escape. As I hit the hardwood floor, Jamie leaps on top of me. Sitting on my stomach, he pins me to the floor. Panic and his weight combine to cut off my airflow. I can barely breathe. Crazed, he continues to deliver blows to my face and head.

What if he kills me? Even if I could scream, no one would hear. Our house is too isolated. I know my energy must be conserved and used wisely.

As Jamie continues to hit me, I feel my left jawbone poke the roof of my mouth. I don't hear the bone break, but I feel my jawbone scrape the roof of my mouth. My left jawbone is pointing inward and up. The metallic taste of blood fills my mouth. I feel it run down my chest. I tell myself to just be calm. I repeat to myself, "Carly...just be calm...think, think..."

Shock prevents the pain from registering in my consciousness. My only thought is that I must not pass out. I must stay conscious; my life likely depends on it. Jamie continues to hit me. I don't know how much blood I have lost, but I am starting to feel faint. I worry I will pass out.

"Jammmmie, pleasssse stoooppp." The words are muffled as though I am talking with a mouth full of cotton. My mouth is a crime scene of blood and broken bone. I attempt to plead with Jamie to stop but can't talk coherently.

The bloody scene finally penetrates Jamie's consciousness, and he stops hitting me. After double digit blows to my head, his hands are bathed in blood. My face and chest are covered in blood as well.

Remaining on top of me on the hardwood floor, Jamie exclaims in horror, "Oh my God, Carly, look what you made me do. I am so sorry." He stands up.

I struggle to my feet, fighting to retain consciousness. Maybe if I stand up I will have a better chance of staying conscious.

Jamie says, "I will take you to the hospital."

I am so angry. The adrenalin is keeping me conscious. "No, I will drive myself."

I hear the panic in Jamie's voice. "You can't drive yourself. We can't tell anyone what happened. You need to say you fell off a ladder."

I need to keep walking, I can't pass out. I fear Jamie will kill me if I pass out. Jamie recognizes that he has brutally beaten me. I sense his fear. He is afraid I will call the police. I need to get to the hospital. I don't want Jamie driving me there.

I am determined that I will not get in the car with him. He is wrapping his apology in an accusation leveled at me for causing the incident, and I know I cannot trust him. No, I need to drive myself to the hospital. I just need to stay calm and *not black out*.

"Just don't lose consciousness," I tell myself. "Keep walking around."

With a history of Jamie intentionally taking my car keys, I have hidden about ten sets of my car keys around the house and in the landscaping outside. If I just keep moving, I can get far enough away from him to grab one of those sets and run out to my car.

I just keep walking around. The first floor of the house is circular. You can walk from the kitchen to the foyer to the living and back into the kitchen.

I continue to walk this circle. Jamie follows, trying to touch me while repeatedly apologizing. On one pass through the living room, Jamie slips in my pool of blood on the hardwood floor in front of the couch.

Realizing he is struggling to get up, I run through the kitchen, grab my purse off the counter, and race outside. I snatch a set of my car keys hidden in the landscape and quickly get into my Mazda Miata.

Without looking back, I speed down the driveway, pushing the small car as fast as it will go. The closest hospital is thirty minutes away. Pulling out of the subdivision, I see headlights rapidly approaching in the rearview mirror. Jamie's truck sits much higher than my car. Oh, God, please don't let it be Jamie. Don't let him catch me.

As I race to the hospital, still bleeding, the vehicle trailing me inches closer, then still closer. As Jamie's truck fills my rearview mirror, I feel my small vehicle lurch as his bumper slams into me. Fear grips me in its vice.

He is trying to run me off the road! He is going to kill me! The only way I am going to survive tonight is to out run him. I push my foot down on the gas pedal, watching the odometer pass seventy then eight.

As I speed toward the hospital, Jamie gains enough ground to pull alongside me. He pushes his truck into my vehicle. My Miata slides off the road. Jamie slows down giving me a chance to swerve back onto the road in front of him. I have to get to the hospital!

Jamie rams the back of my car again! Blood fills my mouth; fear nearly suffocates me. He plans to run me off the road and kill me. I will be just like the man that Russell killed.

I stare death in the face!

Approaching a small suburb east of Nashville, I will soon pass a police station. I need to get there.

After hitting my car for the third time, Jamie's truck starts swaying in the road. I pray my life won't end today.

Arriving in the small town, my foot remains firmly on the gas pedal as I speed right through the red light. If the police stop me, at least then I'll be safe from Jamie.

Jamie, catching up to me again, stops his truck at the light. I continue speeding toward the hospital. His truck fades away in my rearview mirror. He is no longer pursuing me. If I can remain conscious, I will make it to the hospital. Maybe, just maybe, I will live though this.

When I pull up to the hospital, I think about pulling right up to the ER doors. But I don't want to block anyone else, so I park in the parking lot and walk to the ER.

It is now about four in the morning on Saturday. The admitting clerk looks up at my blood-soaked face and shirt, and glancing behind me through the large ER doors asks, "How did you get here? Who is with you?"

"I am alone. I drove myself." The heavy cloak of shame returns, clutching me in its grasp. Broken jaws don't happen by accident. Everyone will know I have been beaten. The fact the perpetrator is my boyfriend further inflames my humiliation.

While putting me in a room, the admitting clerk asks, "How much pain are you in? On a scale of one to ten with ten being the highest."

At that moment, I finally begin to feel the excruciating, white-hot pain. Incredulously, prior to this point, the pain had not registered in my brain. I was most likely in shock. But now I reply, "It's a ten."

Tears of pain and shame form tracks on my cheeks. The clerk quickly says, "Let me go get the nurse." Turning to leave, she stops at the doorway, asking, "Whom can I call for you?"

I shake my head as if to say no and mouth, "No one."

The clerk repeats the question. "You don't have *anyone* you want to call?"

I shake my head, indicating no.

With a look of sadness, the clerk assures me, "I will go get the nurse, and she will get some pain medicine."

In short order, the nurse arrives. "The doctor is on his way." She also asks me to rate my pain on a one-to-ten scale.

"Ten."

"I am going to give you something for your pain." She administers a shot of morphine, and the pain quickly begins to subside. "Do you want to call someone to be with you?"

"No, I don't want to call anyone." I'm too embarrassed to call Lily or Robin. I am ashamed that I have allowed myself to be put into this situation. I can't believe that I am in this condition.

The ER doctor arrives a few minutes later. "Hello, my name is Dr. Hammond. Now tell me who did this to you?"

The tears begin their descent again. I hang my head and whisper, "My boyfriend."

"Well, we are going to have to call the surgeon to look at you. You most definitely will need surgery for your jaws. And we need to call the police. You will need to file a police report, but we are going to take you to x-ray first." My mind is reeling. I don't know if I want to file a police report. I don't know if I can do that. It will be public record then. Everyone will know.

After x-rays while I'm waiting for the surgeon, a representative from a victim's shelter comes into my room. The organization helps women and children in domestic-violence situations.

"Hello, I am Betsy. Do you want to talk?"

"No."

"I understand it can be hard going through something like this."

"I'm okay. I am sorry you had to come out so late." I really don't want to talk about this.

Betsy gently nudges me to open up, to no avail.

Realizing I won't discuss it, she says, "Here is my card. Please call me if you change your mind and want to talk."

The nurse returns to check my pain level. "How are you feeling? Are you feeling any pain now?"

"Yes, the pain is starting to come back."

"Let me see if I can get you some more pain medication." The nurse leaves, quickly returning with another pain shot.

The pain recedes again. She dims the lights. "The oral surgeon, Dr. Lawson, is on his way. You try to get some rest, and we will wake you up when he gets here."

About an hour later, Dr. Lawson walks into the room. "Hello, I am Dr. Lawson. You have some severe injuries, young lady. Both of your jaws are broken, and your left jaw has suffered two breaks. I am most concerned about your left side. Since you have two breaks on this side, you have a free-floating piece of bone on this side. You need to have surgery immediately. I understand that you don't have insurance."

"No, I don't have insurance today. My insurance goes into effect tomorrow. I just started a new job, and I am in the thirty-day waiting period."

"We usually send patients without any insurance downtown to the university hospital."

I have no idea what my medical care will cost. I only know that I don't want to be sent to the university hospital. That's where the indigents go and those who don't have insurance. I would willingly write a check for everything I have in the bank; I just don't want to be sent to that hospital.

With tears welling up again in my eyes, I plead, "I promise I will pay you. I don't have my checkbook with me, but I have my credit card in my purse. I will max it out to pay you a down payment, and I promise I will pay you the rest on a payment plan."

Dr. Lawson smiles compassionately and in a sympathetic tone says, "I will do your surgery. We need to get in the operating room as soon as possible."

I agree to pay the hospital whatever is available on my credit card that night, a small price to pay in order to avoid being transported to the university hospital. The news is regularly filled with snippets of wounded drug dealers and thieves taken to that hospital. The university's vast trauma experience doesn't interest me; my perception of the instability of their environment terrifies me. I will pay whatever it costs to remain at the private hospital.

Dr. Lawson interrupts my dark thoughts. "We will get you scheduled for surgery as soon as possible this morning, but right now, we need to get you into a room. When your surgery has been scheduled, I will come in and talk to you right before we go into the operating room."

"Okay, and thank you, Dr. Lawson."

"You need to talk with the police right away. Do you think you can talk with them before the surgery, while everything is still fresh in your mind?"

I don't respond.

He looks me straight in the eyes. "I can't make you talk to the officer and tell him what happened to you, but I can make sure that you have the opportunity to tell him what happened." He pauses, letting his words sink in.

I remain silent.

"We can't help you if you won't let us," he pleads gently.

"Okay."

After I am taken to a private room, I quickly fall asleep. A uniformed officer wakens me with a knock on the door. As he approaches my hospital bed, a tear slides down my face. "Hello, I am Officer Johnson. Can you tell me what happened to you?"

"It was an accident," I answer with a shaky voice.

"These types of injuries don't usually happen in an accident unless it was an automobile accident. Why don't you tell me the full details of what has happened to you?"

"I really don't want to talk about it."

"I can't make you talk, but if you change your mind, here is my card. You can call me day or night." Politeness dictates that I take his card. I have no intention of calling him. I just want this nightmare to be over.

Dr. Lawson awakens me next. As promised, he arrives to talk to me before my surgery. "I am going to put your jaws straight again. They will be wired shut for six to seven weeks, depending on how fast your bones heal. While your jaws are wired shut, you will only be able to drink, since you won't be able to open your mouth."

"Okay."

He then asks, "Do you want me to remove one of your front teeth so you can get a little bit of solid food in your mouth?"

I look at him in astonishment. "You're not serious, are you?"

"Yes, I am quite serious. Some of the guys that I wire shut want to be able to eat some solid food."

I give him a garish smile. "No. I want to keep my front teeth. I have enough problems. I don't want to add to them by losing one of my front teeth."

Dr. Lawson smiles back. "I understand."

The doctor gives me some information regarding Jamie. "Well that guy who did this to you came into the ER around nine this morning. He was treated for a broken hand. He asked if you were here. We told him you were not here. Since you aren't going to call any friends or family, I am going to put you under an assumed name so if he comes back, he won't be able to find you."

I am embarrassed but agree to the assumed name. I feel safer knowing Jamie won't be able to find me. Coming out of surgery, I return to my private room alone.

"Hello? Are you awake?" The nurse sounds very far away.

My eyelids feel like concrete slabs. Slowly, I nod my head.

"A woman named Misty is at the nurse's station and is asking for you. Do you want to see her?"

"Yes," I rasp through my wired-shut mouth.

"Okay, I'll let her know what room you are in." The nurse turns to leave. A few minutes later Misty, Alan's girlfriend, walks into my hospital room. Her face contorts with concern.

"Oh, Carly, are you all right?"

I speak slowly through clamped teeth. "Yeah, I'll be okay. You shouldn't have come. Alan will be furious with you if he finds out you came to see me."

"Don't worry about me. I needed to come and see you and make sure you were okay. Jamie came to our house early this morning. He told Alan that you had blood all over you and didn't know where you were but that your car was here at Baptist Hospital. He said you weren't here because he had asked for you when he came in to get his hand x-rayed."

"The doctor told me Jamie came to the ER this morning. Is his hand really broken?"

"Yes, it is. Jamie and Alan have already concocted a story that Jamie had come home late and that you jumped him in a fit of rage and he thought you were a burglar and hit you. Jamie is going to say that he didn't realize it was you and that he was only defending himself."

Stunned, I can't believe what I am hearing.

Misty continues. "Alan told Jamie to call the cops and file a complaint against you for attacking him. Alan told Jamie that if you did press charges, it would be easier for him if he had filed against you first. Alan's theory is that whoever files charges second will be seen as retaliating and won't be as credible."

I am lying in a hospital bed with both my jaws broken and Jamie's hand broken, and fear creeps in that Jamie can have me arrested with his false story.

"Well, they are trying to build Jamie's case. Alan and Jamie ripped Jamie's shirt to make it look more like I had attacked him. Alan took pictures of Jamie and his ripped shirt. Jamie also has scratches on his neck. The scratches must have been from where you were trying to fight him off."

I have just survived a vicious attack but am terrified that I might be arrested. I have never seen justice prevail with the police. As a child, I witnessed Russell repeatedly convince the police nothing was amiss when they responded to neighbors' calls about domestic violence. The police always took Russell at his word without further investigation. When the police left, things always got worse at our house.

"Alan is advising Jamie that no matter what he has to do or say, he needs to get you back for at least one year. Alan said the statute of limitations for suing someone civilly is one year. If Jamie can keep you from suing him for one year, you won't be able to sue him later."

Through my tears, I acknowledge my confusion. "I don't know what to do. I am afraid for Indy and Anna. I don't want to leave the Dalmatians at the house with Jamie. If I don't do what he wants me to do, he might hurt them in retaliation."

"Well, you don't have to decide this minute. Where are you going when you get out of the hospital?"

"I don't know. I hadn't even thought about that yet."

"You can stay with Max." Max is Misty's invalid brother. Involved in an accident about twenty-five years earlier, he is permanently paralyzed on his left side. He lives a short distance from Misty's mom, Vivian. Max lives alone. Vivian and Misty share responsibility for Max's care, alternating visits in the morning and evening to bathe and feed him.

"Let me think about it, and I'll let you know, Misty." I am overwhelmed. I can't think straight.

Misty nods knowingly. "Well, I can't stay long. I don't want Alan getting suspicious. I told him I was going to the grocery store. I better go."

"Okay. Thanks for coming by."

"You get some rest, and call me when you can."

As Misty leaves the room, the nurse walks in. I ask, "Can you bring me something to help me sleep?" My mind is racing. I am afraid I will not sleep without a sleeping aid. I take a sleeping pill and am soon sound asleep.

Upon waking on Sunday morning, I immediately start worrying what to do next. Suddenly I realize it is Sunday. I am supposed to meet Ernie in Tennessee for Mom's family reunion. I don't have my cell phone with me. I don't have Uncle Al's phone number to call to tell them I won't be there. I panic.

I finally think to call information to get Uncle Al's home phone number. My speech sounds strange since my jaws are wired shut. So I ask the nurse, "Can you talk to my uncle Al and let him know I won't be able to attend the family reunion today?"

"Sure, I'll let your uncle know you can't make it."

No one answers the call, and the answering machine clicks on. I listen with horror as the nurse says into the phone. "Carly has been admitted to Baptist Hospital. She is recovering from surgery and won't be able to attend the reunion."

There was no need to give any details; she only needed to say I wouldn't be attending the reunion. I am horrified with the details she gave, but there is nothing I could do about it now.

I doze on and off all day long on Sunday. Late Sunday afternoon, the nurse comes into my room. "There is a woman named Robin at the nurse's station on the floor below. She says she is your sister. Robin is demanding to see you. Do you want to see her?"

"Yes, I will see her." I know Robin will not go away, especially after the message that was left on Uncle Al's answering machine. I can only imagine what Robin is thinking since I have been unreachable since

Friday. If my anxiety was high before, it skyrockets now. I fear and dread Robin's judgment.

A few minutes later, Robin walks through the door. When she sees me, her eyes immediately fill with tears.

"What happened? What did Jamie do to you? Why didn't you call me?"

"I just couldn't call you. There wasn't anything you could have done for me." That I must speak through clenched teeth only makes the situation more grotesque.

Robin asks, "Are you going to be okay? They said you had surgery."

"Yeah, I have broken jaws. I have already had surgery. I'm going to be fine. My mouth will be wired shut for six or seven weeks."

"Oh, Carly."

"How did you find out I was here?"

"Ernie went to the family reunion in Tennessee. Uncle Al told Ernie he got a message on his answering machine that you were in the hospital and had just had surgery. Ernie called your cell, and you didn't answer."

My head droops in shame. I am so embarrassed to have my family know that Jamie has beaten me. After all we had endured as kids, here I was repeating Mom's situation. This is the last thing I want to have happen.

"When you didn't return his calls, Ernie called your house. Ernie said Jamie answered the phone, and when he asked for you, Jamie just kept saying you had attacked him. Ernie asked to speak to you but Jamie kept saying you were crazy and that he didn't know where you were. That you had parked your car at Baptist Hospital, but you weren't there. Ernie finally called me to see if I knew where you were or what had happened to you.

"I knew something was wrong when you didn't show up for the family reunion and didn't call anyone back. So I came over here myself to see what was going on. Now tell me what he did to you."

"Jamie attacked me. He came home drunk, and we got into it. He got mad and attacked me. I was able to get away from him and drove myself to the hospital. He followed me and rammed my car a few times. After I had surgery, the doctor told me that Jamie came to the hospital a few hours after I had arrived to get his hand treated. He actually broke his hand he hit me so hard."

"Are you going to press charges?"

"I don't think so. I don't want to be involved with the courts and all that stuff."

Robin says, "Well, whatever you decide, you know you are welcome to come and say with us at our house."

"I don't know what I am going to do just yet. I need some time to think."

"You seem tired. You get some rest tonight, and I will come back tomorrow morning. I can take you wherever you decide to go. You know you shouldn't drive."

"Okay. And please don't tell anyone else that I am here."

"Oh, Carly, don't worry what other people think."

"Don't worry about me. I'll be fine. I always am. I know how to take care of myself."

"Okay, take care, and I will see you tomorrow morning."

"Okay."

Sleep refuses to come. I have no idea what to do or whom to ask for advice. I don't want to press charges against Jamie. I know it will simply increase his anger. I am already deeply afraid of him. I don't want to go to court. Courtrooms hold nothing but memories of fear and threats for me.

My credit card is maxed out with my payment to the hospital. I have some money in the bank, but I will have to pay the entire hospital bill. I know Jamie will never help me pay it.

Can I force Jamie to sell the house? Will I be able to live in the house? Do I even want to live in such a secluded location? Where will I stay? How can I keep Indy and Anna safe?

The questions swirl like a tornado funnel in my mind, scattering my thoughts haphazardly like dust particles. I ask for another sleeping aid. I need to get some rest. I know the next day I must make a decision. Tonight, however, I need to sleep.

The epiphany comes just before I succumb to sleep. I am thirty years old. Two different men have broken my bones. For the second time in my life, I suffer broken bones at the hands of my partners. I am living my mother's life.

In that moment, I realize I need to think differently. I decide therapy is my best solution. To have a better life, I need to change my long-standing patterns of thinking. Until this moment, I've subscribed to the belief that therapy is for weak people—you know, the ones who can't pull themselves up by their bootstraps and keep going.

Experiencing broken bones for the second time in a domestic-violence situation, however, stops me in my tracks. My thinking has shifted. I realize I am the common denominator in these situations. I desperately want a life without violence. I don't know how to make that happen. Maybe therapy can help. I will try therapy.

An action-oriented person, I thrive having a plan. It helps me feel things are moving forward, changing. I slide into slumber, sleeping throughout the night without waking. The next morning, I decide to stay temporarily at Max's. I can earn my keep assisting with Max's care. Only then can I accept lodging from Vivian and Misty at no charge with a clear conscience. It will give me the space and safety to consider my long-term plans. I also want to go see Indy and Anna. I love these dogs so very much. I feel their unconditional love in return, more palpably than I ever have from any human.

Monday is Labor Day. As promised, Robin arrives to drive me to Max's. Instead I suggest she follow me as I drive my car to Max's house. My sense of independence is rigid and nonnegotiable. I don't want to be a burden or allow others to help me. I have always taken care of myself. It is no different now. I drove myself to the hospital under extremely difficult circumstances; I can certainly drive myself to Max's now.

I do not yet know my long-term plans. Tomorrow, Tuesday, however, is a workday and I need to get my plan in order.

I will soldier on. My determination does not waver even under these extreme circumstances.

Once I realized Jamie was an alcoholic, I blamed myself for getting involved with him. I should have recognized his behavior for what it was and never agreed to build a house with him. I tormented myself for my mistakes.

I did not know how to treat myself with kindness, compassion, or forgiveness. I could feel these emotions for others but not for myself. Rather, I felt only shame. Not only had I chosen an alcoholic, I had stayed with him even when I was being abused.

I believe we all have the power to change our internal dialogue. We can do so even if we aren't sure of the changes we need to make. I had no awareness that I was continuing to react from a faulty belief system established in my formative years by watching my parents' dysfunctional, abusive interactions.

I believe that to stop seeing yourself as a victim of abuse, you must stop denying that the abuse occurred. Once you can acknowledge the abuse and have taken steps to end it, it then becomes the problem of the abuser. I had crossed a major turning point in my way of thinking. The first step had been to allow myself to be open to a new way of thinking about my own behaviors, choices, and decisions. In that hospital room, I finally realized that I did not know how to have a life without violence.

Considering therapy to be a viable option represented a significant shift in thinking for me; it cracked my façade. I became willing to open up and become vulnerable. A little bit.

Reflecting on the incident decades later, I easily recognize how shame overwhelmed and influenced my decisions. I was so consumed with hiding my shame that I couldn't see or feel other people's genuine concern and love for me. I can only describe this shame like a dust storm. The thick dust filled every crevice, blocking out all else within view.

It would take years to understand that breaking through this thick layer of shame was the key to unlocking the healing process. I also remained unaware of my deep-seated fears surrounding courtrooms and policemen. I did not consciously make the connection between the horrifying memories of testifying at Russell's trial and my fear of returning to a courtroom.

Pressing charges against Jamie meant courtroom appearances. I did not stop to think about what drove my resistance; I simply would not, at the time, willingly make a decision that would require me to have to appear inside a courtroom. Anything that triggered old fears and feelings related to Russell's murder trial was not a path that I would voluntarily chose. Therefore, refusing to talk to the police about Jamie's assault on me was the only choice I could possibly make at the time.

23. Where Do I Go from Here?

Heavy makeup on Tuesday morning helps to disguise the bruises on my face. I have also practiced talking normally or as normally as I can with my mouth wired shut. If a ventriloquist can talk without opening his mouth, then surely I can master this skill too. Unless you are in front me, you might not even realize that anything is wrong.

I take pride in my determination not to miss work, even though I had undergone surgery on Saturday morning. This small stand offers me the illusion I am in control of the situation.

I borrow Jamie's story, and I explain to my coworkers that I have fallen off a ladder at the house over the holiday weekend. The new house provides a good context. Embellishing the story, I explain that while I was repainting a room, I leaned too far on the ladder, and it toppled over. Trying not to spill the paint from the can I was holding onto the hardwood floor below, I became entangled with the ladder and fell face first on ladder, hardwood floor, and paint can—all unforgiving surfaces.

I don't know if anyone believes me or not. Having significant experience keeping secrets, it is fairly easy to crush prying eyes and further questions. Think what you like, but you won't get confirmation from me. None of my coworkers question the truthfulness of my story.

One hurdle passes.

Since I don't have my cell phone, I know Jamie will probably call me at work.

Right before lunch, the receptionist buzzes me. "Carly, Jamie is on line three for you."

"Okay, thank you." Fear and dread wash over me. I sit in my chair with my hand on the phone. With a click of a button, I will hear his voice. I expect him to be extremely apologetic and remorseful. I am afraid and unsure of what to do.

I know that if I don't talk to Jamie, he will call me repeatedly at the office. This might raise suspicions we are fighting and cast doubt on my story about falling off the ladder.

My hand trembles as I push the button. "Hello."

"Hello, Carly. How are you?"

I remain silent.

"Are you there, Carly?"

"Yes. I am here. What do you want, Jamie?" I struggle to maintain an aloof and disinterested tone.

"You haven't come home. I wanted to know if you are all right."

"I am going to be fine."

"Where have you been staying?"

"I am staying at a hotel." Connecting Misty to this could cause problems for her. A fabricated hotel stay seems the least complicated route.

"Are you hurt? Why was your car at the hospital?"

"I had surgery. You broke my jaws on both sides of my face."

"Did you file a police report?"

I don't want to tell him anything but am also afraid not to answer his questions. My beloved dogs, Indy and Anna, are still at our house. I don't want to reignite his anger for fear he will hurt them to hurt me.

"The hospital called the police. I had no choice but to talk with them."

"Did you tell them you fell?"

"No, I told them you hit me. The doctor told me you came in to the ER after I did with a broken hand."

"I did break my hand. Are you pressing charges?"

"I have not filed charges...yet."

I know Jamie will ask me to meet him; I am so used to his routine after a big blowout. "I think we should meet and talk before you make up your mind."

My main concern is I need to get my cell phone back. "I will meet you in a public place if you agree to bring my cell phone and charger from the house."

"You pick the place and time. I will be there with your phone."

"Okay. Applebee's right across from the mall. Six o'clock."

"I'll be there. And, Carly, I am sorry for my part." Jeez. Don't over-do it. You only broke both my jaws.

"Is that supposed to be an apology?" I ask sarcastically.

"I don't remember what happened."

"Stop. Now you're just lying." I can't disguise my disgust.

Jamie anxiously responds, "No. I haven't told you this before, but I have blackouts. When I drink a lot, I have blackouts, and I don't remember anything." Blackouts? Was he trying to explain away this inexcusable violent behavior too?

"Funny, you never mentioned blackouts before. Seems like a convenient time to have one."

"Please forgive me. I am so sorry this has happened. I know it must have been me who hit you because my hand is broken, but I swear I don't remember anything."

"I don't know if I can forgive you or not."

"Well, we can talk about it tomorrow when we meet."

"Just remember to bring my cell phone. I have to go. Good-bye." I replace the phone with a heavy heart. I desperately want to believe he is a good person and has a good heart. My chest feels heavy.

On Wednesday night, I arrive at Appleby's restaurant just before six. I see Jamie's truck. I walk into the restaurant and see Jamie sitting at a window booth. I tell the hostess, "I see my party over there."

"Okay, have a good evening." I attempt a smile and nod politely, but I think to myself that a "good evening" is not possible in my present situation. I slowly walk toward Jamie.

The first thing I notice is his bandaged hand. He has broken his dominant right hand by pounding on my head. I quickly look away, pushing the dark thoughts aside.

"Hello," he says in his most charming voice.

"Hello. Did you bring my phone?"

"I did." He pulls my cell phone out of his jacket pocket along with the charger. "I even charged it up for you."

"My, aren't you the gentleman? A real prince!" I think to myself. The term *anger* doesn't quite fully describe the intensity of my emotion.

"How are you, Carly?"

"Fine."

"Let's order some dinner."

"No, I don't want to eat anything. I'll just get a Diet Coke." I notice he is drinking a soda rather than beer.

"We have to order something. We can't just take a table at dinnertime and not order something to eat. That would be rude."

Rude? Now you are worried about being rude?

Although I do not recognize it and certainly can't name it, Jamie exhibits the honeymoon stage of the abusive cycle—he is trying to win me back. Negotiating, he offers, "Why don't I just order appetizers?"

I am silent and offer no response. When the waiter arrives, Jamie orders a couple of appetizers and a Diet Coke for me. He misses the obvious; I can't open my mouth to eat. It's a liquid diet for me for the next six or seven weeks.

"Thank you for bringing my phone. How are Indy and Anna?"

"They miss you. I miss you. I have missed you for a long time now."

"Let's not get into it. You broke my jaws. I don't know if I can ever forgive you."

Jamie switches to a reliable tactic. With condemnation, he accuses, "Well, you claim to be such a Christian person. If you are such a Christian, then you have to forgive me. If you can't forgive me, then you are nothing more than a hypocrite."

I don't respond. Confusion clouds my thinking. I believe that good people are supposed to forgive but will forgiveness mean I'm saying it is okay for Jamie to break my jaws? Am I expected to act like nothing happened?

"I think God might see it differently. I do believe in forgiveness, but it's not that simple. You don't just immediately forgive the person who does something so terribly wrong to you and act like it never happened."

Sensing a crack in my armor, Jamie pounces. "Of course it's that simple. What part of 'You must forgive' is so hard to understand?"

I don't have a quick or good response.

"Are you going to come back home?"

"I can't come home right now. I don't know if I can ever come back to you."

Proceeding as though my return is decided and is simply a matter of when rather than if, Jamie retreats to a more compliant stance. "I will start going to church with you if you come home." I focus my gaze at the Diet Coke in front of me as though it contains all the answers to this incredibly difficult situation.

"I know I drink too much. You can help me be a better person just like you promised on our Michigan trip. I know you still love me."

Jamie is an alcoholic, but I can't say this outright to him. He might be apologetic right now, but I know all too well how fast his anger can flare. Like a Jekyll-Hyde personality, he can instantly turn on me for any real or perceived criticism of his behavior. Direct confrontation—even during one of his apologetic, nice moments—is not an option. EVER.

Jamie continues in his softest voice. "You have to believe me. I don't remember anything that happened that night. I have only been drinking so much because I miss you. When you started helping take care of your mom and spending so much time away from home, I missed you. I only drank to take away the pain of not being around you."

"Do you remember trying to run me off the road with your truck?" I ask.

"No. I am just so sorry about all of this."

His words do not ring true as an apology. Rather, they sound more like regret at possibly instigating trouble with the law.

Again, I am confused. The small grain of truth Jamie includes in his comments causes me to hesitate, causes me to question my anger. It is true. My time for him and Allison had been significantly reduced during my mother's long illness. I have some guilt over this. I know that Jamie counted on me to help transport his kids to their school ball games and social events when he had visitation with them. Still, I need some time away from Jamie to process my thoughts.

Jamie doesn't pressure me for a final answer on a possible reunion. He does, however, want my commitment to stay in contact with him. "Will you call me before the weekend and let me know how you are doing?"

"Yes, I will call you before the weekend because I want to come out and see Indy and Anna."

We leave the restaurant, going our separate ways.

I need to think about my next steps. Misty is the only person with whom I openly discuss the situation. I will not confide in Robin, knowing she will pressure me to press charges against Jamie. Even if I don't return to the relationship with Jamie, I will not press charges. I do not want to reenter a courtroom.

I am committed to seeing a therapist. I don't know anyone who has gone to a therapist. No matter—I would never ask anyone for a reference. More secrets. No one can know I am going to a therapist.

On Friday, I call Jamie as promised. I inform him that I want to come to the house to see Indy and Anna this coming weekend. I ask him not to be there. He agrees to be gone, and we work out the time.

As I pull up to the garage on Saturday, I see Indy and Anna. My heart leaps at the sight of them. It is the first good feeling I've felt all week. Happiness floods my body. The feeling is clearly mutual. They are so excited to see me. Their bodies wriggle and twist as they dance around me, twirling so I will pet and hug them from every angle. I miss my dogs. I miss their love.

My cell rings. It is Jamie.

I hesitantly answer. "Hello."

"Hello, Carly. I bought something for you. It is on the kitchen table."

"This isn't a game. You can't just say you are sorry, buy me a gift, and make everything okay." Silence. "I need to go." I quickly end the exchange. He can just keep his stupid gift. I am not even going to go inside the house.

The pattern continues over the next two weeks. I don't see Jamie. Our communication centers on the dogs. He calls me with updates on them. I call him to ensure he isn't going to be home when I plan to visit them.

After a few weeks, I offer an olive branch, telling Jamie, "I will not even considering taking you back unless you go to couples' therapy." I will call the shots on any reconciliation.

"What good is couples therapy if you are about to file charges against me? I need to know if you are going to file charges."

Even though I know I will not file charges, I hedge. "Well, I haven't decided if I am going to file charges or not."

Jamie seizes the opportunity to widen the crack in my weakening resolve. "How can you even consider putting Allison through having her father in prison? Do you want her to experience the same shame and embarrassment that you've experienced? Besides, I don't even remember doing it."

I hadn't considered how the situation would affect Allison. I don't let Jamie know, but he has hit a nerve. I cannot bear the thought of my causing Allison to experience the shame of her father being in prison. Yes, that would be my responsibility.

"I need to go."

Jamie's nice streak continues. This is the Jamie I first met in the bars, the Jamie who was trapped in a loveless marriage to someone else. I know things have to change. We cannot continue as before the incident.

I lay down the law. "I can't even consider coming back unless you agree to three conditions: One, you agree to go to church every week with me; two, you quit drinking; and three, you go to counseling with me.

Jamie agrees to all three. This is the best Jamie yet, better even than the charmer I first met. Maybe things can be better. Two stressors on the relationship are now gone—Mom's illness and building our house.

Returning does not preclude deciding to later leave permanently if necessary. Don't I owe it to myself to find out if Jamie can be the nice and funny guy I knew during our first year? Love is about forgiving each other, right? Loving each other through the good and the bad.

I need some counseling, however, before returning. I select a male therapist from the phone book. I suspect that Jamie will not do well with a female therapist.

Our one and only session does not go well. The therapist asks to see me individually for a follow-up session at the end of our first session as a couple. I am surprised. Can't the therapist see that Jamie is the one who needs help? But I follow through and make another appointment for myself.

Jamie interprets the therapist's request to me alone as confirmation there is nothing wrong with him. He loses no opportunity to express this "truth" to me many, many times.

At my next session, the therapist doesn't mince his words. "I believe you are in danger."

My mouth is still wired shut. The therapist knows that Jamie broke my jaws.

"You should leave this guy as soon as possible. I believe he will hurt you again if you don't leave him."

"What about helping Jamie to change?"

"You can't help someone when they are not ready for help. Forced or coerced therapy doesn't work. Jamie can only be helped when he is ready."

"Okay." I understand Jamie can't be forced into therapy; no one could have forced me into therapy. But should a therapist tell me to leave someone? How can he possibly know the full picture in just one hour? I conclude this therapist diagnoses the situation without all the relevant information. Yes, Jamie broke my jaws; my mouth is wired shut. But there is additional information to consider like my mother's illness, my limited time and subsequent neglect of Jamie and his children, building the house, and the stress of Jamie's alcoholism.

Nevertheless, since I am there, and I'm paying him my hard earned money, I want his opinion on blackouts. "Can someone who drinks a lot actually have blackouts?"

"Yes, blackouts really do happen. And they usually happen only to extremely heavy drinkers."

Jamie certainly qualifies as a heavy drinker. Maybe Jamie is telling the truth about his blackout the night he attacked me. Maybe he really doesn't remember assaulting me. What if Jamie is being honest, and he really does have blackouts? If he is ready to change and reduce his drinking, maybe the tendency toward violence will stop. As a Christian, I feel I should forgive Jamie.

I mistrust my own emotions and thoughts. I know that my thinking, behaviors, and choices have resulted in a life filled with chaos and violence. I know regular violence is not the baseline for many people. I desperately want to understand *how* to avoid continued violence in my life.

If I go back to him, it will be different because at least one thing is changing—I am getting therapy. I selectively choose some truths from the therapist. Ready now with full-blown commitment to learn about the emotional issues, I discount the concerned counselor's warning of danger. Instead, I label the blackouts as the real culprit.

My rationale is that if Jamie stops drinking, the blackouts will go away…and so will the violence.

I don't want to continue to see this therapist. Jamie will be furious if he finds out this guy is advising me to leave. I begin the search for another therapist. Three therapists later, I still have not found one that I feel understands or connects with me.

My determination—both my savior and my nuisance—however, knows no bounds. I remain resolute in my goal to understand and think differently. I am dogmatic in rooting out the right therapist. I decide to go to a center for battered women. Domestic violence is their sole focus. Surely I will be able to connect with a therapist there. If I can't find a therapist there that I feel I connect with, maybe I should just adopt Jamie's aggressive, domineering behavior. Perpetrators seem to get what they want all the time. People like me just tiptoe around them all the time. I am desperate to change my life and get off this emotional roller coaster.

Going to battered women's shelter ushers in a new wave of overwhelming shame. I equate it to admitting I am a victim, which means I do not have control over my life. My options seem limited; if I don't go, I may never have a different life. Fearing life will never improve trumps my humiliation. I schedule an appointment. I tell no one, of course. Not even Misty.

I meet my new therapist, Freda. She is dressed like a leftover hippy from the sixties, and I wonder how this unorthodox woman can possibly help me, but there is more to Freda than her fashion choices. My, oh my.

As I explain my situation with Jamie to Freda, she seems to have already met him. During painful pauses in my stories, Freda begins finishing the tales, perfectly describing Jamie's behavior. How can she possibly know that Jamie doesn't get along with any of my family or friends? How can she know so much about Jamie when she has never met him?

Although I am worried, I am also intrigued. I decide to schedule another session with the hippy. Normally I'm a quick study. I initially think it might take me two or three more sessions to fully understand how Freda has developed this skill set. I definitely want to know what Freda knows.

I feel like I am on the brink of correcting my faulty thinking. Hope returns that I will finally be able to create a life free of violence. I've got this. I can do this.

I still feel ambivalent about how to proceed with a relationship with Jamie. I certainly don't want to hurt Allison.

I decide getting clarity with Freda gives me additional emotional resources. I can move back home with Jamie to see if things get better with our relationship. If things don't improve, I can always move out later.

Having finally arrived at thirty, I am definitely at a crossroads in my life.

My intense shame was pivotal in my agreeing to talk with Jamie after he had broken my jaws. Under no circumstances did I want anyone at work to know my boyfriend had delivered the trauma. I knew if I did not take his phone call at work, he would have come to the office and created a scene. A scene at work would have been worse than Jamie breaking my jaws.

Fear of exposure and humiliation about being judged an ignorant, helpless victim was greater than any physical pain I endured.

Again, I was unable to make any connection between my current mortification and the humiliation I experienced as a child surrounding my violent upbringing. I was unaware I was simply adding to an already abundant source of shame.

While I was lying in my hospital bed, the intensity of the hopelessness I felt drove my determination to make a change. Any change. I knew otherwise I would simply keep on repeating my mother's life—a life filled with violence, strife, and distant, broken, unhealthy relationships.

I had no sense of boundaries for myself. Not allowed to establish emotional—much less physical—boundaries as a child, I had not learned all individuals, particularly adults, have the right and responsibility to delineate and enforce personal boundaries.

I also had no awareness of Jamie's manipulation. His approach to coercing me to talk to him following his unacceptable behavior worked before, and it worked just as well this time. He knew I would take his calls at work. He knew I avoided scenes at all costs. Jamie knew my internal fears would overrule my ability to make rational decisions.

Jamie also played the Christian card to his advantage. I did not understand forgiveness should not displace accountability. In Jamie's argument, accountability, of course, only applied to me—in forgiving him for something he wasn't even aware he had done.

My guilt about not having spent enough time with Jamie and his kids due to Mom's illness was real. I didn't realize my unresolved hurt over Mom's abandonment during my teenage years was influencing my thinking, driving me to irrational conclusions. Incredibly, I equated leaving Jamie—or worse, sending him to prison by pressing charges—with me abandoning his kids, particularly Allison. I simply would not be the cause of another person being made to feel the pain I had experienced from Mom's abandonment of me as a teen.

Once again, I put the aggressor's needs and wants above my own. I did not yet know how to make any other choice.

However, my commitment to pursue therapy never wavered. The hopelessness and subsequent epiphany I experienced lying in that hospital bed made me realize with absolute certainty that I needed emotional help and guidance. I knew I needed to change my thought patterns and didn't know how to do this on my own.

Sheer tenacity drove me to search until I found someone I felt truly understood and connected with me. In this regard, perhaps the intensity of my shame served me well. Had my emotions been less intense, perhaps I would have "settled" for less intrusive conversations with nonprofessionals to process my thoughts. Instead, the intensity of my humiliation drove me to the privacy of a therapist's office—a trusted and competent one—to share my life story, which was to include all the warts of my experiences and how I became me.

My dogged commitment to continued therapy would prove to be the lifeline that guided me out of my dysfunctional thinking and toxic choices.

24. The First Twelve Months

Having interpreted our initial therapist's request to see me alone as an indictment of my emotional stability, Jamie is now off the hook for counseling. But I feel confident that Freda will help me to begin learning how to make better choices. I am hopeful I can begin to understand more clearly the source of our relationship problems. Then I can change myself and subsequently help Jamie be a better person. Jamie and I never discuss therapy again.

I refuse to consider myself a victim. Obviously, it is difficult to deny the physical assault, but all the other usual variables are absent. I have no children. I am not financially dependent on Jamie. I am educated. I can leave at any time.

Continuing to experience ambivalent emotions about my relationship with Jamie, I finally buckle under his incessant pressure to return. I move back to our house. My jaws have been wired shut for five weeks—two more weeks to go.

Because I am only able to consume liquids, my stamina drops. Since I am constantly fatigued, I go to bed almost immediately upon arriving home from work each night. Jamie remains on his best behavior. He stays home, not once going out drinking.

Indy and Anna continue to be a great comfort to me. They are large dogs—Indy weighs 110 and Anna 85 pounds. No one has told Indy though. He thinks he is a lap dog. He loves sitting in my lap, placing his head on my shoulder. Indy seems to sense my emotional pain. It feels like Indy wants to constantly reassure me how much he loves me. I love these dogs with every fiber of my being. I feel Indy and Anna model behavior as nature intends. Show a living thing love, and love is returned.

I take comfort that the natural order of things is right in at least this one arena. Jamie cannot distort my dogs' affection toward me. The dogs are beyond the reach of Jamie's manipulation. He cannot persuade the dogs to modify their behavior toward me. I wish all of my life could be as simple as my relationship with Indy and Anna.

I meet with Freda one hour every other week. About six months into our meetings, Freda asks, "Carly, are you aware that you reschedule or are late to every other session we have?"

I hang my head in embarrassment.

Freda continues in a kind voice. "I am telling you this because I think that you are subconsciously trying to avoid the pain of talking about your past."

I instantly recognize the truth of what Freda is saying and know she is right. Opening the lid on the stuffed emotions from my past is terrifying. I am not consciously aware I have been rescheduling or arriving late to our appointments. I refocus my determination. I will attend all appointments...on time.

It shocks me to realize I have subconsciously sabotaged my own healing! Nuts. This feeling—understanding and learning about one's behavior—is tougher than I expected. Why can't it be easy? However, I remain dedicated. I want to understand my behavior and what drives my choices. Freda concentrates on emotions and events attached to the Russell era, also known as my childhood. I want to change my current situation: eliminate the violence and constant arguments with Jamie. I want to understand why Jamie and I can't get along.

I cannot recall Russell ever living full time, or even for an extended period of time, with the rest of the family. Interactions with Russell, although intense, have always been sporadic. Russell was always mean. I do not have a single memory of Russell being kind or gentle. In my mind, this distinguishes Jamie from Russell. I know that Jamie can be nice, funny, and charming. I've experienced Jamie's warmth and friendliness.

The ability to connect the behavior of Jamie and Russell could provide me with the motivation to leave Jamie. But I just can't see that Jamie is anything like Russell.

I have also never witnessed Russell express any desire to become a better person or change his hate-filled behavior. Jamie, in contrast, has asked me on multiple occasions to help him be a better person. Everybody makes mistakes. Jamie recognizes his and wants to improve.

Jamie's ability to switch behavior quickly keeps me in a constant state of emotional upheaval. Should I refuse forgiveness to someone begging for it? Does that make me a bad person for not allowing others to make mistakes?

As I talk through my thoughts with Freda, she helps me become aware of behavior patterns of abusers. Common abusive behavior includes isolation from family and friends, complete financial control, elimination of any social activity not involving the abuser, increasing demands regarding the abuser's wants, and often extreme jealousy.

Slowly, ever so slowly, I begin to see the pattern of Jamie's ongoing abusive behavior. I begin to slowly distance myself from Jamie emotionally. Meanwhile, about seven months pass since Jamie broke my jaws. He his mostly still exhibiting good behavior, and his anger only flares occasionally. The outbursts always end quickly, immediately followed by an apology.

I want to believe that he is changing.

I start reading lots of self-help books. My perspective begins to shift. The new insights make me feel I am actually on the right path. My interest is sparked. I can't get enough.

Jamie condemns my reading choices. He certainly doesn't support the changes in me and is quick to challenge any new information I share. I quit sharing my thoughts with him. Once again, I keep my thoughts to myself. I am in no way, however, dissuaded from continuing to expand my reading sources.

Around this time, Lily breaks up with her boyfriend, Billy. Lily discovers Billy is cheating on her with another woman. Although he is not physically abusive to Lily, I don't feel Billy is good for her. I don't think Billy treats Lily with respect—and he didn't, not even during their initial, get-to-know-you dating period.

Lily and I begin to share our self-help books and insights with each other. We swap books, sharing our perceptions and new understandings. Very strong, well-respected women in our individual careers, we support each other's emotional growth in our personal lives. My insights continue to strain on my relationship with Jamie. Jamie increasingly vocalizes his aversion to the self-help books. The stories, however, present me with a lifeline and break my isolation. I begin to realize I am not alone in my suffering. The stories give me strength and encouragement, so I refuse to change my reading choices.

I am slowly realizing my past experiences hold me hostage. I am frustrated I simply cannot shake the hold these horrific experiences have over me. I persist in thinking there is something wrong with me in my relationship with Jamie. I am determined to fix whatever is wrong with me.

Jamie just doesn't understand his abusive ways. He doesn't want to read the self-help books. He thinks they are nonsense. I get it. It is very uncommon for abusive men to admit that any of their actions are wrong.

Nonetheless, I am determined to help not only myself but Jamie as well. I purchase tickets to an event by John Gray, author of *Men Are from Mars, Women Are from Venus.* The event will be held at a small, remodeled, stately historic movie theater in the downtown area. A beautiful building, it is one of Jamie's favorite places to go; we have attended many concerts there during our six years together.

When I tell Jamie that I've purchased tickets to go there, he asks, "Who is playing?"

"Oh, I want it to be a surprise." He does not press me for details.

The night of the event, I begin to worry. I am afraid Jamie will get mad when he finds out whom we are going to see. We plan to eat dinner out beforehand. Getting ready to go out for dinner, Jamie says, "I am going to fix a drink. Do you want one?"

My heart starts to race. I have not seen Jamie drink since the night he broke my jaws. I reply as nonchalantly as possible, "No, I don't think it is a good idea to drink before the event."

"I haven't had a drink in a long time, and this is supposed to be a fun time tonight. I am going to have a drink." I don't respond; he prepares his drink. As we are leaving the house, he mixes a second drink for the road.

I am quiet at dinner. Jamie consumes two more drinks during the meal. As we are leaving the restaurant, he turns back. "Wait, I am going to the bar. I want one for the road."

"No, we're going to be late," I complain.

"So what? We will be a few minutes late. Why are you getting so uptight about it?"

I decide that arriving late is better than fighting with Jamie. I wait as he downs his fifth drink within a two-hours period.

Finally we are on our way to the theatre, and my stomach twists like a pretzel. Serious doubts arise in me about the wisdom of such an outing. Jamie is drunk; I worry about how he will react upon discovering we will be attending a seminar rather than a concert. We are in Jamie's truck. He has asked me to drive because he knows he is going to be drinking. I am anxious about how the evening might progress, so I double-check to ensure I've stashed enough cash in my purse to take a taxi home if necessary.

Going out with Jamie requires emergency taxi money. I never want to call anyone to come and pick me up. Emergency taxi money is simply part of my wardrobe when I'm going out with Jamie.

We pull into the parking garage next to the theatre, and Jamie notices the marquee. "Who is John Gray?"

I respond, "He is an author."

"This isn't about one of those stupid self-help books that you read?"

"I have read his book, and I think he can help us to understand each other better. Maybe we won't argue so much."

Jamie is furious. "What a stupid thing to spend your money on! We should just leave right now!"

"Well, since we are already here, I am going to go in."

I hope he doesn't follow me inside as I walk toward the theater, but he does. Arriving inside, Jamie heads straight for the bar, and I follow him without a word. He downs the first drink and orders an immediately orders another one.

With resignation, I state, "I am going to go sit down."

"Give me my truck keys." This is not a good sign. I reach in my purse and hand his truck keys to him.

"Let's go," he commands with a smirk, heading for the auditorium doors.

Everyone is seated, and John Gray is already on stage and speaking. We proceed to our seats in the second row. Upon purchasing the tickets, I was excited to be seated in the second row. Now, I long for remote seats in the balcony or the back row.

As we stand at the end of the aisle waiting for people to stand so we can take our seats, John Gray attempts some humor, saying to us from the stage, "I hope you aren't late because you were in a fight."

Jamie spews venom. "As a matter of fact, we are. What makes you an expert on relationships?"

The popular author responds lightly. "Well, I think you are in the right place, and hopefully you will learn something tonight."

The comment enrages Jamie. He shouts back, "You don't have anything that I want to hear." He storms off, heading to the entrance.

Embarrassed, I no longer want to remain. Instead, I follow Jamie—not because I want to talk to him, but because I can't leave fast enough. How could I have been so stupid to think Jamie would listen to this speaker? Jamie's willingness to create an ugly scene in such a public arena shocks me.

Upon entering the lobby, Jamie swings around and yells, "What did you think, that I would stay and listen to some idiot who thinks he knows everything tell me what I am doing wrong? How stupid are you?"

I silently but determinedly walk toward the women's restroom. I remain there about twenty minutes. I want to make sure Jamie is gone when I exit. I reassure myself I am okay, grateful for my emergency taxi fund.

Exiting the theater, I don't see Jamie. I hail a cab and go home. Jamie arrives home in the wee hours of the morning.

I wonder if Jamie has been faking his good behavior. I am more familiar with tonight's behavior. Maybe he has been fooling me into thinking that he is changing.

However, the next day, Jamie apologizes profusely for his behavior. "It was the alcohol. Next time I won't drink so much. I am not perfect, but I am trying. I have been really good for several months now. This was just a slip up, and I'm not perfect. I love you."

I am unsure of his apology and suspicious about his motives. I decide to talk to Freda about the event.

I was in a constant state of confusion. Old denied emotions from my childhood were stuffed inside me, clamoring for release. A geographical move had not allowed me to outrun these feelings. These unprocessed emotions were contaminating my thinking.

I wanted Jamie and me to get along and be happy. By intentionally hiding the fact that we were going to a seminar, something I instinctively knew he would disapprove of, I was unknowingly exhibiting a form of controlling behavior. My intentions were irrelevant; my actions were simply controlling. I couldn't force Jamie to do anything, even if I believed it was for his own good.

Jamie's behavior upon arriving at the seminar was clearly out of line. Mine, however, was also out of line in that I was attempting to manipulate him into attending.

It is difficult, if not impossible, to change something about which you are unaware. I wasn't aware that I was attempting to control abusive behavior. I did not realize that I had the right to set boundaries in a relationship. I was very upset with the way the night at the seminar had ended, but I wasn't clear on why it had gone so wrong. I just knew that this relationship was draining me.

Freda helped me understand that negative or toxic relationships drain you and deplete your strength. I was beginning to understand that relationships are the cornerstone of our mental health. One's relationship with a partner can add light or cast a shadow over your entire life.

I was trying to fix something outside of my control. An overdeveloped sense of responsibility drove me to fix my relationship with Jamie. An unchallenged lie becomes your truth. And my unchallenged belief was that Jamie's behavior was not the behavior of a perpetrator or abuser—I believed that the consumption of alcohol contaminated Jamie's behavior. Therefore, alcohol was the enemy, not Jamie.

With Freda's guidance, I began to question my own behavior as well as Jamie's. I began to recognize the manipulation in my own behavior in my attempts to get Jamie to attend the event. Of course, Jamie blamed the alcohol—and me—for the sour turn of events. But I wasn't so quick to buy into his argument anymore. I recognized my manipulation in securing his attendance, but I also knew that his subsequent acting out at the event was not my fault.

What was right and fair in a relationship was still a little fuzzy though.

I was trying very hard to determine my role in these events. I knew I could choose my behavior regardless of how Jamie acted. I just needed more clarity on how healthy relationships should work.

In the meantime, I was determined to never invite Jamie to another function. On that, I was very clear.

25. Breaking Point

It is more than a year since Jamie broke my jaws. The statute of limitations now protects Jamie against any civil suit that I might try to file against him for breaking my bones. Jamie, almost to the one-year anniversary date, renews his heavy drinking, partying into the wee hours of the morning. I am sad but not completely crushed or angry like I was during his earlier binge drinking.

Not a single friend or family member of mine will tolerate Jamie. His frequent demeaning, abusive verbal assaults on me embarrass everyone, keeping others at bay. Even Jack, who frequently hunts, subcontracts work with Jamie, and attends many of our cookouts in the back yard, begins distancing himself from Jamie.

One cold night in February, Jamie enters the house, stomping snow off his boots with significant force. Startled, I ask, "What is wrong?"

"Jack has been avoiding me for weeks now and won't return my phone calls. So I stopped by his house to ask him why he was avoiding me. You know what he said?"

"No, what did he say?"

"He said he doesn't want to be my friend anymore."

"Did he say why?"

"He said it was everything."

I understand Jack's decision. I think to myself, "Maybe it is because you are so mean."

"What the hell does that even mean? I tried to get him to tell me one thing I had done, but he couldn't."

"He wouldn't tell you why he doesn't want to be friends?" I ask, attempting to show some expression of sympathy rather than expecting a logical answer.

"No, but he is a stupid SOB. He will see. I gave him a lot business. He will be sorry he did this to me."

Jamie is clearly upset Jack no longer wants to be friends with him. I have never seen Jamie so upset. I do feel sorry for him. This is reminiscent of the Jamie I experienced during the Michigan trip when he had asked me to help him be a better person. His sensitive display of emotional pain reminds me that he is human, capable of feelings, regrets, and sorrow.

Jamie's emotional pain reveals his own woundedness. I recall the Al-Anon phrase "Hurting people hurt other people." Jamie is just another wounded soul trying to figure out this life, perhaps not so different than me.

My conversations with Freda convince me that the path to a better life lies in processing my thoughts and emotions surrounding my childhood experiences. Maybe Jamie just needs to do the same thing.

I talk to Freda about Jack having ended his friendship with Jamie. She asks me how I feel about it. I admit I think it is unusual. Freda encourages me to focus on myself and my own choices. I argue Jamie needs help too. I need to figure out a way to help him because otherwise everyone who cares about him may ultimately abandon him and he may never "get it."

Freda gently but repeatedly encourages me to focus on myself. I decide to actively work on establishing some personal boundaries in my relationship with Jamie.

Freda urges me to begin by setting small boundaries. With small victories under my belt, I can then work toward setting and maintaining larger boundaries. I decide that my first small boundary will be to no longer ride with Jamie as a passenger. He is a consistent speeder, and I feel like Jamie takes unnecessary risks while driving. I am always worried—if not outright terrified—for my safety while riding with him.

Maintaining the boundary is easy at first because Jamie does not realize the change. This gives me my first small victory: eliminating the terror of riding with him without the negative feedback I will surely encounter when he realizes I have set this personal boundary. As predicted, Jamie is furious when he realizes I will no longer ride with him. However, my mind is set; I will not budge. Repeated arguments do not sway me. It feels good to take a stand for myself. A small decision in the grand scheme of things, the decision to honor this boundary boosts my self-confidence enormously.

The dynamics of our relationship are shifting. We rarely see each other. With each encounter, I endure Jamie's meanness and cruelty. I emotionally distance myself from him a little more each passing day.

A lot of changes are happening in my life. I am learning to set personal boundaries, and I started a new job about six months ago. During my last job search, I contacted a recruitment company specializing in accounting and finance placements. Rather than place me with one of their clients, they offered me a position as a recruiter.

"If you decide you don't like working here, you will know which of our clients is hiring, and you will know who has the best benefits," they said.

This makes sense to me. Recruitment work often entails late evening hours to interview potential candidates. The schedule offers me a plausible excuse to avoid being home.

It is now early spring, and summer and the annual Country Music Association festival are just around the corner. I am optimistic about my future. The CMAs in the past have been a time when Jamie and I had parties with our friends and enjoyed the week-long festivities.

But this year is different. I don't want to attend anything with Jamie. I don't want to risk him getting mad and causing a scene. So I attend the CMAs with my friends. On the way home after leaving the CMAs, I realize I only have fun when Jamie isn't around.

I sadly think to myself that I need to find my way back to the place where I have fun in my life again. Recalling my pleasant experiences working in Colorado years earlier and longing to get away, I plan a solo trip to Colorado for the second week of June. When booking my flight, I look forward to the trip. I don't share my plans with Jamie.

Although sharing the same house, we live separate lives. My office and a guest bedroom are located in the walk-out basement. I began sleeping in the guest bedroom shortly after the one-year anniversary of Jamie breaking my jaws. We hardly talk and rarely see one another.

One morning, a few weeks after the CMAs, Jamie walks out of the master bedroom and confronts me in the kitchen while I'm making myself breakfast.

Standing in front of the microwave, I hear the door to the master bedroom open. I cringe. I don't want to talk to him. Just let me escape back downstairs.

Entering the kitchen, Jamie accusingly snarls, "Aren't you even going to say hello? What about 'Hi, honey'?" I don't respond. I don't turn to look at him.

He yells, "You have to stop treating me like a criminal. You act like you are so much better than me. You just need to stop it. And I mean stop it right now."

I turn, looking him straight in the eye. "I don't want to talk to you. I've changed my mind. I don't want breakfast after all." I move to step around him, heading toward the stairs and the sanctuary of my office.

Jamie taunts me. "Well, maybe to get your attention, I just need to get something of yours. Maybe then you will pay attention to me."

He heads downstairs. I dare not follow. I don't want to be in his crosshairs.

Quickly returning, he waves my laptop carelessly above his head. "I'll bet you will pay attention to me now."

"Give me my laptop."

Jamie mocks me. "Oh, now you want to talk to me. I have your attention now, do I? I am going to smash this laptop to a thousand pieces."

I try to pull my laptop from his hands. He slams the laptop down on the kitchen counter, grabs me, and throws me down on the hard slate kitchen floor.

I am once again on the floor, about fifteen feet from where he broke my jaws. It is now eighteen months later, and I can't believe I am here again. The realization strikes me as vehemently as Jamie's previous blows that nothing has changed. My relationship with Jamie remains the same as it was on that fateful weekend he broke my jaws.

When I hit the floor, I have a flashback to my very first memory of Russell. I vividly see Mom lying perfectly still on the pavement, absorbing Russell's assault. While I am lying on the floor, time moves as though in slow motion.

Mimicking my mother, I lie perfectly still. I know I am no match for Jamie's aggressiveness. My passivity conveys my unspoken message to him that he wins; there is no need to keep hitting me.

This moment is forever stamped in my mind. This is the moment I finally fully understand the emotional, mental, and physical toxicity of this relationship. I must escape this man. I finally understand what Mom was attempting to do that horrific night so many years ago; her command that we should remain quiet was an attempt to protect her two children in the backseat of the car. Now in this moment, as I lie on the floor of my own kitchen, I so desperately need the same protection again, and I feel Mom's spirit with me. She is right there beside me on the kitchen floor, while Jamie beats me yet again.

This is my moment of clarity—my crystalline glimpse into what must be done. I will leave Jamie for good. My mind is made up.

Jamie finally stops his barrage, stands, and glares at my lifeless body. I remain motionless. I am as limp as an abandoned doll, but even so, he kicks me one final time to see if I am conscious.

I remain still.

I intuitively know that I need to remain still—lifeless. If the perpetrator thinks I am dead, he will feel victory and stop the attack.

Jamie walks into the kitchen to lean against the counter. Now about seven steps from me, if I can make it to the stairs and into my office, I can lock the door. If Jamie tries to break down the door, I can exit through the exterior door in my office, reach my car and escape.

I am finally finished with this relationship. I will call the police and report Jamie's attack. Having never called the police before, I know the call will irrevocably damage the relationship. I am ready to end this partnership.

I make a run for the steps. Surprisingly, Jamie doesn't follow me.

Reaching my office, I dial 911 on my cell phone. I am quite sure that Jamie has no idea that I will call the cops. In our six-year relationship, I have never called the cops. But this time I have finally had enough.

"911. What is your emergency?"

"My boyfriend has just attacked me. Please send the police now."

"What is your address?"

"896 Fiddle Lane." With a Sumner County address, law enforcement from that county is dispatched to the scene.

I anxiously wait in my office for the police to arrive. Jamie is still upstairs with my laptop. There is no turning back. I am terrified. I wonder if I should call anyone to come and help me. Shame keeps me from reaching out to any friends or family for help. How can I explain that once again Jamie has attacked me? My friends and family have repeatedly warned me they feared this day would come.

No. I will handle this on my own. I wonder where I will go from here.

About thirty minutes later, the Sumner County police arrive. From my office door, I see the police cruiser pull through the trees into the clearing on the driveway. As soon as the officers get out of the car, I open my office door to meet them.

Jamie walks out onto the deck, directly above my office. He is standing right above me and the police officers.

Jamie yells down from the deck, "Officers, she is on medication. She lost her mother a couple of years ago, and she has not been in her right mind ever since then."

Shock ricochets through my body like echoes in a canyon.

He continues. "She has been taking all sorts of pills and is probably high right now."

The police officer responds. "Ma'am, let's step inside the house, and you can tell me what happened here this morning."

I am afraid to go in the house. It doesn't matter to me that there are two police officers present. Terror consumes me because Jamie now knows I have called the police.

Finally, one of the officers takes Jamie into an upstairs room of the house, so he can't see me. I begin to slowly calm down. The second policeman and I remain outside.

"I went upstairs to fix myself some breakfast this morning. I basically live downstairs, and he lives upstairs. This morning he got up while I was in the kitchen and threatened to destroy my laptop. When I attempted to get it back from him, he attacked me. He threw me down on the kitchen floor and started hitting me."

I show the policeman the cuts on the inside of my mouth from Jamie's blows.

"We are going to arrest him."

"What will happen from here?" I ask with tears in my eyes.

"He will be taken to the local jail. He probably won't get out for a day or two. You should call an attorney and file for a restraining order."

Jamie is handcuffed and put in the back of the cruiser. The police and Jamie drive off. My mind is numb. What should I do?

I will file a restraining order to keep Jamie away from me. I decide to wait a couple of hours to calm down before I call an attorney. I don't want to start crying and become emotional when I talk to my lawyer.

About an hour later, Misty calls me. Jamie has called Alan from jail seeking advice. Alan has vast experience in these situations.

These are my goals: to divide what Jamie and I jointly own, ensure we go our separate ways, and if at all possible, avoid court. I want to move on with my life without Jamie. I don't want to stay in the house we built. The house is too secluded; I am too easy a target for Jamie.

I need to find someone who can keep my dogs, someone with whom Jamie will not have any communication. There is absolutely no way I will leave my precious Indy and Anna behind.

I know there is no turning back. I'm afraid that I am now facing the biggest fight of my life. Dividing our belongings and financial assets is going to be a nightmare.

In an attempt to avoid court, I naïvely think I can convince Alan into talking logic to Jamie. We can work out a mutual agreement and untangle our finances without involving the court system. Surely Alan will see that this is in Jamie's best interest. Surely Alan doesn't want Jamie to have to go to court over this latest assault. Although a rough character, Alan seems the lesser evil compared to the court system.

The decision proves fatal, like a lamb calling the wolf to come and slaughter it.

Alan isn't concerned about being fair or doing the right thing. Alan is only concerned with helping Jamie get out of trouble and winning big, crushing me in the process.

I leave the house we built together.

And so the battle with Jamie begins.

I desperately wanted to believe that Jamie was not an abuser. Convincing myself he wasn't, I returned to the relationship after he had broken bones in my body. Jamie's fear of a civil suit for his physical attack on me motivated him to maintain our relationship and walk the straight and narrow as best he could.

The marked change in his behavior toward me almost immediately following the one-year anniversary of the attack substantiated his true motivation. Free from the threat of a lawsuit from me, Jamie once again became violent and aggressive.

Ongoing therapy helped me begin to change and learn how to establish personal boundaries.

My flashback to the vision of Mom lying lifeless on the road felt surreal. In that instant, I knew if I didn't get away from Jamie, my life would never change. It was a deep, internal, unquestionable knowledge that I cannot explain. The imprint of the image of Mom lying lifeless on the pavement and the unshakable realization I had to escape for good was as real as the air I was breathing.

At that moment, in slow motion, I foresaw repeated attacks for the rest of my life, until one day when I simply would not survive. Having finally decided to leave Jamie, I was resolute. Jamie's accusation that I was using drugs shocked me. An occasional Tylenol was the extent of my medicine consumption. I should not have been surprised. With multiple prescriptions, mostly for anxiety, Jamie had tried on multiple occasions to get me to try them. I had always refused.

I was still very naïve. It was hurtful to hear Jamie telling lies about me. I simply could not understand why he would lie about me. Even though I had lived with people who used and abused their mates, I continued to try to understand their behavior by using logic. I simply could not comprehend how or why they could engage in such egregious behavior. It didn't make sense.

It was June 1998, and I was discovering that my thirties were not turning out to be so great. But I thought I could still get my life back on track. I just needed to stay in therapy and get a new home—a home I owned by myself.

I continued to be unaware of the enormous amount of fear I harbored regarding the courthouse experience from my childhood. Unhealed, these childhood wounds and residual raw emotions would continue to influence my current choices without my awareness.

You can't change your history, but you can change your responses to external factors.

SECTION V

CHOICES AND CONSEQUENCES

---

26. Jurisdictions

I feel so alone and afraid. I fear that no one will believe the extent of Jamie's manipulation or cruelty. This vulnerable mind-set weakens my thought processes. As a result, I make hasty decisions that unintentionally support Jamie's distortion of the truth.

I hire Mr. Knight to represent me in the case against Jamie. Mr. Knight represented Jamie's ex-wife during their divorce, so I feel this particular attorney might have some insight into Jamie's character. At the very least, he should be aware of Jamie's penchant for spinning small grains of truths into outright lies. Mr. Knight's office is located in the high-rent downtown district.

The mahogany-lined walls, plush carpets, and partner portraits on the walls all scream money—money I can't afford to pay. These thoughts and the fear of not being able to pay my legal bills swirl through my head with increasing velocity as I sit in the cool leather club chair. The young receptionist seated at the front desk is dressed for success. Her soft black-leather stilettos perfectly complement her gray skirt and white blouse.

The critical voice in my head increases in volume, berating me for not working things out with Jamie. Grasping for calm, I reassure myself that the situation will be settled quickly.

The receptionist ushers me down the long portrait-lined hallway leading to Mr. Knight's corner office. With each step, I feel my sweaty palms and racing heart. The attorney's enormous desk resembles the deck of a battleship. Glass walls behind him offer an impressive view of downtown Nashville. Standing like the captain of a ship, he makes the journey around his desk, offering his hand in greeting. "Hello, Ms. Lee."

"Hello," I squeak, trying to discreetly wipe my hand on my pants before stretching it out.

"Have a seat and tell me what seems to be your trouble today, young lady."

"Well, as I said on the phone, my boyfriend beat me up yesterday. I called the police, and they came and arrested him."

"Okay...this boyfriend of yours, Jamie, he is in jail right now?"

"Yes, he is in Sumner County jail. Our house sits in Davidson County, but the driveway and mailbox are in Sumner County. When I called 911, since it was a Sumner County address, Sumner County officers were sent."

"Interesting. There might be a jurisdiction issue. We will have to wait and see what Sumner County does with the current charges against him." His brow wrinkles. "Tell me more, Ms. Lee, about your relationship with Jamie."

"We have been living together, and Jamie wanted to build his 'dream house.' I never trusted him, and that's why we never married. Because I, too, wanted a home of my own, I agreed to build a house with him after we had a legal partnership agreement drawn up to protect us both in case one of us wanted out of the partnership or if one of us died. The agreement spells out how the property will be divided if we decide to go our separate ways."

"I see. Who drew up this agreement for the two of you?"

"An attorney Jamie knows."

"Did you get a second opinion on this partnership agreement?"

"No," I respond softly as the critical voice in my head shouts, "Why didn't you think of that then?"

"Did you bring the agreement with you?"

"Yes." My hands are shaking as I retrieve the contract from my bag.

Inspecting the document, Mr. Knight informs me of next steps. "Well, because he was arrested on domestic abuse, he will be ordered to stay away from you. In a few days, you will have a court date, and the judge will decide who will get to stay in the house."

"I am afraid to stay in the house. The house is surrounded by woods and is very secluded."

"You need to fight for the house. If he gets possession of it, he might not agree to buy you out or put it on the market. You will be stuck in a situation in which you cannot force him to sell or move."

"What about our partnership agreement? Can't I make him sell based on the terms of our agreement?"

Mr. Knight explains, "This agreement states you both agree to live there and maintain the property fifty-fifty."

"But he beat me up—again. I can't live there with him. He has tried to kill me more than once. If I stay, I believe he will kill me."

Mr. Knight repeats, "Well, the partnership contract states you agree to live there and pay half of the maintenance. The agreement doesn't list exceptions for these conditions. You need to fight for possession of the house."

How can I have been so stupid? Why didn't I get a second opinion? I have not protected myself, and now I will have to pay for it.

"I will need a retainer fee. If you can pay that today, I will represent you in Sumner County on your next court date for the property issues. You won't need me there for the criminal charges. These are charges against your boyfriend. The county prosecutor will represent the state's side."

Stunned but unsure what else to do, I write a check and leave. My mind is swirling. I can't stay in the house; I am too afraid. What about my dogs, Indy and Anna? There is no way I can leave them with Jamie.

The thought of being homeless terrifies me. I feel sure Robin or Lily will let me stay with them until I figure out my living arrangements—but I don't want to have to stay with either of my sisters. They will take me, but asking for my dogs to stay would just be too much. Pondering my situation, it occurs to me to call Jack, Jamie's former business associate and friend. Jack has a large yard; he might agree to keep my dogs. It is a lot to ask, but I don't have many options.

I drive to Jack's house so I can ask him in person. His vehicle is in the driveway. Good, he is home. I hate asking for help, but I have no choice. I must protect Indy and Anna.

I pull up beside Jack's van and get out of my car. I slowly walk toward the back porch and knock on the screen door.

Jack answers right away, dressed in his contractor flannel shirt, jeans, and work boots.

I see the curiosity on his face. "Hi, Carly. How are you?"

"I'm okay. I stopped by to ask a favor. You don't have to say yes, and my feelings won't be hurt if you say no." I pause and look away. I am embarrassed to ask for his help. I take a deep breath, look up, and continue. "I thought of you because I know you no longer talk to Jamie."

"Okay...what is it?" he asks with a gentle voice.

"I am leaving Jamie, and I need someone to keep Indy and Anna for me until I find another place to live. I know it is a lot to ask."

"Of course I'll keep your dogs. I'll keep them for you as long as you need me to."

The detested tears burn behind my eyes as relief floods my body. "I can't tell you how much I appreciate this. Can we keep this between us? I don't want Jamie to know where the dogs are—or where I am, for that matter."

"No, you don't have to worry about anyone finding out; I will not say anything to anyone. If you don't mind me asking, what happened?"

Shame engulfs me. Dropping my head, I look away. "Jamie and I had a huge fight, and it got physical. This time, I called the cops, and he was arrested. There is a court date in a few days in Sumner County regarding the criminal charges against him."

"I'm not surprised by Jamie's behavior. Are you sure I can't do anything else for you?"

"No, making sure Indy and Anna are cared for is my biggest worry right now. I don't know when I can bring them by, but I'll be in touch soon."

"Just call me."

"I can't thank you enough for this."

"You're welcome. Just be careful and stay alert. Try not to go anywhere by yourself."

"Okay. Thanks again for keeping my dogs." I leave Jack's house with an enormous sense of relief. I know my dogs will be safe.

Terror does not adequately describe my emotional state regarding the upcoming court date. Scared and alone, I make a very, very bad decision. In an attempt to avoid a courtroom appearance, I am thinking about calling Alan to see if he can help me work out an agreement with Jamie. I can't call Jamie directly as there is a no-contact order between us, and if I do, I am afraid Jamie will have me arrested.

My attorney has advised me not to talk to anyone about the case, most certainly not to Jamie or his family. Mr. Knight counsels me to handle everything through the courts; however, he has no idea of the extent of my terror about returning to a courtroom.

Although Jamie is in jail, I am afraid to go to our house by myself. I ask my friend Karen to accompany me to the house to feed Indy and Anna. Karen agrees and invites me to stay with her for a few nights.

As I sit alone in Karen's spare bedroom, I decide calling Alan to work out an agreement with Jamie is my only option to avoid a court appearance.

The next day Misty, Alan's girlfriend, calls me. "Hi, Carly."

"Hi."

"I just wanted you to know Jamie is staying with us."

"Is he furious with me that I called the cops?"

"He is worried about court. Alan advised him to get a female attorney because she will make him look more sympathetic to the judge."

I share with Misty that I am considering calling Alan. Misty doesn't think it's a good idea; she encourages me to follow my attorney's advice.

"Whatever you do, Carly, stay away from Jamie. He is going to really hurt you if you don't stay away."

"No, I can't ever go back. It is really over between us. I am only concerned about ending our financial partnership. All I want is to get my stuff and equity in the house. Then we never have to see or speak to each other again."

"Be very careful, Carly. I am concerned for your safety."

"I don't want to press criminal charges against him. I just want it to be over."

"You shouldn't be alone right now. Are you going to stay with one of your sisters?"

"No. I'm staying with a girlfriend for the next few days. I don't know where I am going to stay long term yet. When Jamie was arrested, there was an EPO issued, so he can't come around me right now. When we go to court in a few days, the judge will decide if this EPO will be turned into a permanent restraining order. I'm assuming Jamie and I will have to agree on which one of us is going to stay in the house until one of us buys the other one out or we sell."

"I don't believe he will be fair, so make sure you get a very good attorney."

"I hired Jamie's ex-wife's attorney, the attorney she used in their divorce. I don't know how good he is, but I know at least he is not going to be on Jamie's side or a friend of Jamie's. I think I will call Alan tomorrow to try to work something out with Jamie. I'll keep you posted on my whereabouts."

"Take care of yourself, and good luck with court and everything."

The next day I call Alan. As his phone rings, I wonder, "Am I doing the right thing?"

"Hello, Carly."

"Hello, Alan."

"Are you doing okay?" he asks.

"I'm doing the best as can be expected given the situation."

"Have you been to the hospital?" I think this is an odd question to ask me.

"No, I haven't been to the hospital."

"So you aren't hurt then?"

"I will be okay."

"Well, Carly, you know you should try to work things out with Jamie. You know you don't have any experience with going to court. Court is expensive."

I am silent.

"You really don't want to be in court do you? You don't want all your dirty laundry aired in public, to be on display for the entire world to see? What will people think of you?"

"Alan, I want to work out an agreement over the house without using the court system. That is why I am calling you."

"I think that is a smart move on your part, Carly. I always knew you were a smart girl. I have to go right now, but I will call you back tomorrow, okay?" I feel hope return. Maybe I can work out a financial arrangement with Jamie through Alan and avoid court after all.

As promised, Alan calls me the next day. "Hello, Carly."

"Hello, Alan."

"So you aren't hurt, is that right, Carly?"

"Yes, I am not hurt. Things are awful the way it happened." Why does he keep asking me that?

"So you are sorry that you called the police on Jamie?"

"No, I am not sorry that I called the police. I just don't want to go to court. I am afraid to go to court."

"So you are afraid to go to court because you lied to the police?"

"I didn't lie to the police. Jamie hit me, and I know he won't quit hitting me. That is why I called the police."

"Okay, Carly. I have to go, but I will call you later tonight."

I can't understand why Alan calls me only to say he has to go and will call again later. Is Jamie listening to our conversations?

Alan calls me later that night. He starts the conversation the same way. "So you aren't hurt, are you, Carly?"

"I am physically okay, Alan."

"So the only reason you want to talk with me is to get money out of Jamie. And if Jamie gives you money, you will drop the charges against him."

"I want Jamie to agree to pay me my half of the equity in our house and reimburse me the cost of my medical bills when he broke my jaws. If we can agree on the dollar amount, I will drop the criminal charges."

"So if Jamie pays you money, you will drop the criminal charges?"

"I don't want to press criminal charges against Jamie. I only want what is rightly mine."

"So what is the amount of money you want from Jamie?"

We discuss the appraised value of the house and the equity value in the house. I sum up our conversation. "So splitting the equity in half and adding my medical expenses from my broken jaw, I agree to this amount. If Jamie pays me this amount, I will sign the house over to him."

"So what you are saying is if Jamie pays you the amount you just calculated, you will drop the criminal charges, and you will both go your separate ways."

"Yes."

"I need to let Jamie know, and I'll call you back tomorrow."

It is two days before we go to court. I am nervous because time is running out. The next day, Alan calls me. "Hello, Carly."

"Hello, Alan."

"So are you hurt, Carly?"

What is going on? Why does he keep asking me this? "I'm okay."

"So you are saying that you will drop the charges against Jamie if he pays you money?"

"Yes, but it has to be the figure we discussed yesterday. I also want my personal belongings from the house. I don't want to fight with

Jamie or go to court. If Jamie pays me the amount we agreed to yesterday, I will drop the criminal charges."

Alan asks me again, "So if Jamie pays you the money you are demanding, you will drop the criminal charges?"

I repeat myself. "Yes, if he agrees to pay me the amount we agreed to yesterday, I will drop the criminal charges in Sumner County."

Alan quickly responds, "I'll have to get back to you." I hear a click on the other end of the phone. Alan doesn't even bother with a good-bye this time.

I wonder why Alan called. We simply repeat everything from our previous conversation. I will find out the reason for his motives the next day in court.

Our court docket is set for one o'clock. By 11:00 a.m., I still have not heard from Alan. I call him to see why he hasn't called me with Jamie's response. Alan's phone rings repeatedly and then goes into voice mail.

Alan is not answering his phone.

I sense that something is terribly wrong. With apprehension and dread, I drive to the Sumner County courthouse. I go by myself. I remind myself Mr. Knight said this is not a big deal. The prosecuting attorney will be there for my side. Jamie is the one facing the criminal charges.

Jamie stands confidently near the front of the courtroom, sandwiched between Alan on his left and Amanda McMillian, his attorney, on his right. Alan holds a tape recorder.

Amanda proceeds to tell the judge, "This isn't a case of domestic abuse but rather a case of blackmail. We have evidence to prove that Carly is trying to get money from Jamie, and she only called the cops as a ruse to have something with which to blackmail my client."

I connect the dots. Alan's repeated phone calls and incessant questioning—"Are you hurt, Carly?"—suddenly make sense. They needed me to say the right words in the right order so the taped conversation would match their manufactured story line. Amanda continues. "The proof of blackmail is a conversation between Alan and Carly yesterday, with Carly agreeing to drop the criminal charges against Jamie if he will agree to pay her a lump sum of money. This is nothing more than a clear case of blackmail against my client."

My unexamined, internal intense fear of court led me to a decision that perfectly supported the perpetrator's deceitful, manipulative plan. Jamie and I certainly had our problems, but I never dreamed anyone could or would intentionally devise such a cold, vicious, manipulative attack.

I feel numb; the event seems surreal.

Amanda continues. "The court does not need to review the evidence because as a matter of law, Jamie should be released. Sumner County officers unlawfully arrested Jamie because they did not have jurisdiction to be on the property. The house is located in Davidson County. When Ms. Lee called 911 and gave the physical address, the Sumner County police were dispatched incorrectly. My client, Mr. Goffy, is in fact a resident of Davidson County. Therefore based on the legality of the matter, the criminal charges are unlawful and should be thrown out."

I am on emotional overload, and it is hard for me to fully take in what is happening. Everything is twisted and warped; the truth is no longer recognizable.

As I am alone and without legal representation, I simply do not know how to fight against Amanda and Jamie. The judge declares, "The Sumner County officers did not have the jurisdiction to arrest the defendant. The criminal charges are hereby dismissed. The defendant is free to go."

What is happening?

The EPO is dismissed. However, a no-contact order for ninety days between the two parties is issued. The judge informs us, "This is not a restraining order because domestic violence has not been proven. This is simply a mutual no-contact order between the two parties."

Amanda responds, "Thank you, Judge, for the court's time."

Amanda, Jamie, and Alan turn to leave the courtroom. As I stand aghast and alone, Amanda turns around, stares directly at me, and strides purposefully toward me. Oh, God. What is she going to do now? I shrink back as if anticipating a physical blow.

Shoving documents into my hand, she informs me with a hard voice, "Carly, you have been served."

As Amanda, Jamie, and Alan leave the courtroom, I stand motionless in shock. I walk to my car like a robot.

In the privacy of my car, I take deep breaths, trying to slow my heartbeat and regain my composure. As I sit behind the steering wheel, I become aware of the throbbing pain in my head. My chest feels like it will explode at any moment.

In the safety of my car, I begin to cry. I am emotionally overwhelmed. I wonder how it could have turned out this way.

I must get away from this place. I will myself not to think about what just happened. I simply focus on getting away from this building.

I find my keys, put them in the ignition, and pull away from the building. Driving down Main Street, I turn down the first side street. Pulling into a gas station a few blocks away, I slip into an empty parking space.

With trembling hands, I retrieve the documents that Amanda thrust in my hands. I take a deep breath and start to read. Jamie has served me to take sole possession of the house. Claiming closer proximity to his employment, Jamie argues that his ten-mile commute outweighs my purported sixty-mile commute to my employer's home office in Lafayette. I work from a home office, not the company's Lafayette office. The Lafayette address is, of course, the address on record for my employer.

The second motion files a civil case against me for ownership of our house. How is this even possible?

The experience solidifies my confusion and mistrust of officials and court in general. Fairness and facts don't matter. Those are simply trivial matters to be manipulated to support any story the bully wants to manufacture. I don't know how to successfully navigate these waters.

I call Mr. Knight to update him on the turn of events. He advises me, "Go to your house and remove all your personal items from the house."

"I can't do that. Jamie will be furious if I move anything out."

"If you don't, he might take everything, and you will end up with nothing."

"I'm afraid of Jamie. And we bought some of the furniture together. He will kill me if I take anything out of the house."

"My advice as your attorney is to take everything. Possession is nine-tenths of the law. You can later give back what is his if you decide to do so."

"Okay. I will call you if I need you today; otherwise, I will call you in a couple of days to find out what I need to do next."

"Take care and call me when needed."

My fear of Jamie outweighs anything anyone can say to me, including my attorney. However, I don't want to walk away from my personal possessions, and I need my stuff from my home office.

I need help, so I again decide to call on Jack. Jack knows Jamie; Jack is the only person I can call for help. I want to keep others from knowing what has happened until I have a place to live. Once I am stable, I can decide then if I will share any of these crazy events with others.

Jack again agrees to help me without hesitation. His solitary request is that we enlist another male to help him remove my things from the house.

"I can call my brother."

"That will help. Just let me know what time. I will be ready."

Reluctantly, I call Ernie; I simply loathe dragging someone else into my chaos. But he agrees to help me immediately. We agree to meet at Cracker Barrel in two hours, giving me time to rent a U-Haul.

Arriving at Cracker Barrel two hours later, Ernie is already there waiting for me. Leaving his vehicle, he walks around to the driver's side of the moving truck.

"Hey, sis, are you okay?"

"Well, I've been better."

"Do you want me to drive?"

"If you don't mind, that would be great. I will call Jack. I need to let him know we are on our way to pick him up."

"Yep, let's get this show on the road. The sooner we get this over with, the better. I am so glad you are going to be rid of this loser."

I do not respond. What can I say? While I am very grateful for Ernie's help, it is difficult to absorb what feels like an I-told-you-so speech.

Ernie and I pick up Jack. Even with two trusted men with me, I am terrified. Since the EPO is no longer in effect, Jamie does not have to stay away from the house. In the U-Haul cab, there is complete silence. As Ernie slowly maneuvers the cumbersome vehicle down the winding drive, we keep our thoughts to ourselves. As we emerge into the clearing, I realize Jamie's truck is not in the driveway. Relief washes over me; I suspect my companions appreciate the reprieve as well.

Ernie, Jack, and I enter the house. I begin to cry; the men, however, focus like a laser on removing the items I want and exiting as soon as possible.

Standing in the living room, I try to decide what is most important to me. I think about my office. Since I work from home, my office items are probably the most important things I should load first. I tell them, "Let's start with my office."

"Why don't you tell us what you want from the living room and we can start loading, while you go pack the stuff in your office?"

I point out a few things I want to take and then head downstairs.

My laptop is sitting on my desk. Strange…I last saw my laptop when Jamie slammed it down on the kitchen counter right before I called the police. Since that day, I have only been to the house to feed the dogs but have not gone inside. Jamie must have brought my laptop down here, but when?

Perhaps out of habit, I open the laptop. There is a note from Jamie on the keyboard. "You better not take one thing from this house or else you will be sorry."

There is no signature on the note, but I don't need his signature to know it is from Jamie.

It is apparent Jamie came to the house immediately following court this morning. I begin to cry. Running upstairs, I shriek, "You guys, stop. I can't take anything. He left me a note in my laptop. He says I can't take anything or else!"

"Or else what?" Ernie asks indignantly.

"Jamie is furious with me. If I take anything, he will kill me." I am an emotional wreck, incapable of making rational decisions at the moment.

Jack tries to calm me down. "He is not going to kill you, Carly."

"You don't know how mad he can get. I just want to take Indy and Anna and leave."

"This is your last chance. Are you sure you want to leave all your stuff?" Jack asks.

"Yes, let's just get the dogs and go."

"Okay. I'll load the dogs," Jack replies.

I return downstairs to retrieve my laptop cord. I exit the house from my office, and I meet Ernie and Jack at the U-Haul. The dogs are safe inside. I climb in, hugging my precious Indy and Anna. I never spend another night in that house.

Ernie needs to get back to work; Jack and I drop him off at his car.

Before heading to his vehicle, Ernie turns and asks, "Are you okay, Carly?"

"I will be."

"Where are you staying?"

"I am staying with a girlfriend. But I think I will get a hotel room. I need some time alone to think about what I need to do and where I am going to live."

"Okay. Promise me you won't talk to him if he calls you."

"I promise."

"Call me tomorrow."

I turn to my brother. "Thanks, Ernie, for your help today. I hated to call you, but I didn't know who else to call."

"Don't sweat it, sis. What is a big brother for if he can't help out a little sister?"

"Thanks. Hopefully, the worst of it is over."

"Just remember, call me if you need me. Don't do like you did when this jackass put you in the hospital and not call anybody."

"Okay. Thanks again." I hug Ernie with gratitude.

Jack and I drive to the storage unit I've rented. It is only when I raise the overhead door on the moving van I realize I failed to get any of my clothes. We haven't taken much from the house. Jack and I put the few items in the storage unit.

What do I do now? Do I go to Colorado next week as planned? Experiencing similar feelings as when I was lying in the hospital bed, I decide any decisions should be postponed at least until tomorrow.

I am still reeling with shock from the court experience earlier in the day. Right now I need to decompress from the day's events. Once I calm down and can think coherently, I will develop a plan of action.

It is now clear Jamie will stoop to any method to cheat me out of my equity in the house. With Alan as his mentor, I fear I do not stand a chance against them. I am in exactly the type of situation I promised myself I would avoid as an adult.

How can I fight people like Jamie and Alan? I vow to myself my next home will be in my name only. It will be a safe home—a safe place for me and my dogs.

Still unaware of any connection to my past, I did not realize my fear of returning to court was connected to the terror and trauma I experienced when testifying against Russell at his murder trial as a young teenager. I never discussed that experience with anyone, not even my mother. I locked the painful feelings and memories away, certain I would never have to revisit the horror again. Thus far, I had succeeded; nearly twenty years had passed since Russell's murder trial.

At this point in my life, I had no awareness these unexamined, unprocessed fears and emotions held me emotionally hostage, rendering me incapable of making intelligent, rational decisions in my legal fight with Jamie.

Shame only fueled my problems. Keeping secrets kept my shame at bay in the short run, but ultimately proved fatal by influencing my most important life decisions.

The tentacles of shame were far-reaching. I was ashamed of my lack of judgment about becoming involved with Jamie in the first place, trusting him with the partnership agreement, not leaving him sooner, allowing him to alienate me from my family, being involved in a domestic-violence situation (just like my mother), and now being involved in the court system. I again wondered how I could have ended up in this situation. I was self-sufficient in so many ways. My mind simply could not grasp how I had allowed myself to end up in this position. I could not understand what I was doing wrong or how I was making such poor choices.

I was also not aware that my intense desire to protect my dogs was an unconscious desire to protect myself. I did not have the self-esteem or self-love to understand that I was worthy of protection.

It was so difficult for me to ask for help. Asking for help would make me vulnerable to criticism, reproach, and disapproval. And no one could be more critical of me than myself. I didn't need another person telling me how stupid I was or how I had made the absolute worst choices. I reminded myself of those facts daily.

So just as I had done when I was a young girl, I was going to take care of this myself. I had gotten myself into this crazy mess; I would figure a way out.

27. Emotional Vulnerability

Stunned by the dismissal of the criminal charges against Jamie in Sumner County, I spend the next few days in a daze. It is clear I am in for a nasty court fight with Jamie. My attorney, Mr. Knight, recommends I press charges against Jamie in Davidson County for the assault, going directly to the district attorney's office to explain the jurisdiction confusion. He also advises me to file for a domestic-violence order against Jamie in Davidson County.

I listen, assuring him I will consider his advice. After the fiasco in Sumner County, however, I am hesitant to act immediately on this new advice regarding criminal charges against Jamie. After what I have been through after taking Mr. Knight's advice, I am not so ready to act immediately on his counsel.

I decide to proceed with my plans to take a trip to Colorado. I need a change—of scenery, of people, of everything. I meet Bruce in Denver. A funny, robust guy, he is very interested in me. He is a nice distraction from the chaos unfolding back in Nashville, and I am flattered by the attention. It feels nice after enduring Jamie's abusive behavior and regular insults over the last several years. However, romance is not on my agenda at the moment.

Returning to Nashville, I am anxious to see my Dalmatians. Leaving the airport, my first stop is Jack's house. Pulling into Jack's driveway, I see Indy and Anna in the back yard. Hearing my car, they excitedly run to greet me. Stretching my arms wide to make room for both their large, wriggling bodies, I welcome them with hugs. It is pure joy at the reunion: a jumble of black-and-white spots, cooing, barking, and sloppy kisses. The heartfelt emotion overwhelms me. Why can't everything be this easy? Jack hears the commotion and comes outside. "Hello, Carly. When did you get back in town?"

"Just now. This is my first stop."

"Welcome back. Where are you staying?"

"I don't have anywhere to stay permanent just yet."

"You are welcome to stay here. I have a spare bedroom. Lola and Grant won't mind you being here."

I know Jack has four bedrooms, and his kids, Lola and Grant, are nice. I waver, but I can't accept his gracious offer. He is single. People might get the wrong idea.

"Thank you so much. It is very generous of you to offer, Jack, but I don't think it is a good idea."

"Where are you going to live, Carly?"

"I don't know. I would like to find a place to buy, something small. Maybe something I can restore."

"What about an old farmhouse? There is a place like that not too far from here if you're interested. It's right around the corner, an old place, completely surrounded by woods. Wanna see it?"

"Really?"

"Yes, of course."

Jack and I hop in my Miata. About a half mile down the road, we turn into Maple Estates. At the top of the hill, we turn right onto an old gravel farm road. With the top down on my Miata and the warm summer wind blowing through our hair, we round the bend on the gravel road.

And there it sits—as though quietly waiting for me—a two-story, dilapidated, lap siding, seasoned farmhouse.

Three hundred acres with mostly wooded areas surround the structure on three sides. A newly built brick home sits on the fourth side of the farmhouse. It is a private location, a peaceful location—I am intrigued.

The property appears abandoned, and uncut grass stretches past the top of my little Miata. There are broken and missing windows and a sagging front porch complete with an equally drooping roof. Worn, peeling shingles warn of squatters not of the human species.

Intent on seeing more, I turn to Jack. "Do you think it is okay for us to get out and walk around?"

"Well, there sure isn't anyone here to tell us not to."

"Good point."

Getting out of the car, I walk through the tall grass to the front porch and stop. A strong sense of peace settles over me, and an intense feeling of belonging envelops my body and spirit. I feel suspended in time.

Jack's presence and the sounds of nature around me slowly seep into my awareness again. The sense of belonging lingers. This brief moment of peace offers salve for my deep wounds—a glimpse of hope amid the swirling chaos of my deepening legal battle with Jamie. I feel a glimmer of hope that I will someday put the mess with Jamie behind me. Then I will finally have the life I promised myself—a life free from violence and constant fear.

I wonder if I have finally found my safe place.

I fall in love with the farmhouse. I love the privacy—no prying eyes, no unwanted questions. I can hide from the world, and there is plenty of room for Indy and Anna to roam at will.

Feeling a kinship with the house, I am drawn to the challenge of returning the structure to its original glory. Like me, the building has clearly weathered some hard times…but it's still standing. I want to save her—to restore the esteemed lady to her former splendor and upgrade her to her future potential.

I look at Jack. "I love this place. I wonder who owns it."

"I don't know. I ride my four-wheeler over here in the evenings to watch the deer in the fields."

"Well, if you find out who owns it, will you let me know? I'd like to know if it is for sale."

I know I will need to get my property settled with Jamie before I can buy anything. But I am definitely interested in purchasing this serene place if it is for sale.

Jack assures me, "If I hear anything, I will let you know."

We return to Jack's house. I hug Indy and Anna close, lingering to whisper into their ears how much I love them. Finally standing, I tell Jack, "I'm going to visit my sister. I'll call you tomorrow to check on the dogs."

"Okay. Be safe and be careful." As I pull out of Jack's driveway, it strikes me again that he is a genuinely nice, down-to-earth guy.

For the first time since calling the police on Jamie, I feel hopeful that I can have a good life once I untangle my finances from him. Should I dare dream of having a safe life and a safe place to live? Can it really happen?

I drive to Robin's house. Robin and her husband, Derek, live about twenty minutes from Jack. They live in a subdivision closer to downtown Nashville with their two small boys. Although Robin would let me stay with them until I figure out where I am going to live, it is not an option I consider. Robin never disguised her disdain for Jamie; the inevitable "I told you so" constantly lurks like an ominous cloud over our conversations.

Staying in a hotel feels the same as being homeless—transient and uncertain. And it is certainly out of my budget for the long term. These feelings only add to my high levels of anxiety and fear. I face the exact situation I promised myself as a young girl I would never be in: *homelessness*. For now, staying in a hotel that offers long-term arrangements is the best alternative for housing I can find.

Since returning from Colorado, I receive multiple daily calls from Bruce. I am not interested in a romantic relationship, but the attention feels nice. Every conversation involves some version of Bruce asking when I will visit Colorado—and him—again. Bruce's interest in me increases my sense of value—in stark contrast to the emotions evoked by the ongoing lawsuit with Jamie.

My appointments with Freda continue. She helps me process my emotions over my breakup with Jamie.

Freda warns me that I need to prepare myself for a malicious court fight with Jamie. She suspects he will want revenge and will use intimidation and scare tactics to get all of the equity in our house. She encourages me to use the legal system and follow my attorney's advice.

Freda tells me that I have an obligation to press criminal charges against Jamie. She says perpetrators usually escalate; the next time, he could actually kill someone. She reminds me that someone could likely be me. Freda explains it is highly unusual for perpetrators to change their behavior on their own; abusers require professional help to make lasting behavioral changes.

I feel stuck in a no-win situation. I don't want to press charges against Jamie. I do not want to be involved in a criminal case with him. I don't want his daughter, Allison, to feel the shame of her father serving prison time. Conversely, part of me does want Jamie to suffer the consequences of his physical assaults on me.

My intense determination to have a different kind of life—a life free of violence—consumes my thinking. Freda tells me that learning how to protect myself is the path to the kind of life I want. My determination to find the life I want combined with a sense of responsibility and obligation to do the right thing finally outweigh my feelings of shame and desire to protect Allison.

I decide that I will file criminal charges against Jamie in Davidson County.

I felt like I had been swept up in a tornado funnel cloud. As I was unwilling to confide in my friends or family, Freda represented the extent of my emotional support system.

Accustomed to a limited or nonexistent emotional support system, this time somehow felt different. My own actions and decisions—my life choices—led to this situation, not just something I witnessed.

The shame I felt reappearing in court crippled my ability to make rational decisions. Abandonment issues from my childhood years compounded unprocessed emotions lingering long after Russell's murder trial. But any suggestion of abandonment issues would have only angered me at the time.

I equated abandonment issues with weakness—someone who was looking to be rescued or to blame her problems on others. This was definitely not me. I would never adopt either persona. I was scared, but I also knew I was resilient.

I certainly didn't *need* anyone.

I wanted as few people as possible to know about the battle between Jamie and me. This desire kept my armor of silence and segregation firmly in place. My isolation was fortified, thickening my walls of concealment with each chaotic experience.

I just needed to learn how to make better choices. Therapy was helping me to do that by thinking about things differently. I was willing to learn; I was slowly, but steadily, changing.

It was a major internal hurdle for me to reach the decision to press criminal charges against Jamie in Davidson County. By making this decision, however, I felt like I was learning to take my life back.

I was determined to learn how to avoid becoming a victim—again. However, my old behaviors were ingrained at a young age; I had honed them to perfection. I would not let them go easily. Instead of seeing a red flag with Bruce calling me every few hours, I felt flattered by the attention. I interpreted Bruce's frequent calls as care and concern for me. The attention made me feel like I mattered, like I was important.

My unrecognized, unresolved abandonment issues gave abusers leverage to take advantage of me.

Unaware of my emotionally vulnerable state, I remained exposed to becoming a victim yet again.

28. A New Beginning: A New Perp

Finding a place to live is my main priority and immediate goal. I continue to stay at the extended-stay hotel for the next couple of weeks but know I need to find a permanent, cheaper place to live. Unsure of how long it will take to settle the court case with Jamie, I need to be conservative with my money.

Feeling ongoing therapy is critical for my mental health, I cannot sacrifice that expense. Without my therapist's help, I fear I will keep repeating my bad choices. I continue to see Freda every other week. Her lack of judgment of me about my life choices creates the emotional safety for me to continue to open up to her on a deeper level.

It is a Friday evening, and I am grateful to have the weekend ahead of me. I am seriously going to look for a place to rent this weekend. For tonight, however, I am going to go and visit my Dalmatians and then head back to the hotel and go to bed early.

When I arrive at Jack's house, Indy and Anna and I complete our usual rambunctious greeting. It's a beautiful summer evening. Jack invites me to join him for a drink under a large oak tree in his backyard. We don't say much but just sit there and watch the dogs play.

Within a few minutes, a car pulls into the driveway, and an elderly man gets out, slowly approaching us. "Hello there. My name is Rudy Sweets. I live up the road, and my two cows got out. Just wondering, have you seen them walk by?"

Jack responds with a compassionate smile. "No, we haven't seen any loose cows."

"I've got to repair that fence. It's just been so hot, and I haven't been feeling very well lately," says Rudy.

Jack says reassuringly, "Well, if we see them, I will let you know. Where do you live?"

"I'm at the corner of Tyler and Williamson Road, the house with the red tin roof."

"Have you lived around here long?" Jack asks.

"I have lived around these parts my whole life," Rudy responds.

"Then you probably know who owns the old farmhouse down the street, just past Maple Estates."

"Why, yes, I do know who owns it. Why do you want to know?"

"I know someone who might be interested in buying it."

"Oh yeah? Who would that be?"

I chime in. "I am going to be selling my house soon, and I might be interested in buying the farmhouse. Do you know how to contact the owner?"

"Yeah, as a matter of fact, I do. You are speaking to the owner."

I can't believe it! What a coincidence—the owner of the old farmhouse has actually found me.

Rudy offers some history on the place. "The farm has been in my family for generations. My brothers and I inherited the farm from our parents. The farm was just a little over three hundred acres. I got the farmhouse and twenty-five acres as a sole owner. The remaining farmland I own with my two brothers. The county has a contract to purchase the acreage tract. The county wants to put it in a land trust as a nature preserve."

"So the land will never be developed?" I ask.

"Not the acreage the county is buying. They may have a park with walking and hiking trails, but no ball fields, just a passive park. The only tract left to sell is the one with the farmhouse. It sits on ten acres."

"So you have sold your other five-acre tracts?"

"Out of the twenty-five acres, I sold one five-acre tract to a doctor, another five-acre tract I gave to my nephew, and a third five-acre tract I sold to a police officer over a year ago. The police officer paid a thousand dollars for a contract for deed and has not made any payments since then. I really need to talk to the guy and find out when he can start making payments."

"Did your nephew or the doctor build the brick house?"

"That belongs to my nephew. The doctor just bought the property as an investment. He never intends to build on his five acres."

"So how long has it been since anyone has lived at the farmhouse?"

"About twelve years. I was the last person to live there. As you can see, the house is in pretty bad shape. I lived in the camper behind the house." My intrigue grows. "I would like to sell the old farmhouse to someone who is interested in restoring her. The house was built in 1812; she is almost two hundred years old."

"I would love to restore the house." I wonder to myself if I can figure out a way to buy this property. I feel a quiver of excitement run through my veins.

Rudy says, "Stop by and see me in a couple of days. We can talk money."

"May I look around the farmhouse?"

"Sure, look all you want."

I anticipate it might take six months, at worst a year, to get my equity from the house I own with Jamie.

The next afternoon I stop by Rudy's house. As I pull into his drive-way, I see the same red Isuzu trooper that had pulled into Jack's drive-way when Rudy was looking for his runaway cows. Junk surrounds the garage and occupies most of the space on the front porch. He must be a pack rat.

Rudy opens the door. "Hello, Carly. Come on in."

"You know, Rudy, I haven't been able to stop thinking about your farmhouse since Jack took me to see it."

"Well, young lady, I will sell it to you for market price."

"That sounds fair, but I can't buy it until I sell my house. To be quite truthful, I own a house with my ex-boyfriend, and we are fighting over it in court."

"Ah. Court can be messy and take a long time sometimes."

"Well, I am hoping it won't take longer than six months, a year at the most, to get my equity. I just don't think I can get financing on the farmhouse because of its current condition. I don't have enough money for a down payment and repairs."

"Would you be interested if I offered you owner financing?"

"That would depend on the terms you offer."

"Well, I would need you to pay me something every month. The policeman only paid a thousand dollars as a down payment, and he is not making any monthly payments. I am going to have to go see an attorney about that."

"I can pay you monthly if we can agree the monthly payments will go toward the purchase price."

"Would you mind having a half-black policeman living beside you? He hasn't built a house yet, but I know that is his plan eventually—to build a house on the five acres he has a contract on."

"No. It doesn't really matter to me who lives on the other five acres. I just want my privacy. I am not interested in knowing any neighbors."

"To help you out, I can break the farmhouse tract from ten into five acres and that would reduce the selling price."

"That would definitely make it more feasible for me. If we agree on something, I also might be interested in buying your camper."

"Are you going to live in it?"

"I was thinking if it's livable, I could use it until I make the farmhouse suitable to live in. Since it is just me and my Dalmatians, the camper will work for a while."

"There is nothing wrong with the camper. But the well on the property doesn't work anymore. There is no running water on the place. You will have to haul in your water."

"Maybe I can get the well running. A big draw for me is my Dalmatians will have the yard space to run."

"And," I think to myself, "I will have the privacy and safety to begin to heal emotionally." From my perspective, the positives far outweigh the negatives.

"I want to ask Jack to look at the camper. I want to get his opinion on the electrical stuff. I'll check back in with you in a day or two."

"Okay, young lady. I will wait for you to stop by soon."

Leaving Rudy's, I call Jack. "Hey Jack, I am just leaving Rudy's house. He is offering owner financing on the farmhouse. He is even willing to divide the ten acres the farmhouse is on into two five-acre tracts to give the farmhouse a lower selling price. So I can swing what he is asking for a monthly payment on the farmhouse and five acres. It would cost me as least that much to rent a house, and why not spend my money on something that I am buying instead of renting. What do you think?"

"I think it needs a lot of work...I mean a *lot* of work. But I can help you."

"I am headed over to look at the camper. He said he lived in the camper twelve years ago. I'm going to go see if it's livable now while I work on renovating the farmhouse. Do you want to ride over with me and look at it? I would love to get your opinion on the electrical stuff."

"Sure. I'll go with you."

"Okay, I'll pick you up in a couple of minutes."

I know Jack is a competent carpenter and home remodeler. I trust and value Jack's opinion on the camper's condition and what it will take to restore the farmhouse.

The camper is laden with dust, dirt, and more junk. Rudy is definitely a pack rat. Emptied out, though, the recreational vehicle might be livable…just maybe.

Jack says, "Well, it seems the electrical system is intact, but I can't know for sure until we try it."

I feel anticipation and hope start to build inside of me. Maybe this can be my new home, my new start. It seems meant to be. After all, Rudy found me…and he wants to sell the property…and he is willing to subdivide the tract to lower the price…and provide owner financing.

Rudy and I enter into a verbal agreement. I will buy the farmhouse and five acres and make monthly payments to him until my house with Jamie sells or Jamie buys me out. I also buy the camper from Rudy, and I am able to pay cash for the camper.

Oh, life is so good. I am on cloud nine. I have a home! Granted, it doesn't have electricity or running water, but it is safe, and Indy and Anna have lots of room to run and play. Hope and joy fills me.

I call Jack with my exciting news. He responds with optimism wrapped in realism. "Looks like you have a lot of work to do. Need some help?"

"Oh, that would be great. Where do I start? There is so much to do."

"Well, you need to mow the grass to get rid of all the snakes. I can bring my mower over, and we can get started on the yard."

"Ugh! Don't talk about snakes. I am afraid of snakes."

Jack just grins and raises one eyebrow.

I sheepishly say, "Okay. And thanks, Jack, for all your help. You've been great. I really appreciate all you have done for me."

I meet Jack at the farmhouse, and we attack the overgrown grass. As the sun sets, we stop to take in the beauty surrounding us. My heart swells with gratitude to have a place of my own at last. Jack doesn't say anything; he just sits quietly beside me. I feel his compassion for my situation with Jamie; thankfully, I do not feel any judgment from him.

We leave the property as the sun slowly gives up its last rays of light and sinks behind the horizon. Jack returns to his house. I return to the hotel. I plan to ready the camper for move-in by the weekend.

With daylight savings time in summer, I can get by without electricity for a while. I purchase a water cooler and picnic supplies. Seeing the glass as half full, I think that I won't have to worry about doing dishes for quite some time.

I am unable to stay away. I drive out to the farmhouse by myself the following day. Picking up some trash around the camper, I bask in the peaceful environment. I glance up to see a stocky-looking man walking purposefully toward me. His demeanor is what I would call "puffed up"—like a turkey puffs up when it is mad or getting ready to fight. I recognize that strut. Jamie used to walk that way. Fear runs through my veins, and the hair stands up on the back of my neck as he crosses over the property line and approaches me. He sticks his hand out. "Hello, my name is Detective Sugar."

I tentatively shake his hand. "Hello, my name is Carly."

"So Rudy tells me you are going to buy the farmhouse and restore it."

"Yes." I think to myself, "I do not want anything to do with this guy." I see the warning signs, and this time, unlike with Jamie, my radar is up. I am listening to all the signals with my full attention. I just wish he would go away! IMMEDIATELY!

"So I hear you are single. Do you have a boyfriend or family to help with restoring the farmhouse?"

How can I get away from him? Like right now. I respond casually, "I have friends who are going to help. I wasn't planning on being here long this evening, so I had better get going." I move toward my car to indicate that I am leaving.

"Just let me know if I can do anything for you. I'll bring my grill over, and we can grill out together and have a few beers. It'll be an outdoor date."

"I have a lot to do. I won't have time to grill." I walk toward my car as he follows me, encroaching on my space.

"Well, you have to eat. I am not going to take no for an answer. We are neighbors after all. We will be seeing a lot of each other," he predicts enthusiastically.

Barely glancing at him, I respond quickly. "I'm really busy. Gotta go." Chills run down my spine as I get in my car and drive off. Detective Sugar is still standing on my property.

Gratitude for my ongoing therapy grew exponentially the first time I saw Detective Sugar walk across the yard to introduce himself. Therapy had taught me I had the right to choose whom I let into my life. These choices were my first baby steps in setting personal boundaries and a giant leap toward self-care. Detective Sugar was definitely not going to be invited into my life, and I was not going to allow him to barge in either. He was someone I wanted to avoid at all costs.

But unlike when Jamie charged into my life and kept seeking me out, I was both elated and scared about Detective Sugar. I was elated because I had grown enough through my therapy to recognize at the beginning someone I should avoid. And I was scared because Detective Sugar was going to be my neighbor and a cop, so it might prove difficult to avoid him.

I had been through so much, and I was going to err on the side of caution. Cop or not...neighbor or not...I simply did not want to interact with him. I did not want to be friends, nor did I want to fight. I just didn't want to engage with him on any level.

What I didn't realize is that with some bullies, avoiding them is not an effective strategy for dealing with them. I had not yet learned that I would need to go on the offensive to protect myself. I was a long way from learning to fully protect myself, but I was making progress.

Oh, the progress I would make in the coming years...

29. New Legal Battles

The following day after work I return to the farmhouse to finish cleaning the camper. Jack has cut the grass earlier in the day, and the lawn looks beautiful to me! I drive my Miata through the freshly mowed yard, parking next to the camper. A short time later, I see Detective Sugar's vehicle approaching on the gravel road that accesses both our properties.

I hope he doesn't come over to see me again. Rudy indicated that although the policeman did not have a house on his property, he often drives out just to sit there. Surely he's just coming to check on his five acres and enjoy the peaceful setting.

A few minutes later, Detective Sugar parades confidently toward my property. Seeing him approach, I quickly go inside the camper, hoping to avoid him. Moments later, immediately outside the door of the camper, Sugar calls my name.

"Hello, Carly. Carly—are you in there?"

"I'm here, but I'm kind of busy. Got a lot to do."

"I need to talk with you."

I can't image what he needs to talk to me about. We have nothing in common. I can't understand why this detective won't just leave me alone. I certainly do not want him coming inside my camper uninvited. I have enough courage, self-worth, and self-esteem to know these simple camper walls delineate my new boundaries. Nothing is going to invade my new home—my safe place. I step out of the camper.

"So you have something you need to tell me?"

"Well, I just want to let you know that you are safe here."

I am puzzled by the odd comment. "You don't have to worry about Jamie Goffy, you know—your ex-boyfriend who broke your jaws on both sides of your face." The blood drains from my face. Stunned and shaken, I wonder how he can possibly know that. As Detective Sugar continues, I wonder if, in my surprise, I asked the question out loud.

"I ran your car tags. I saw you had filed criminal charges against Goffy. I know you are a victim of domestic violence. You don't have to worry about him down here."

I am horrified and afraid. I'm pretty sure it's illegal for him to run plates just because I am his neighbor and he wants information on me, but I am afraid to remind him of this legal tidbit. He's the officer of the law, after all. I just want to get away from Detective Sugar as soon as possible.

He continues undeterred. "I know it is a dead-end road, but Goffy won't get past me. I will protect you. You can rely on me."

"I can take care of myself. I don't need any help." Fear keeps me from being more assertive in communicating to him that he has crossed the line. Clearly, Detective Sugar does not apply the law to himself.

Undeterred, he stakes his watchdog status. "Well, I will be watching you."

This guy gives me the creeps! I don't want him looking out for me, looking at me, or even talking to me. He doesn't have the right to run my plates. I've done nothing wrong. I don't want or need his help or protection. But I also don't need trouble with a detective. I decide that avoiding Detective Sugar is the best approach. Evading shouldn't be that difficult.

"I need to go." I head toward my car.

"Well, when you have some time, maybe we can hang out together and get to know each other better. Like a date even."

"I'm very busy and don't have much time to talk."

"Well, we are both single adults, and we are going to be neighbors, so we already have something in common."

"I've got an appointment; I have to go." I am determined to get away from him, even if it means leaving the property.

"Okay. I hate that you have to rush off today, but I will see you tomorrow."

Frustrated and disappointed at having my cleaning time cut short, I get in my car and leave. I will stop by Jack's house to see Indy and Anna. If Jack isn't home, I can visit with the dogs until he arrives. Maybe we can ride back to the farmhouse together.

I always feel better when I'm around Indy and Anna. I vow not to let this Detective Sugar ruin this property for me.

Maybe I can ask Rudy to tell Detective Sugar that I am a very private person and one of the most attractive features of the property is the privacy and seclusion it offers. I want to be careful because I intuitively know I don't want to anger Detective Sugar.

Jack and I drive back to the farmhouse a couple of hours later. Thankfully, Detective Sugar is gone. Jack works on the yard while I clean the camper. As the evening light begins to fade, Jack and I stop to watch another beautiful sunset.

It dawns on me that I've never taken the time before to enjoy sunsets. I decide I like watching sunsets with Jack.

I smile to myself and think this is just the place to "find myself" again.

The court date for a ruling on possession of the house is quickly approaching. I am fearful because of the craziness of the last court ruling. I am also terrified of seeing Jamie again.

The Sumner County judge awards Jamie temporary possession of the house. My lack of understanding of the court system leaves me feeling confused and helpless. I did not think I could feel more helpless than I did in my initial court appearance against Jamie, but I am wrong. Why won't anyone listen to me? I simply cannot understand how this can happen in a court of law.

After being awarded legal possession of the house in Sumner County court, Jamie files a new motion in Sumner County claiming I stole his belongings from our house.

It is difficult for me to comprehend this is actually happening. How is it possible for Jamie to legally file criminal charges against me for taking what is mine while charges for his physical assault against me have been dropped? And how can he claim I have deserted the property?

I ask Mr. Knight, "How can Jamie file anything claiming ownership of the property when it is in both our names and I paid for half of it to be built?"

"They are basing their motion of his ownership on an old desertion law. This desertion law dates back to the first settlers. Decades ago, desertion laws were instituted so the government could legally take back land when settlers abandoned property for which they had been given land grants. Although rarely used, the desertion laws are still legal. Since you are refusing to live on the property, he is claiming that you have deserted the property."

This is crazy. I just cannot understand how I can own a house with Jamie, get beat up by him, call the cops on him, and now lose the house and everything in it because I refuse to live there with him.

I have not done anything wrong. Jamie broke my jaws and lied in court.

Freda is right. The criminal charges of theft against me are completely bogus. Jamie employs intimidation tactics to increase my fear of him. His strategy works. Continuing to fear for my physical safety, my anxiety now extends to protecting my financial well being.

A couple of months and several court filings later, my attorney gets the criminal charges against me dismissed without requiring another court appearance from me. It is a relief and small win, but I remain on pins and needles, anticipating what will come next in this court battle. It is clear there is no place for the truth in the motions Jamie's attorney files.

I have no way of knowing that my legal woes have just begun.

What you don't know *can* hurt you. Not knowing the court system or having an understanding of how things worked, or should I say how ruthlessly people will use the court system to cause anguish and turmoil, made me vulnerable. I was up against Jamie, who was ruthless himself, but I was also battling Alan's decades of experience with the criminal court system. To sum it up, I was like a lamb ready to be slaughtered by the big bad wolf.

As a law-abiding citizen, I could not outguess or outthink some-one as corrupt and cold-blooded as Jamie. Although I feared Jamie would be unfair, I didn't know that the court system could be ma-nipulated so easily.

Maybe if I did not have so much shame inside of me, I would have reached out for more moral support. Instead, I let the committee in my head, which had led me to where I was in this point in my life, make my decisions. I had not learned to seek out trustworthy people. To be truthful, up to this point in my life I had not trusted any au-thority figure, other than my therapist, with whom I had shared my feelings. And my relationship with my therapist was only two years old at this point. It wasn't like I could call her up and ask her questions on a daily basis.

Usually the first authority figures we come into contact with are our parents. If your interactions with your parents or caregivers en-courage you to share your feelings and emotions at a young age, you feel supported. This provides the perfect environment for an indi-vidual to learn to trust—not only to trust others, but also to trust one's own judgment. However, this was not my childhood experience.

My earlier experiences taught me to be quiet and not to cause waves, or the result could be more violence. In short, I learned to be submissive to avoid violence. So this was exactly what I was doing with Detective Sugar—avoid and don't confront.

However, with my therapy, I was changing. I still wasn't strong enough emotionally to change my outward behavior of avoidance when confronted with a bully, but my internal dialogue had evolved. I knew it was okay for me to not be friends with Detective Sugar. I knew this didn't make me a bad Christian or a bad person.

My life experiences were slowly dragging me, kicking and scream-ing, onto a path of self-love and self-protection.

30. Intimidation

Working on the farmhouse property keeps my mind off the court case with Jamie. The late afternoon sun is warm as I continue the cleanup effort, enjoying the peaceful setting. I glance up at the sound of a car approaching to see the detective driving down the road. Not again! I hope Rudy has talked with him. I don't want him on my property.

Moments later, Detective Sugar parks his car and struts across the grass, approaching the camper where I am cleaning. I have nowhere to hide. The best course of action is to tell the detective I am extremely busy…again.

"Hello, Carly. Are you working hard?" He talks with a bit too much familiarity in his voice.

"Yes. There is a lot to do."

"You must be working up an appetite by working so hard. Do you want to join me for a cookout? I can bring out a grill, and we can grill some burgers. Who knows, maybe one day we might combine our tracts and have the only ten-acre tract down here."

The statement frightens and repulses me at the same time. Apprehensive about offending the detective, I answer casually, "I am just so busy, and Jack usually brings me something to eat."

This is clearly not the response he anticipated, and he looks at me for several long moments—not quite angry but provoked. He hesitates a moment longer and then turns around and begins walking toward his car.

Without turning to look at me again, with his back still to me, he speaks in a very loud voice. "You know, eventually, you will have to make time for me as I am not going away."

I wonder if that is a threat.

"You win again today, but I'll catch you later, and you can take that to the bank," he states with a slightly angry tone in his voice.

I lied. Jack is not coming over with food, but it makes me feel safer to indicate Jack could arrive at any time. Jack does spend a lot of time helping me. I enjoy his friendship. When Jack does stop by later, I tell him about the detective's repeated unexpected, unwanted visits and admit that Detective Sugar gives me the creeps. Jack points out that the detective only drops in to see me when I am alone.

Interesting. I wonder why that never occurred to me before.

I decide the next time Detective Sugar shows up and I'm alone, I will leave before he has a chance to walk over to my property. I can always drive over to Jack's house. He lives right around the corner. Jack has given me a key to his place to use in case of an emergency. If needed, I can stay at Jack's until he gets home, and then the two of us can go back to the farmhouse together.

Jack warns me to be careful around the detective.

Jack's unquestioning support provides a great source of comfort. Jack understands how the ongoing court battle with Jamie devastates me and how apprehensive I feel about my neighbor, the detective.

Jack is well aware of Jamie's vile character. He has witnessed Jamie's ruthless and dishonest means of conducting business with others, including Jack himself. I vividly remember Jack breaking off the friendship while Jamie and I were still together. Jamie's lack of integrity led Jack to end not only their friendship but also any communication or business dealings with Jamie.

I feel comfortable with Jack. More importantly, I feel safe with Jack. I share my disappointment and hurt over Jamie, the trial, and my own stupidity for getting involved with Jamie at all. All the while Jack listens quietly and patiently...without judgment.

Meanwhile, Bruce continues to call, constantly asking when I will come see him again. It has been about three months since I have last seen Bruce. Maybe a visit to see Bruce will provide some respite from the craziness of my legal battle with Jamie.

So I return to Colorado. Bruce is very attentive and charming. As coowner of a construction business with his sister, Bruce sets his own schedule. He does not work during my entire visit to Colorado. We go to dinner and concerts. He even takes me to Aspen. Colorado is a beautiful state. Aspen is spectacular!

It is an exciting time. I am unaccustomed to this level of attention. Bruce never shows any anger or aggression, just intense interest in me.

The problem is after a couple of days, I feel a little smothered by the constant contact with Bruce. I question my emotions, however, wondering if my feelings are skewed. Isn't this the kind of intimacy and excitement people talk about having with their partners? I recognize that the craziness of my life doesn't exactly lend itself to developing a normal view of relationships.

As my "relationship résumé" consists of two men who broke my bones, I am certainly no expert on intimate relationships. If someone strives to be nice to me and wants to talk with me all the time, maybe I should feel flattered rather than suffocated. After all, I am valiantly trying to change my thinking, behaviors, and choices.

I determine that my feelings of being smothered by Bruce's intense attention fall outside the norm. I vow to ignore them. I recognize I have a hard time letting others do things for me. The self-sufficiency skills that helped me to survive in my youth no longer serve me well. I am determined to change my thinking. No matter how difficult or uncomfortable the challenge poses, I will learn to let good, kind people get close to me.

After a four-day weekend in Colorado, I return to Nashville. I feel my chest tighten as the plane touches down on the landing strip. The ability to relax and enjoy activities in Colorado contrasts sharply with the stress of maintaining a fearful vigil, looking over my shoulder in Nashville. I live in continual fear and dread of Jamie's prolonged intimidation tactics, anticipating he will stop at nothing to coerce me into signing over the house free and clear.

My fears prove well founded. Jamie's intimidation campaign continues unabated like a raging storm. Adding pressure to the pending desertion motion regarding our house in Sumner County, Jamie begins stalking me.

Jamie never calls me directly; rather, he leaves subtle clues alerting me he is there, watching me.

My abrupt departure from the house that Jamie and I owned together warranted leaving behind most of my personal belongings, including a box of childhood mementos and family pictures. Jamie broke my jaws just three months after Mom died. My life is a sea of crises following her death. The photos of her that I left at the house feel like my only remaining connection to her.

When checking my mail at the farmhouse a couple of days after I return from visiting Bruce in Colorado, I find an unmarked envelope in the mailbox alongside some junk mail addressed to me. The blank envelope contains a picture of Mom—torn into little pieces. This picture of Mom was kept framed on a table in the living room at the house I shared with Jamie, so he is the only person with access to the picture. This is a warning. Will I ever be safe?

Warily, I get back in my car and call the police. I know they will do nothing, but I want to leave a paper trail. I want someone to know what I am experiencing.

The police do not think I should file a report. I insist. They finally consent when they realize that I won't take no for an answer. A report is filed.

I continue to see Freda every other week. My sessions with Freda help me to understand things from a new perspective. I begin to see red flags with others' behavior. I begin to learn not to expect others to react the way I would react.

Some see it as common sense, but protecting oneself is unfamiliar thinking to others. For some people, if you aren't a cheat, you don't expect to be cheated and therefore don't know how to protect yourself from cheats—unless someone teaches you or you learn through the school of hard knocks. Lacking healthy parental role models, I am determined to stop learning my life lessons the hard way—through tough life experiences. Instead, I want to think things through, make solid judgments, and then act accordingly. Sessions with Freda help shift my thinking toward learning how to protect myself and my interests.

The trial for Jamie's assault is set in Davidson County. Again, using jurisdiction as her argument, Jamie's attorney, Amanda, claims the criminal charges are unlawful. Simply reversing her jurisdiction argument, now arguing the case in Davidson County, she claims Jamie is a resident of Sumner County.

I cannot believe what I am hearing! Can an attorney legally argue a case like this? How can this be happening? Amanda argued that Jamie is a Davidson County resident to get the case dismissed in Sumner County on jurisdictional issues. Now, in Davidson County court, Amanda is arguing that Jamie is a Sumner County resident to get the same charges dismissed in Davidson County.

To say I feel further victimized by the legal system is a massive understatement. Jamie's attorney is knowingly protecting someone who broke my bones; she is helping Jamie steal my half of the equity in the house. Our yearlong battle in the Sumner County court system over the house is still ongoing, and there is no end in sight.

I despise feeling so vulnerable. My indignation and frustration grows with a court system that allows this type of legal manipulation and abuse to occur.

The jurisdictional issue protects Jamie from the jail time for assaulting me. Davidson County court will not call the Sumner County officers who responded to the 911 call to testify in Davidson County.

I feel like I've been beaten up all over again! Frustrated and feeling like I have no other options, I agree to a plea bargain. Jamie pleads guilty to lesser assault charges and serves no jail time. The judge orders him to pay my medical bills, go to anger-management classes, and serve a three-year probation period. Thankfully, I also have a three-year protective order. If Jamie contacts me directly in any way during the next three years, he will be arrested.

It is not the punishment I feel he deserves. However, I'm trying to hold Jamie accountable, a bold step toward self-protection compared my previous passive behavior.

Not quite a victory, but it still feels good. Somebody believes me.

The judge instructs me to carry the court-order document with me at all times.

Leaving the Davidson County courthouse, I catch Jamie glaring at me. I freeze. His stare tells me everything I need to know—his rage is red hot.

Fear consumes me! What have I done? Have I made a mistake? Have I pushed Jamie too far? I know there is no way for me to undo what has been done in court today. I don't really want to undo it, but I am terrified.

An avid hunter, Jamie owns a lot of guns. His probation terms do not allow any guns in his possession. But I know Jamie, and I know that a paper document will never make Jamie give up his guns. I just hope he will never use one of them on me.

That night back at the farmhouse, I wonder if I should just move to Colorado. I don't feel like I will ever win in court with Jamie. He is too cunning and manipulative with the court system. I will never get a fair hearing in court against him.

Jamie's subtle threats continue. A few days following his guilty plea in the criminal case, I receive another "message."

Living together, Jamie and I kept family photos on a table in our living room. When he was angry with me, he would turn my family photos face down.

A few days after the criminal case is heard, I return to the camper to find a picture of Indy and Anna kept on a small ledge behind the sofa turned face down. Jamie has found a way into the locked camper.

I feel my body start to tremble. What else is he going to do? Will he hurt my dogs? With shaking hands, I call the police to file another stalking report. When the officer arrives, he refuses to file a report.

The officer argues the pictures could have accidentally been turned over. Since I have not witnessed Jamie at the camper, there is nothing he can do. The officer suggests I call him back if anything else happens. I know Jamie is stalking and harassing me. I fear for my life, yet there is nothing the police can or will do—I'm not sure which.

I feel like target practice for Jamie.

When the police officer leaves, I call Jack. I don't want to drag anyone else into this chaotic storm, but I need to talk with someone.

Jack recommends I carry a gun for protection. Afraid of guns in general, I also fear Jamie could easily take a weapon away from me and shoot me with my own gun. No, I am not ready to get a gun.

It feels like the conflict with Jamie will never end.

I dedicate all my free time to working on the farmhouse. The physical labor tires my body and mind, keeping dark thoughts of the ongoing court case with Jamie at bay.

Maintaining the historical integrity of the farmhouse during renovations will be costly and time consuming. To avoid an extended stay in the camper, I decide to build a small carriage house on the property. I will live in the carriage house while I take my time restoring the farmhouse, which at this point might take a couple of decades.

Jack agrees to build the carriage house, and I can help as a labor hand to keep costs down.

Unsure of the outcome and timeframe of the civil court case with Jamie regarding the disposition of our jointly owned house, my plan for the farmhouse property lacks a specific timeline. It's totally dependent on finances and how much this legal battle costs. Nonetheless, it feels good to be developing a plan for the future.

Despite the ongoing chaos of the court case with Jamie, I see glimpses of a possibly normal life following the settlement of the court case.

Watching sunsets with Jack, I allow myself to occasionally daydream that the court case is over and life is normal. I'm just a girl watching a sunset with a trusted friend.

I am thirty-three, and I still have much to learn.

Pressing criminal charges, trying to hold Jamie accountable for breaking my jaws, was a gigantic step for me. Granted, it was a year and a half after he had broken my bones, but I was finally at an emotional place where I could file the criminal complaint.

For me, it wasn't just trying to hold Jamie accountable for his violent actions; it was also about saying that I matter. I am important enough, and I count. You can't just mistreat me and suffer no consequences. Those days are gone.

Holding the bully accountable and making him actually endure the consequences of his actions helped me to heal on an emotional level. And while having the protection order didn't make me feel physically safer, I did feel that if Jamie did anything to me, the chances of him getting caught and having to answer to the authorities for his actions were greater because of the protection order. Just maybe it would make him think twice before he lashed out at me.

Being new to taking a stand for myself against a bully, I wasn't very good at it, but practice makes you more skilled. What I did know for sure now was that no one was ever going to hit me again and get away with it. I would file charges immediately if that ever happened again.

But what I really wanted to know was how to avoid those situations and men like that in the first place. It's not like you date a guy and then you think, "Oh, I like you enough, you can hit me." No, it's not like that at all. In the beginning, you have no idea the guy is even capable of that kind of behavior. They come on slow and test you to see how far they can push or mistreat you. They are testing your tolerance level for mistreatment.

Oh, it was still confusing for me, but sometimes in Freda's office, it made sense.

The first big realization I had about protecting myself was when I had the strong feeling about Detective Sugar, the feeling that I wanted to avoid him completely. I wasn't confused about that at all. I saw the glaring red warning signs from the first moment I laid eyes on him. The only difference was he was a cop. That made me nervous.

But in all this I felt that someone—God, maybe a guardian angel, Mom, someone—was looking out for me. It was almost as though the old farmhouse found me. And I had a place to live that, while not perfect (no running water or electricity and the cop neighbor thing), it did have the things I craved most: peace from Jamie, privacy, and a place for my dogs.

When I left Dalton, I thought I had finally figured out a way to a great life. Well, now in leaving Jamie, I knew I didn't exactly know the way to a great life…yet. But with therapy, I was going to find out. I was not going to let this court battle ruin the rest of my life. I knew I was in for some rocky times, but I constantly kept reminding myself that eventually this would pass.

31. Picking My Battles

I do not believe the desertion claim will hold. I incorrectly assume it falls into the category of just another legal maneuver to wear me down, a nuisance to prolong the legal battle and gnaw at my emotional stability.

However, my worst fear is realized. The court awards Jamie legal possession of our house. He refuses to sell the property or buy out my share. Incredibly, Jamie has now filed a motion demanding I sign the property over to him free and clear, using the desertion claim as his legal position. I would walk away from my half of the equity in our jointly owned property if I sign the house over. No, I have to fight this legal battle even though this fight will cost me money I don't have.

Six months have passed since I left Jamie, and it's now November. I am making progress on the farmhouse property. I have installed a temporary electrical pole on the property and have electricity in my camper. I have a building permit to build the carriage house.

Technically, the camper does have electricity, but I have to select which appliances get juice. Using the electric skillet requires unplugging the heater, a minor inconvenience to have Indy and Anna with me every day. My daily routine consists of a series of electrical trade-offs. I eagerly anticipate move-in day for the carriage house.

Water is a different tale. Running water remains elusive, and the old well is still not operational. A cooler filled with water suffices, although water rations are in effect during the winter months. As with most outdoor enthusiasts who stay in the great outdoors, my bathroom becomes the closest tree.

I keep a shower bag in my car. I shower at the local gym, Jack's, or my sister's house. Colder months present interesting challenges. If left in my car overnight, my shampoo freezes in my gym bag. I quickly learn to remember to bring my gym bag into the camper at night in the colder months.

Not an ideal situation, but doable.

Christmas arrives. Completion of the carriage house reaches the halfway point. I anticipate a settlement on the court case with Jamie by the following spring. The long, drawn-out process is frustrating and confusing. The Sumner County court denies all my motions, including three separate motions requesting an appraisal on the house. My attorney warns me, "Jamie's stalling tactics are keeping the case tied up in court. You might be in for a very long battle."

I continue my sessions with Freda. With her gentle guidance, I gain clarity of the possessive and abusive patterns in my intimate relationships with men. I better understand and recognize common behavior traits of abusive men: jealousy and a desire to control their partner's friendships, family relationships, and finances, and the ever-present threat of triggering their anger.

Freda helps me realize just because a man *acts* nice doesn't mean he is nice.

A year after leaving Jamie, I begin to filter Bruce's behavior through my new understanding of abusive patterns of behavior. I recognize the now-familiar pattern: constantly wanting to know my whereabouts, who I talk to, trying to select who I am friends with, and trying to gain control over me financially. I end the relationship and reach a new level of gratitude for my therapy. I am finally taking the right emotional steps to create the life I want. Only Indy and Anna surpass the importance of my therapy.

Jamie begins a new attack strategy in court. He files motions to force me to pay half of all the monthly maintenance and other household expenses. The new motion claims our partnership agreement legally obligates me to pay half of the household bills regardless of where I reside.

This is a new level of crazy. How can the legal system be so twisted? Has everyone forgotten Jamie beat me up and broke my bones? My attorney tells me I am being hometowned in Sumner County court.

"Explanation, please," I question my attorney.

He interprets. "Sumner County court is trying to railroad you into giving the house to Jamie." He recommends I secure a Sumner County attorney."

I feel overwhelmed. I wonder if this will ever end. Will I ever get my equity from the property? What should I do? Do I continue to use an attorney who has communicated he can't help me? Do I hire a Sumner County attorney? How much money can I continue to spend on this?

I can't let the bully win. I will not walk away from my half of the equity in our jointly owned property. So I decide to hire a Sumner County attorney.

I need to let Rudy know the court case with Jamie may not be resolved any time soon. I have a contract to buy the farmhouse, and construction on the carriage house is well underway, but the deed remains in Rudy's name.

Belatedly, I realize starting construction of the carriage house without the property in my name and only a signed purchase contract is not one of my better decisions. Maybe Rudy will provide permanent owner financing until a settlement with Jamie is reached and we can transfer the property into my name.

Thankfully, Rudy agrees to transfer the property to my name in exchange for an increased monthly payment. I can live with that.

Two weeks after getting the deed in my name, Detective Sugar files his first formal complaint against me with Davidson County building-and-code enforcement. The complaint states that I don't have the right to build a carriage house on the property.

The timing is no coincidence. Detective Sugar waits until the property is in my name before filing the complaint. Having rebuffed

Detective Sugar's romantic advances on multiple occasions, I am fully aware he is now trying to make my life difficult. I can only conclude from his word choices and behavior that he is angry because I continually refuse to have any relationship with him—whether intimate or as a friendly neighbor. That I own property as a single female simply fuels his anger. He, in contrast, is unable to afford payment on his five-acre lot and construction of a house by himself. Maybe he is jealous that as a woman I am doing this on my own. Or maybe it is something altogether different. I don't know and don't care.

But the complaint he files infuriates me. However, I remain determined to take a stand for myself and to not be intimidated by Detective Sugar. I finally understand I am worthy of this basic human right.

Building and zoning had already issued the permit to build the carriage house. How can they subsequently issue a code violation for the very thing they approved? I make an appointment to meet with representatives from the code-enforcement office at the farmhouse.

Through it all—the criminal and civil court proceedings with Jamie, the zoning complaint with Detective Sugar, and ongoing renovations to the farmhouse—Jack continues to offer steady, consistent, nonjudgmental support. He remains calm and collected, someone I can count on...always. One day it occurs to me—isn't this a good foundation on which to build a relationship? Jack is the kind of guy I need.

I've known Jack four years now. I love watching sunsets and gazing up at the moon with him. I wonder if I can fall in love with him.

Do I even know what real love is?

I decide to ask Jack if he wants to date. I intuitively know Jack will never be physically abusive of me. I know that I always have fun with him.

I wonder why I have never considered dating him before.

Today, the thought of dating Jack makes me smile. The familiar quietness and peacefulness of shared sunsets with Jack settles on me.

My feelings regarding Jack were in stark contrast to the constant attention Bruce showered on me in the beginning of our relationship. Bruce's nice act initially fooled me. Two months after meeting me, however, Bruce asked me to marry him. I found this peculiar. Of course I was not going to marry Bruce. I didn't really even know him; besides, I had no intention of marrying anyone ever again.

Therapy helped me see the red flags in my relationship with Bruce. Fortunately, I was able to recognize his abusive patterns of behavior before I invested too much in the relationship. I felt intense gratitude for the knowledge that allowed me to recognize these warning signs, avoiding what would have most certainly been my third abusive relationship. I am confident I dodged a bullet by choosing to end my relationship with Bruce.

I had heard the Al-Anon slogan "It's progress, not perfection" countless times. While I wasn't quite ready to believe this advice extended to me, hearing this philosophy repeated over and over was beginning to have a positive impact on me. I was not as critical of myself for having dated Bruce. Until you date someone, how can you possibly know?

I was determined my next relationship would not be with an abuser. I wanted a relationship with a man like Jack.

At the same time, I also deeply wanted to understand myself and why I had stayed with Jamie for so long. I was desperately yearning for as much understanding and progress as I could get and as fast as I could get it. Free from Jamie's controlling behavior for a year, I was struggling to understand my reasons for staying so long. Why had I not left earlier?

As my gratitude increased for my newfound knowledge regarding common behaviors and traits of abusers, so also did my shame for having stayed in the relationship. How could I be getting emotionally better but feeling worse? Sometimes the emotional work was just too damn hard and confusing.

However, the payoff of doing the difficult work of unraveling my tangled emotions was well worth it. For me, I was beginning to recognize the people who were trustworthy and those who were not. This knowledge was helping to make better decisions in my life. It wasn't perfect, but I felt I was headed in the right direction.

32. Endings and Beginnings

Jack and I officially start dating. It's late September 1999, and the leaves have just begun to turn.

We work on the carriage house and celebrate our hard work with bonfires on the farmhouse property in the evening. I love the fires. I find solace and peace while listening to the crackling and popping sounds while the smell of a campfire wafts through the evening air. The intrigue of the dancing flames, the warmth of the fire, and watching a log finally burn through and drop further down into the embers offers a bubble of momentary safety and distraction from the chaos of the court cases with Jamie and Detective Sugar.

Some things in this life are transparent—they are what they appear to be, like sunsets and fires. These are the exact opposite of the crazy court battle that rages on with Jamie.

On the legal battlefront with my neighbor, the carriage-house construction complaint is dismissed, and I am allowed to continue building the carriage house. In spite of it, Detective Sugar files several additional complaints against me—all baseless.

He files complaints with multiple county agencies. He leaves no investigative agency out of the loop: the health department, code enforcement, building, planning and zoning, even animal control.

Detective Sugar files complaints against me at least twice a month. Rather than redirect resources to hire an attorney—money I don't have—I meet with county officials of the agency he has chosen to file a complaint with to remediate or disprove whatever the current complaint is about.

At one point, Detective Sugar calls the health department, complaining my septic is leaking and contaminating his water supply. A health-department officer arrives to serve me the complaint and investigate.

Sam, the health-department inspector, confirms the septic tank does not leak but wants to test my water supply. With the old well on the property finally operational again, Sam draws some water to test.

Sam is a nice man, and he offers some empathy. "I have dealt with neighbors who don't get along for many years."

"I just want my neighbor to leave me alone."

"Well, there don't appear to be any violations here, but policy requires I submit the water for testing. You should get the results via mail in about four weeks."

"Okay, will you call me when they come in?"

"I will mail a copy to you. Good luck with everything here."

"Thanks, I appreciate it." Maybe now Detective Sugar will leave me alone. What else can he possibly try?

Almost two years have now passed since I moved to the property. With the carriage house complete, I am eager to move in and put my camper days behind me. Incredibly, Detective Sugar tries to block my certificate of occupancy for the carriage house. He files a complaint stating that I don't have the authority to have the carriage house on the land and demands either the carriage house or the farmhouse be demolished. The planning and zoning agency refuse to grant me a certificate of occupancy with an open complaint against me. Detective Sugar files a complaint of his choice every month, ensuring that I always have an open, active complaint against me.

Jerry Robertson is in charge of planning and zoning. His counterpart in code enforcement is Charles Parker. Jerry calls me requesting I meet with him and Charles on my property. I agree.

Jerry and Charles share with me that they are in a difficult position. They explain that every citizen has the right to file a complaint against a neighbor, and every complaint must be investigated. They inform me there is no limit to the number of complaints that a person can file against someone, regardless of whether or not even one complaint is found to be valid in nature. Jerry and Charles suggest that my neighbor is using their agencies to harass me. Unfortunately, there is nothing they can do.

"Have you ever thought about suing the guy?" Jerry asks.

Charles chimes in. "It seems the number of unfounded complaints would make a good case for harassment. Maybe that would put a stop to this."

They have no way of knowing that I will never initiate a lawsuit of any kind against my neighbor, regardless of his harassment. I know only too well the court system can be manipulated and is not always fair. I am more terrified of the court system then I am of Detective Sugar. "I don't want to be involved in a court case with Detective Sugar. I just want him to leave me alone."

I attach my extreme fear of the courts to the insane legal battle I'm having with Jamie for my rightful share of our jointly owned property. No way will I ever initiate another legal battle. No matter what this detective does, I simply do not have the emotional energy to fight in court against him. It doesn't matter that I am right, and every complaint he has filed has been found unwarranted.

Meanwhile, the battle over the house I own with Jamie in Sumner County intensifies. Sumner County rules I must pay half of the bills that Jamie produces for the maintenance of the house since I "abandoned" it.

Jamie produces several thousands of dollars in maintenance bills for the past two years...in addition to the mortgage payment. Of course, these maintenance bills consist of invoices mostly billed by Jamie's company. But the judge orders me to pay one half of these bills, which is several thousand dollars I do not have.

And it doesn't stop there.

Additionally, I am ordered to pay half of all future property maintenance. For the first time, I consider signing the house over to Jamie. With this ruling, Jamie has no incentive to change anything regarding our house.

I'm in shock again.

Detective Sugar's continual bogus complaints are difficult to manage but pale in comparison to Jamie's new legal onslaught. I wonder if my life will ever be normal, including the government agencies that one would think should make sense.

Finally, every inspection has been approved: electrical, HVAC, plumbing, and building—all that remains is occupancy approval. The only requirement to get your occupancy permit is to have all these four inspections passed and then to apply for your occupancy permit. With all four inspections passed, my occupancy permit should be a rubber-stamp formality.

But my application is denied, and no reason is offered.

I am at a loss as to what to do.

The detective's ever-increasing bullying and intimidation tactics begin to exhaust me. Rudy tells me Detective Sugar was furious when he first found out I was dating Jack. The detective told Rudy, "Well, if she can date a carpenter, then why couldn't she date a detective? I guess it's because I am half black."

"Rudy, I just didn't want to date him. It doesn't have anything to do with him being half black," I insist.

"Well, young lady, you just need to pray about it. All things are possible with God."

I don't want to have the religious conversation, so I don't respond.

"I'll talk to him and see if I can help smooth things over between the two of you."

"I just want him to leave me alone."

"Let me see what I can do."

"Thanks, Rudy."

About a week after this, I come from work, and there is a ticket on my front door. Detective Sugar has written me a ticket for my dogs being loose. There is a county ordinance that all dogs must be restrained. I have five acres and have an invisible fence on my property. I know from previous conversations with Rudy that the detective doesn't like my dogs running loose on my five acres and wants me to have them on a chain or penned up. But I refuse to chain or pen up my dogs. So he has written me a ticket. I guess he thinks he is animal control now. It sure feels like he is taking his anger or bitterness toward me to the next level. I read the ticket, and I will now have to appear in Davidson County court. I am beginning to feel it's not safe for me to be outside when I am home alone. I am now fearful for my physical safety and my dogs' safety around this detective.

I am still seeing Freda on a biweekly basis. She is helping me gain understanding regarding my previous romantic choices in men. I haven't spent much time talking with her about Detective Sugar because I was never in a romantic relationship with him, and I believe that my behavior has no impact on the way he has treated me. But I will definitely have some discussion with her about this latest event.

Freda has helped me to finally understand my part in my relationship with Jamie. My part was that I agreed to stay. After each fight, I analyzed our argument to try to figure out how I could have prevented it. After each violent episode, Jamie slyly managed to show remorse while also continuing to blame me, suggesting I had "provoked" him. Shame prevented me from discussing the relationship with anyone else, so I never entertained other perspectives. It was always the same committee in my head that led me to the same conclusions.

Even if I didn't fully believe it was my fault, I rationalized if Jamie thought my behavior was the source of the fight, then I just wouldn't do whatever it was that he said caused us to fight. Surely this would prevent future fights. That's logical, right? Isn't there supposed to be give and take in relationships?

My go-to consolation was always "it's not as bad as Mom and Russell." I wasn't living in poverty. Life isn't perfect. Shouldn't you take the good with the bad?

The shame surrounding my violent relationship with Jamie kept me locked in silence. Jamie didn't have to ask me not to tell anyone; I willingly built thick walls of silence. Shame is a powerful force and was my prison. I was a long-term prisoner held captive by shame.

I slowly lost who I was or even who I hoped to be by refusing to defend myself against Jamie. Never having been allowed to stand up for myself against a bully as a child, I didn't understand that I had value and had the right to stand up for myself.

Freda helps me see how my childhood experiences shape the way I currently see the world, forming my expectations of relationships and influencing my current decisions.

My relationship with Jack is so different than any other I have experienced with a man. He is kind and considerate.

The first argument with Jack is something that will change me forever. Being fiercely independent and never wanting to feel trapped in a relationship again, I come and go and don't always tell Jack where I am going. Not because I have anything to hide—I just don't want him to ever feel he can tell what I can and can't do.

One evening, I go over to Karen's to visit with her, and we have a few drinks. It gets late, and I decide to spend the night rather than drive home. It is very unusual for me to spend the night away.

When I come home the next day, I decide to lie down and take a nap. A couple of hours later, I hear Jack come into the camper. I rise up from the bunk and say, "Hello."

"Well, nice of you to come home."

"Why are you mad?"

"Don't you think you should call and let your boyfriend know where you are and that you are okay?"

"Stop it. I won't have a boyfriend who is jealous. I have lived that life and won't do that again." I walk out of the camper and toward my car.

"You are so insensitive. Can't you even think how I felt last night, worrying if you were okay?"

I am heading for my go-to response: escape. I head to my car to leave.

Jack follows me and grabs my arm. "Don't go, Carly. Let's talk."

"Let go of me, you son of a b———!"

Shocked, he immediately releases me and backs away.

I get in my car and speed down the driveway and away from the house. I stay away for several hours. When I return home, Jack is gone. I am glad. I don't want to see him for a while. I had been feeling that I knew this was too good to be true. He is just like all the other guys.

He returns the following day and claims his boundary. "I don't care how much I love you. If you ever call me names again, I will never have anything to do with you. Even though you don't know it's not okay to call me names, no matter how mad you are, I know it's not right."

I hang my head in sorrow. He is right.

"I know you have been treated badly by Jamie, but that doesn't give you the right to treat me badly or call me names when I'm only concerned about you because I didn't know where you were."

"I am sorry. You are right. I just got so frightened when you grabbed my arm and I needed to get away."

The incident exposes my fears and behavior and makes me sad. I realize I am allowing past experiences to dictate my current—inappropriate—responses. I am ashamed that I lashed out at Jack with such demeaning language.

I resolve to never denigrate Jack again.

Almost as though talking to himself, Jack admits, "I don't understand you, but I do love you. I know you have a good heart and are kind, but sometimes your behavior just seems bizarre to me."

I cringe inside. Will I ever be "normal"?

Keeping people at a distance offers me the illusion of being normal. The incident with Jack, however, confirms to me that I am not the "normal" I long to be.

I wonder if my emotional wounds can ever be healed. Without a doubt, the ongoing court battle with Jamie hinders, and perhaps prevents, my emotional healing. The property settlement court case fuels, rather than reduces, my continual emotional distress.

With Detective Sugar showing no signs of slowing his harassment, Jack gently inquires, "Would you ever consider moving away from the farmhouse property? You certainly have a lot of stresses on you, and maybe this is one stress that is in your power to end."

"No, I am not going to let Detective Sugar run me off from this property." Selling the property feels like I'm letting him win. I am desperately trying to learn how to stand up for myself against bullies. If I sell, it feels like I am just running away, and Detective Sugar wins.

"No, I will not sell."

I will no longer acquiesce to appease the bully. There will be no running away or backing down this time.

Therapy had helped me learn that I had the right to set boundaries, and that I didn't need others' permission to enforce those boundaries. I also didn't have to feel guilty about setting those limits on others. But the line between my boundaries and sensitivity to Jack's needs were still very confusing to me. The line between my boundaries and Detective Sugar was just as confusing to me.

When Jack was concerned and couldn't reach me, which had never happened in our dating relationship to this point, rather than be understanding, I wanted to escape. Because it was so out of character for me to be away from home overnight, Jack was concerned for my safety. At the time, I didn't want to engage with him due to his being angry. I was afraid. I had not learned that it's okay to be angry. Up to this point in my life, all of my experiences with a love partner getting angry with me had resulted in physical violence toward me. So if this was my experience, then I couldn't image it having any other outcome for me but physical violence. My past experiences were heavily influencing, if not outright controlling, my present behavior.

Thoughts, attitudes, expectations, and behaviors are hard to change. I was also not used to having others ever worry about me. At the time, it had not occurred to me to call Jack and let him know where I was or that I was going to spend the night with my girlfriend. And when he questioned me, my immediate thought was that he was jealous. When Jack grabbed my arm to try to get me to stay, I immediately freaked out and assumed he was going to hit me. My learned response—fear—kicked in. I was in full fight-or-flight mode. And I was choosing flight; I was going to get out of there no matter what the cost.

In order for me to see my part, the best thing that could have happened was for Jack to do exactly what he did—call me out for calling him names. That behavior was what I had seen and experienced, except this time I was the one doing the name-calling. Although I didn't want to be physically abused ever again, I also did not want to be this person either.

I wondered if there were somewhere in the middle where you could be angry, where you could not want to talk, and where you could just be left alone for a while. Never having seen a couple argue fairly, I didn't know how that looked or felt. But I wanted so desperately to learn.

I was so confused. How could I be more gentle and compassionate in my relationship with Jack but learn to defend and protect myself against Jamie and my cop neighbor?

33. Letting Go

My Sumner County attorney is making some progress for me. He gets the judge to allow for an appraisal of the house. Jamie and I will each get our own appraisal. Once both of these appraisals are filed with the courts, the judge will then rule on the value of the house.

I feel that this is at least a step in the right direction. So maybe the desertion claim is not going to work for Jamie after all. I am still fighting the several thousand dollars of maintenance fees that Jamie claims I owe for the house since I have been gone from the property. This number will only continue to increase each month as the court battle drags on.

Meanwhile, the court date for the dog ticket is coming up. I decide that I am not going to use an attorney for this since Detective Sugar doesn't have the right to write me the ticket in the first place, and besides, it is bogus anyway. I am hoping it will get thrown out. I have been to court more times than I can count about property complaints and trumped-up building violations, and I feel I should not waste my hard-earned money on an attorney for this stupid dog ticket. How hard can it be? I mean after all, I have proof I have an underground fence.

The night before the dog court date, I cannot sleep. I am not exactly afraid but very apprehensive. I have not done anything wrong. It is legal to have your dogs restrained by an underground invisible dog fence. But my court experience has taught me that courts and judge rulings don't always seem fair.

I have taken off work to go to court. I have to be there at 1:00 p.m. I call Jack before I leave the house at 11:00 a.m. to let him know I'm leaving.

"Hi, Jack."

"Hi, Carly. Are you getting ready to leave the house?"

"Yeah, just wanted you to know I was heading downtown to the courthouse."

"Are you sure you don't want me to meet you at the courthouse?"

"No, I don't want you to have to miss work over this stupid ticket, too. This is just crazy. I'll be fine. I'll call you when I get home."

"Okay, just remember, he can't hurt you."

"Thanks for the pep talk. Bye."

"Bye, Carly."

I give Indy and Anna hugs and kisses. "Now, kids, you know I love you. I will do anything to protect you." A small tear rolls down my face. My resolve is fierce. I will not let the bully next door run over me and my dogs. He should not be allowed to give me tickets that are in direct opposition to the actual law. And this is, after all, a ticket about dogs not being restrained, and he is a narcotics detective. Maybe the judge will impose a penalty on him for writing me this crazy ticket.

The Davidson courthouse is about thirty minutes away. As I drive the familiar route, my heart starts to pound faster. I can feel my blood pressure rising.

I have to do this. And I don't really have the money to hire an attorney to go with me. I tell myself I will be fine.

I arrive downtown and park my car in the parking garage adjacent to the courthouse. I walk into the courthouse, and I start to get dizzy. I grab hold of the wall. I am afraid I am going to faint. I take a seat on the chairs lined up against the wall. I tell myself I will be okay.

I am afraid I will see Detective Sugar coming in. I have no way of knowing if he is already here or not. I must get up and walk through the metal detectors. I don't want to run into him here. I stand up slowly and walk to the back of the line. As the line moves ever so slowly, and I get closer to my turn to walk through the scanner, I begin to feel like I am very small. Like a little girl. I am afraid—no, terrified. I am all alone. I don't know if I will make it through these metal detectors without breaking down and crying. I don't know if I will be able to walk into the courtroom alone.

I have been in this very courthouse many times over building and code complaints. But this is different. I am trying to protect my beloved dogs.

I close my eyes and picture Indy and Anna. I will do anything to protect them. They are innocent. Don't they deserve protection from this bully?

With my eyes closed and all my concentration on trying to calm myself down, I don't realize the line has moved forward. I feel the person behind me push my back.

"Hey lady, the line is moving. You need to go on."

I am pulled out of my trance. "Sorry," I mumble under my breath and walk forward.

Whew! I finally make it through and don't set off the alarm. The elevators are just around the corner, and I walk that way. As I walk up to the elevators, the middle door opens as if on cue. I get in and push number six. I am due in courtroom 601A. As the elevator doors open on the sixth floor, I again become very anxious.

I close my eyes. I tell myself, "You can do this."

I walk into the courtroom and take a seat in the back row. The courtroom is packed. I look around and don't see the detective. That's a relief. I savor the thought of him not showing up and this going very smoothly. One can wish, right?

After about ten minutes, the judge, bailiff, and court reporter come into the courtroom. The bailiff barks, "All stand."

As I stand up, I see Detective Sugar walk through the same door the judge just walked through. Well, that figures. He is a cop, so I guess he can come in the back way. I sure hope he isn't friends with this judge. I hope this isn't another rigged courtroom.

Since my last name is Lee, I am thinking that it might be a while before my name is called to go in front of the judge. But I am wrong.

Detective Sugar is standing by the prosecutor. The prosecutor is shuffling through a stack of papers on the table in front of him. He finds what he is looking for and yells out, "Carly Lee, all present for case 345-AB, step forward."

The moment of truth arrives. I stand up, wipe my sweaty hands on my pants, and step through the half swinging door that separates the courtroom floor from the public rows.

"I'm here. I'm Carly Lee."

"Stand over there, ma'am." The prosecutor points to the defense table.

I walk to the table and put my purse on the table.

Judge Walter is a stern-looking old man. He looks at me and asks, "Do you have an attorney?"

"No, Your Honor, I do not."

"Well, what is this all about, young lady?"

"Your Honor, my neighbor, who is a narcotics detective, doesn't like the fact that my dogs run loose on my five acres. I have an invisible dog fence, but he wants me to chain my dogs up. I don't want my dogs on a chain; that is why I put in the invisible fence. Animal control states that an invisible fence is sufficient for dogs to be considered under the owner's control."

The judge looks over at the prosecutor table. "Detective, what is your side?"

Detective Sugar stands up. "Your Honor, my neighbor lets her dogs run outside her five acres all the time. She simply will not keep them on her property."

This is a lie.

The judge looks my way. "Is this true, Ms. Lee?"

"No, Your Honor, it's not true."

"Detective, do you have any proof of Ms. Lee's dogs running outside of her property?"

"No, Your Honor, but as an officer of the court, my word should take precedent over her word. And I am telling you, her dogs run loose all the time off her property."

"Your Honor, he is lying."

"Now, Ms. Lee. You can only speak when I ask you a question."

Not again! Not another rigged courtroom!

"Now, Detective, I don't know why you feel you had to write Ms. Lee a ticket personally and not call animal control. They are the appropriate agency to handle a matter of this nature. The fact that you don't have sufficient proof that Ms. Lee's dogs were off her property means I am going to dismiss this ticket and case. Next time, call animal control."

I can hardly believe my ears. The truth is actually going to win today.

Judge Walters looks at me. "Ms. Lee, good luck to you."

"Thank you, Your Honor." I remain where I am because I am not sure what I should do next. I know the detective will be furious, and I don't want to do anything to make the situation worse.

The judge looks at me and with a sympathetic smile says, "You are free to go."

Afraid my voice will crack with emotion, I nod my head as if to say thank you to the judge.

I grab my purse and walk briskly out the courtroom doors. I want to get out of there as quickly as possible.

I can hardly believe it—a judge who actually listens and rules with common sense.

As I leave the courthouse and walk to my car, I call Jack to tell him the good news. I dial his number, and when he answers, I shout out, "I won, I won!"

"That's great! What happened?"

"The judge threw out the ticket. He didn't think the old boy detective should have written the ticket, and he told him next time to call animal control."

"Ha! I bet he was mad as a bull in a china shop."

"I didn't stick around to find out."

"Well, let's celebrate. Meet me at the pizza place on Bourbon Street in thirty minutes."

"Okay, see you there."

So *this* is what it feels like when things go the way of justice in the court system. I am not used to this.

After eating a late lunch with Jack, I head back to my house. When I pull into the driveway, I see papers scattered all over my front yard. I stop my car and get out. I walk over to the closest paper and bend down to pick it up.

It's my mail. Someone has taken my mail out of the mailbox and thrown it into the front yard!

No, not someone—the detective. I quickly pick up my mail scattered in the front yard and head inside. I guess he is super mad about losing in court today. I know there is nothing I can do about this. If I call the police, they will tell me there is nothing they can do. I am not even going to waste my time doing that. But I know stealing someone's mail is a federal offense. I am sure the detective knows that. If he feels he can do this and get away with it, maybe I shouldn't be outside unless Jack is home. I feel less safe knowing that the detective is becoming bolder.

Jack arrives home later that evening, and I tell him what the detective did with my mail.

"Carly, do you think it's safe for you to stay here?"

"I don't feel safe, but if I move, I will always feel like I am running. I can't always run from everything."

"This isn't everything. It's a detective who writes you tickets and takes your mail from your mailbox and throws it across your yard. You are just pissing him off more and more."

"I know. I wish I knew what to do."

"Sell your house."

"But I don't want to have to move from here!"

"Well, let's not talk about it anymore tonight. You beat him in court today, so for today, you are the victor, regardless of whether he took your mail or not."

I walk over and hug Jack. I so appreciate him being supportive of me.

For the next few weeks, I don't have any interaction with the detective. Thankfully, I don't run into him on the shared road leading to our adjoining properties.

About a week after the dog-ticket incident, planning and zoning finally grant my occupancy permit for the carriage house. I receive notification in the mail that I have been approved.

This calls for another celebration with Jack. I feel life is moving toward the normal zone—if only I can get the court case with Jamie settled.

About a month later, there is substantial progress on that front. My appraisal is completed, and my attorney files the report with the court. A month after that, Jamie's appraisal is filed. My attorney's secretary calls me on a Friday to let me know she will be faxing me a copy of Jamie's appraisal.

I am on pins and needles. The appraisals are a big deal. I feel the end of this lawsuit might be in sight.

When I read Jamie's appraisal, I am stunned. I knew Jamie would get an appraiser who would give a lower appraisal value than the real value, but I didn't expect this. His appraisal is less than half of what the bank appraised it for when we finished building it six years earlier. Jamie's appraisal is about 40 percent of the amount of my appraisal. Jamie's appraisal is obviously a fake. We paid for almost one half of the construction costs out of our own pockets. There is no way Jamie's appraisal is reasonable.

I call my attorney and tell him Jamie's appraisal states that the house was built in a substandard manner and thus the property is less valuable than other homes in the area. I ask if this is a legal appraisal, and my attorney tells me it is.

My attorney's strategy is for us to go in front of the judge and ask for the court to not consider Jamie's appraisal, as it seems out of line with the bank's appraisal six years earlier.

As I hang up the phone, I wonder how I ever let my life get into such a mess. There are times when my current life is good, really good—like if I haven't seen my bully neighbor in several days and I haven't had any court interaction regarding the house settlement with Jamie.

Yeah, without those two things, my life is pretty good. My work is good, my love life is the best it's ever been, and I now have my occupancy permit for the carriage house. I can feel normal for a few days at a time.

I simply must get things settled with Jamie, but if I quit now and just sign the house over to him, I will actually owe him money because of the maintenance-fee ruling by the judge. I just don't want to keep fighting him in court and spending money on attorneys. It's a financial drain.

A year and several court filings later, my attorney is successful in getting the maintenance fees dismissed. However, the appraisals, both mine and Jamie's, are considered valid, and we are waiting on the judge to make a ruling on the house value. It's been over a year, and there is nothing I can do. I just have to wait.

Meanwhile, I still meet with Freda. She knows that we are waiting on the judge to make a final ruling on the house value, and then hopefully the case will be settled soon after that. Freda recommends that I join a group at the battered women's shelter. It will be with other abused women who have gone through individual therapy too.

I don't know. It is one thing to talk to a therapist and quite another to talk openly in a group with other women. I tell her I will think about it.

On my next visit, Freda presses me on attending the group. Freda tells me that I am experiencing good days, actually several good days in a row, as long as I don't have to deal with any court issues from Jamie and the detective.

Common sense tells me that I have to continue to push myself if I want to continue to make progress with my emotional healing. That means taking the advice of my therapist even when I really don't want to. Man, this healing, growing, and evolving emotionally is tough stuff.

So I relent and agree to go to group. We will meet once a week. I secretly think meeting once a week for group session is a little too much meeting, but I agree to give it a try.

The next week I am anxious because I still don't like to talk about abuse with anyone other than Jack. Just because I agree to come to the group doesn't mean I agree to talk in the group.

For the first couple of months, I don't speak at all during the group meeting. Finally, the therapist leading the group asks me to share. I don't want to be rude to the others as they have shared so freely, but I am not ready to dive very deep. No, this is one onion that has many layers, and, being a master of secrets, even sharing a little is tough.

I close my eyes and think. I want to be totally honest but am not ready to be totally open. So I say, "I really appreciate this group. This is the first time I have ever felt like I was not being judged for my poor choices. You can't know what you don't know, and I didn't know when I began a relationship with my former boyfriend that he would physically abuse me. You guys get that.

Our stories have so many common threads that I feel I don't need to share the details of my stories and take up your time. I guess for me now, the big question I have for myself is, 'Why did I stay for so long?' You guys get it. You understand that leaving an abusive relationship is sometimes like going up and down a ladder. You go up the ladder and make some progress but think you need to take a step down or backward because you love him or for other reasons that sound very

CARLY LEE

logical to you at the moment. I like to think of my final decision to leave my abusive relationship as my own personal *leaving-ladder* experience. I think of it as the leaving-ladder experience because you may travel over the same rungs or experiences—forgive his bad deeds, reconcile with him, get your heart broken again, forgive his bad deeds, reconcile with him, and so on—many times. And thus up and down the leaving ladder we go

At that moment, my logical thinking regarding my intimate relationships is confused. I wondered if I could even make a rational decision. I was desperately hoping for a change. I was hanging onto the belief the man that I fell in love with would show up again. The man who was nice, caring, charming, and said he loves me. I haven't had many people in my life tell me they loved me, and the abuser had confessed his love for me many times. Often in the beginning, he showed me more affection than anyone else had in my entire life. Wasn't this worth trying to fix?"

The rules of therapy were you could not give anyone advice. We were there to listen to each other. I felt no judgment—nothing but compassion.

After I had finally spoken in the group, I did feel different. I was no longer in a vacuum of silence. Granted, there were only seven other women in that room, but I had shared with others my intimate feelings about my previous abusive relationship. This was a whole new level of releasing my shame and secrets and allowing a deeper level of emotional healing to occur.

And it felt good to let it out.

I wanted more of this good feeling. I was so drained from all the court fighting with Jamie. It had now been one and a half years since Jamie and I submitted our separate appraisals to the court. I was hoping it would be over soon.

And then the day finally comes. I receive a call from my attorney.

"Hi, Carly."

"Hello."

"Are you sitting down?"

"Should I sit down?"

"Yes."

This can't be good. "Okay, I'm sitting down."

"Well, the judge has ruled the house is worth what you owe the bank."

"What? How the hell can that be?"

"Don't worry. We will appeal this. This value is 50 percent what the bank valued the property at almost seven years ago. Maintained properties don't go down in value in a stable real-estate market."

Since I had now been in this court battle four and half years, I am a little more experienced at knowing what questions to ask. "So what is our strategy to fight this?"

"We will file a motion asking for the courts to appoint an appraiser. We will require an independent value. We will argue that the judge is not a qualified resource to make property-value determinations."

"But wouldn't that be the judge ruling against himself?"

"We will need to research case law to strengthen our position."

"Let me think about it."

"There is no other alternative."

"Just let me think on it. I'll call you next week."

I am the one who is spending the money, and I need to think. The phrase "throwing good money after bad" comes to mind. How much longer could/should I fight this battle with Jamie?

It has never been a matter of right versus wrong in the legal system. If I continue in this court battle, I am going to keep spending money and constantly be distressed about the legal maneuvering of Jamie and his lawyer. And I may never recover a penny of the money I have spent trying to get my half of the equity. It isn't fair, but it's a financial gamble to continue fighting, and there is definitely an emotional price to pay.

Spring will officially start next week. I love springtime: the new flower buds, the fresh air, and the longing for summer days.

The weekend rolls around, and I put a mental deadline of Sunday at 6:00 p.m. for making my decision to either continue the court battle with Jamie or to end it. It's Saturday morning, so I am not going to decide today. Today, I am just going to let my thoughts wander wherever they take me.

I decide to work in the yard. As I am digging in the soil, I feel inspired by the warm sun and how every year my favorite flowers, black-eyed Susans, grow back. You can't see the flower roots in the ground during the cold winter months, but these beautiful flowers grow back every spring.

Flowers that don't get enough water or sunshine don't do as well, and I can sympathize. I felt I haven't gotten what I needed so far in my life, and I haven't done as well as I should have. But I have survived. I know that my future will be based on the decisions I make today. How can I do it differently so that two, three, or five years from now I am living the kind of life I wished for as a little girl?

I know what a good life for me will look like: a safe home, a good job, a loving relationship, and no court battle. I have all of this except the "no court battle" thing.

This dark cloud of legal conflict with Jamie and Detective Sugar is overshadowing all the good things in my life. I can't roll back time and undo getting involved with Jamie. But I can stop this battle with Jamie.

With my hands in the dirt, I decide right then and there to sign the house over to Jamie. My sanity is worth more to me than continuing to fight a court battle where I might ultimately lose. And this will stop the financial drain of having to pay attorneys to keep fighting this lawsuit.

I become filled with hope and strength, not only because of the new spring air but also because I feel the hardships will soon be in my rearview mirror. I wouldn't wish this experience on my worst enemy, but I have survived and am stronger for having lived through the experience. I feel I will never willingly choose a path of violence again. I definitely will never remain silent about it again. No, my eyes are definitely open, and I am aware of the methods of perpetrators. I finally feel in control of my destiny.

For me, learning that my choices sometimes had long-term consequences made me pause. I had always known that I would have to work hard to get ahead in life, and I was okay with that. What I had not realized is that working hard, doing the right thing, and always taking financial responsibility for myself were not the only *key ingredients* to having a successful life. Maybe this belief would not have been challenged for me if I had met, fallen in love with, and married a good guy the first time around.

But that didn't happen to me. My life's journey was to be along a much rockier path, and my beliefs would be challenged to the point where they would be broken down. I would try to make sense of my shattered beliefs and faulty thinking.

As a young woman, I was very naïve and fell prey to a street-smart man who exploited me to his advantage. After finally leaving Jamie, I was desperate to learn how I could have allowed myself to replicate the victim role that I had witnessed my mother play.

From my earliest memories, I had vowed to not be dependent on a man or to be vulnerable. I would take care of myself and not rely on others. To me, this represented the way to avoid being a victim. I didn't discuss my formula with anyone; I simply came to my own childish conclusions (beliefs) on the matter. As an adult, I only challenged these beliefs when it became crystal clear to me that they were not accurate, and sometimes that took a painfully long time.

I was faithful to my beliefs for a very long time. I believed that you should keep your word—and then I learned its okay to change your mind. I believed that you should forgive as a good Christian should—and then I learned that forgiveness does not replace accountability.

I believed that you should take the bad with the good—and then I began to think I might deserve better.

And then I spoke out during a group-therapy session. I didn't want to speak out in the beginning, but I slowly opened myself enough to follow Freda's advice. When Freda said that in her opinion, group would be good for me, I went to group. When I was encouraged to speak up in the private and confidential setting of this group, I finally did. The results were transformative for me.

The committee in my head was getting new information to make decisions, and these new decisions were starting to create pockets in my life that were good. The changes didn't happen overnight but little by little I was changing what I allowed into my life. And these changes help me to think differently, which in turn changed my beliefs and resulted in me changing my actions. Then I could finally experience different outcomes in my life.

My new goal was to expand the good pockets of life so they would cover my entire life. I wanted to cut strife and turmoil out of my life completely. The main source of this quagmire was anything connected to Jamie.

When I made the decision to sign the house over to Jamie, I finally felt free. This feeling of freedom was different than when I felt free of Dalton. When I untangled myself from Dalton, I was grateful to be free, but I had not yet learned that I needed to protect myself from other predators. However, being done with Jamie and the court battle was freeing—and I had now earned the knowledge that I need to protect myself from predators.

With my newfound emotional freedom and the ability to spot a violent predator, I finally felt liberated. I thought I knew how to protect myself from all predators.

But you can't know what you don't know. Specifically, I didn't know there were many forms of predators. And I didn't quite realize or understand that a predator with a badge can inflict a unique form of abuse.

EPILOGUE

Today as I sit here in my home with my beloved dogs snuggled up to me, I reflect on letting go of my shame, embarrassment, and humiliation of what I have experienced in my life, both as a child and as an adult. I would never have imaged a decade ago that I would be willingly to share my story publicly and willingly expose myself to the judgement of others.

But today, I feel free and dare I say open to being vulnerable and un-afraid of releasing my secrets. Knowing that I have learned many great lessons on how to protect myself from those that wish to control, manipulate or use me has given me the freedom to share what I have experienced. For in telling my story I am taking my power back and courageously defeating shame and the binds that hold me emotional captive.

In defeating shame I will no longer keep silent when misdeeds occur. Quite the opposite, I will tell the world what I see and know. As I continue to write about how I have learned and grown from my abusive experiences, I am constantly amazed how my own beliefs, self-love and respect continue to grow.

My life is far from perfect but I am a million miles from where I was a decade ago. And I believe that when I finish my next book, I will be a million miles from where I stand today.

I wish everyone who reads this book to grow in self-love, courage, trust and belief in yourself. For I truly believe if I can do it, anyone can do it.

ABOUT THE AUTHOR

 It is with first-hand experience as a victim evolving to a survivor that Carly writes *Why Do You Stay*.
Carly Lee holds a bachelor of science degree in business administration with computer information systems. She works as a project manager for a health services and innovation company in the health care industry. Lee lives with her husband, Jack; three Yorkies; and a collection of rescue cats.
Lee hopes that sharing her story of overcoming a life marred by domestic violence will offer hope and inspiration to other victims and those who care about victims: friends, family, therapists, and others who want to understand better *Why Do You Stay?* She is now writing a follow-up to *Why Do You Stay?*

STAY CONNECTED

To stay connected with Carly visit her blog at CarlyLee.blog.

To learn where she will be appearing, signing books or speaking, visit her website at Carlylee.net.

Made in the USA
San Bernardino, CA
17 July 2019